APPLYING
DATA
STRUCTURES

APPLYING DATA STRUCTURES

T.G. Lewis
University of Southwestern Louisiana

M. Z. Smith
IBM Corporation

HOUGHTON MIFFLIN COMPANY, BOSTON
Atlanta · Dallas · Geneva, Illinois · Hopewell, New Jersey
Palo Alto · London

Printed in the United States of America

Library of Congress Catalog Card Number: 75-25004

ISBN: 0-395-24060-3

To Brian and Madeline

Green meadows
turn to August gold.
You are the rain.

CONTENTS

vii

PREFACE

The study of data structures emerged as a central computer science course in university undergraduate curricula because of its imperative prerequisite nature. Data structures are an integral part of programming, both at the application program design and implementation stage and at the basic structural stage of underlying techniques used to construct programming systems. Compilers, operating systems, and text editors, for instance, use data-structure techniques presented in this book.

One must use data structures to develop techniques for system implementation and for applications programming. Therefore it is an application-oriented topic. We have used application examples to present techniques, tradeoffs, and usefulness of a variety of data structures.

Data is structured in order to be manipulated. The type of structure depends on the desired manipulation. Conversely, the efficiency of manipulation algorithms depends on the appropriateness of the data structure. To structure data effectively, it is essential not only to know techniques but also to know when to apply certain techniques. We present basic data manipulation: searching, sorting, and updating, and special-purpose algorithms that are linked to a particular data structure, e.g., stack processing and sparse lists.

In early chapters we pursue an intuitive development through examples. Chapter 5 presents, as gently as possible, a formal basis for data structures. The book develops each topic by appealing to the reader's natural intuition. We use mathematical formalism only where it improves clarity of presentation or gives exacting tools to measure algorithm performance. Chapter 10 deals with data structure applications and may be used to reinforce concepts throughout the book. We hope that this method of presentation will gradually lead to a formal study of data structure.

Chapter 1 presents a few examples that rapidly motivate the reader to study data structure. You will notice that we take an independent approach to programming language. Algorithms are treated in semiformal English phrases wherever possible. We adhere to a stepwise, modular style of algorithm presentation reminiscent of structured programming. Programming languages (PL/I and SNOBOL) are given only as an enrichment.

Chapter 2 starts the study of data structure by presenting unstructured data, that is, strings. We include some PL/I and SNOBOL to show how strings manifest themselves in a high-level language. These topics have been expanded and placed in Appendix A and Appendix B. String operations of concatenation, separation, substring, index, and replacement are shown to lead to problems of data organization. These problems are in turn resolved by techniques developed in Chapter 3.

Chapters 3 and 4 cover all linear data structures: lists, stacks, deques, and queues. The denseness of a list is shown to be a measure of its compactness and therefore its storage efficiency. The operations of insert and delete are costly unless restricted as shown in Chapter 4.

Chapter 5 begins the formal theory of structure through graph theory. The general nature of a graph encompasses all linear and nonlinear lists and, in particular, models tree structures through restrictions placed on the graph.

Chapter 6 completes the study of structure with a presentation of data structures stored on auxiliary storage devices. Such external structures are called files. A discussion of single-key and multiple-key file structures shows that there is little difference between a file structure and a multilinked list.

Chapters 7, 8, and 9 cover the basic data-manipulating algorithms. Sorting is an expansive topic, so we present only the most significant techniques. Searching is also a large topic, so we discuss only the most obvious algorithms. The book is unique in deriving the average number of comparisons in the binary search technique. Because memory management has many ramifications, we concentrate on the most frequently used methods, and present for the first time in a textbook an analytical model for memory management.

Chapter 10 contains ten applications of data structures. These applications may be used to demonstrate a particular point or may be considered a final chapter on applications. The chapter progresses from program design to program development, and finally to program execution; yet any application may be treated separately.

Chapter 11 is a further formalization of the graph theory model presented in Chapter 5. Chapter 11 is recommended only for the mathematically mature reader.

Appendixes A, B, and C may be used to enrich a computer science course that uses PL/I for programming. Through examples, we demonstrate the constructs of PL/I that are useful for list processing and memory allocation.

We feel that the book is unique in several aspects. The notation is selected to more accurately represent the concepts we want to reference. In Chapter 2 we use concatenation to mean joining of two strings. Unfortunately, there is no comparable word that means disjoining, so we use separation in place of uncatenation, discatenation, etc.

We treated the concept of list density in Chapter 3. This is a convenient way to measure storage utilization and also to name packed lists. The use of atom to indicate a unit of a linked list and of NIL for the end of a list are borrowed from LISP. You will notice that in later chapters we prefer the terms node and vertex. Terms such as pointer, link, or thread are commonly accepted, but chain (for linked list), shelf (for queue), and heap (for stack) are still questionable.

We dropped the contemporary usage of pre-order, post-order, and end-order for tree search algorithms in favor of descriptive names. For instance, in place of pre-order, we use root node-left-right-recursive (NLR-recursive). The reason for this is that, when using current terminology, we could never remember which node of a tree to begin a search.

We use simple probability and calculus only where the use of analytical methods provides a distinct improvement in understanding formulas. In general we give performance formulas without confusing the reader with derivations requiring mathematical sophistication.

Algorithms are in English and algebra. They are written as top-down modules that may be readily applied to a programming language implementation that uses structured programming techniques. Experienced programmers will readily recognize the approach, while a novice programmer will form stylistic habits early in his or her career.

The authors have taught data structures for several years. In writing this book, our motivation was twofold: to provide a single source for topics relevant to data structures, and to provide a readable book. We studied available literature in depth and decided what should go in this book and what should be read in its original form. The pertinent literature may be found listed under References.

We achieved our second goal through the assistance of several waves of students who used our early manuscripts as textbooks. Their contribution was great, and we frequently employed their suggestions to improve general clarity.

For their valuable assistance, we would like to thank the following individuals who reviewed this book during its developmental stages: David R. Musser, University of Wisconsin (Madison); Sara R. Jordan, The University of Tennessee; Daniel P. Friedman, Indiana University; Victor B. Schneider, Purdue University; and Edward Katz, University of Southwestern Louisiana.

It is also a pleasure to acknowledge the assistance of University of Missouri-Rolla students and faculty, University of Southwestern Louisiana students, and the flawless typing of May Heatherly. In addition, we thank Terry Walker, John Hamblen, Bob Flandrena, Ray Ford, Ed Runnion, and Brian Smith for their help.

T. G. Lewis
M. Z. Smith

APPLYING
DATA
STRUCTURES

1
WHAT IS A DATA STRUCTURE?

1.1
An Intuitive Approach

Novice programmers usually work with small amounts of data and are not concerned with efficient ways to store information. Instead, they choose a method that is either easy to program or a method with which they are familiar. When tackling a complex problem or one involving large quantities of data, programmers must organize the problem-solving procedure or they will waste valuable computer time and storage.

Following the classical von Neumann model, most computers have a sequentially ordered memory. This means that we may picture memory as a sequence of locations, each with a unique numerical address as shown in Figure 1.1.

Putting data in memory usually causes no problems as long as we do not erase values we wish to keep. Difficulties begin to arise, however, when we try to use the data and realize that perhaps we should have been more orderly in our organization of storage. For example, suppose we have a group of names, some of which are listed last name first and others, first name first. To make things easier, let us also imagine that each name fits into one memory location. In reality we may need several locations per name, but would still have the problem of organization. Upon examining Figure 1.2, we discover that alphabetizing the names is not easy because we must first locate the last names.

It is easier for a person than for a computer to find the last names because the person knows that Bill, Martha, and Ann are first names. But how do we tell this to a computer? And what about the last person on the list? Is his name Sam Paul or Paul Sam? Anybody would have trouble

1

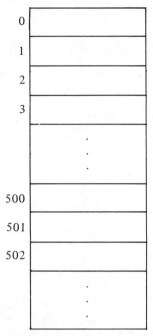

Figure 1.1 Diagram of a memory area

alphabetizing this list, unless it could be assumed that all last names appeared first.

Structure is a relationship between the individual elements of a group. Governments, universities, and businesses all have their defined organizations. In computer science the relationship between data items is a *data structure*. Does the idea of structure apply to some abstract quality, e.g., the way we picture the data or the way we reference it? Or is it the way in which the items are stored in a computer's memory? In this book we will present various data structures, introduce their terminology, and discuss their storage. We will present numerous pertinent examples which illustrate applications of the data structures. For now, let us discuss several types of structures with which you are probably familiar, though you may not realize that they are classified as data structures.

Lists, such as the one pictured in Figure 1.2, are a type of data structure. The items are related in two ways. First, they are all names, and second, they are stored in sequential memory locations. In order to refer to the list, we need to know its beginning and either its end or its length.

Lists have some basic problems that arise when we begin to add or take away items. For example, adding to a grocery list or a client list is a simple matter of including additions at the end. If we add a name to an address

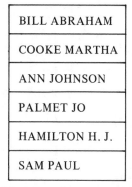

| BILL ABRAHAM |
| COOKE MARTHA |
| ANN JOHNSON |
| PALMET JO |
| HAMILTON H. J. |
| SAM PAUL |

Figure 1.2 A list of names to alphabetize

list, we may try to keep the names in alphabetical order. Thus we may be forced to write in the margins or to write smaller as shown in Figure 1.3.

Deleting items from noncomputer-type lists is equally simple. We need only to draw a line through the element. Adding or removing names from an unordered list may not be difficult provided we have enough paper. However, if our list is ordered, insertion and deletion may be more of a problem. In the case of an address book, where names are added, removed, or corrected, we have limited space to make changes and to maintain the alphabetical list. In fact, every so often we may be forced to get a new address book and start a fresh copy.

A list is fairly easy to store in computer memory because in its simplest form a list is a sequence of items. It corresponds naturally to the sequential nature of computer memory. Contrasted to a list, a table (or *matrix*) is two-dimensional. As an example, consider the table in Figure 1.4 which gives prices for items purchased in units of 1, 3, or 12. Assuming a memory location holds only one entry, the 4×7 entry table requires 28 locations.

Most high-level languages have built-in procedures for storing tables. To reference a single item, programmers need only to give its row and

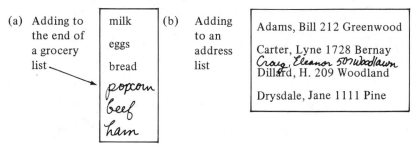

Figure 1.3 Adding to lists

	Price for these quantities		
Item number	1	3	12
1062	.99	2.84	10.50
1048	1.88	5.60	22.38
1175	1.29	3.17	13.76
1287	2.35	7.01	25.11
1296	10.12	28.92	118.05
1408	5.06	14.32	58.73
1450	7.21	20.86	80.90

Figure 1.4 A price table

column number. Thus to find the cost of 12 units of item 1175, we would reference row 3, column 4 and find 13.76. Working in an assembly language or in a language that does not automatically store tables, we would need to provide our own scheme. Usually tables can be stored by column or by row (see Figure 1.5). If we know the exact size of the table (number of rows and columns), we can compute the location of any item (see Exercise 3).

When working with tables, we must consider such topics as inserting or deleting items, ordering the table with respect to item numbers, or search-

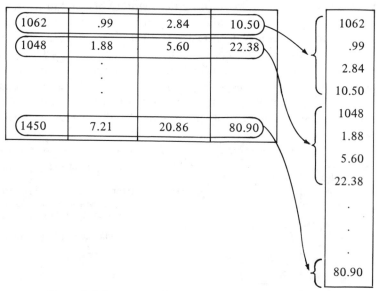

Figure 1.5 Storing a table in sequential memory locations

ing the table for a particular item number. These considerations present unique problems that will be discussed in later chapters of the text.

Another type of data structure is the file. A *file* is a collection of records that is usually stored outside the computer's memory on magnetic tape or disk. The common analog of a file would be the contents of a filing cabinet. The information in each folder is a *record*. Since files are usually voluminous, only portions of them can be read into memory at a single time. Their size also makes organization important so that access time will be minimized. Some files, such as the reservation records of an airline, are dynamic. People frequently make or cancel reservations and thus the file constantly changes. Other files are more or less static and require less attention; e.g., census data changes only every decade.

Another data structure which is more complex in form is the *tree*. Trees are frequently used to represent the organization of elements into a hierarchy. Figure 1.6 illustrates the order in which tasks must be completed in the assembly of an airplane. The highest level (level 1) is the finished product; the lowest level (level 4) contains assembly-line tasks that may be completed concurrently. Tasks at level 4 (ribbing, sheet metal, electronics, and turbine) must be completed before tasks at level 3 (fuselage, wings, and engines) can be started. Therefore in this example we are working from the bottom to the top of the tree.

Trees are also used in playing games to represent valid moves. For example, in a tic-tac-toe game in which we have the privilege of going first, our first choice would be to place our mark in any of the nine squares. After our opponent has played, we are limited to one of seven squares. Thus in a single game, we would be going from level to level using only a small part of the tree.

Examine Figure 1.7 and imagine that you are "X" and your opponent is "O." At the beginning, you may choose to mark the upper left square, the left square, the center square, the upper right square, or . . . . Suppose you start by marking the left square. Since you have chosen to follow the center branch of the tree, your opponent now has retaliation potential (at

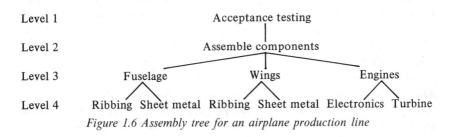

Figure 1.6 Assembly tree for an airplane production line

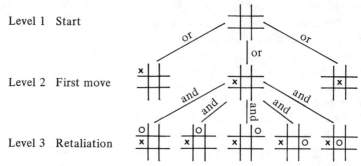

Level 1   Start

Level 2   First move

Level 3   Retaliation

Figure 1.7 Partial tic-tac-toe game tree showing only symmetric moves possible. A player selects an "or" move and an opponent replies by selecting an "and" move

level 3) of upper left, upper center, upper right, right, and center. The symmetry of the tic-tac-toe board allows us to simplify the tree shown in Figure 1.7 and yet account for all cases.

The game tree spreads out as increasingly more and/or branches are shown corresponding to subsequent moves. An optimal game strategy can be used to decide which "or" branch to select. For example, in tic-tac-toe an optimal strategy is to select the "or" branch that renders the maximum number of ways to win. At level 1 the maximum ways of winning is given by the "or" branch that leads to the "X" in the center (upper left allows only three straight lines, left allows only two, but center allows four straight lines).

In both examples of a tree, note that a hierarchy is created. This is an important feature of trees. The hierarchy expresses either what is more important, what must be done first, or what is more general. It is a conceptualization of *single-path structures:* Each item at the lowest level may be reached by one and only one path from the item at level 1. For *multiple-path structures* an organization called a *graph* is needed.

We can think of a graph as a road map which shows cities and the connections between them. Frequently if we wish to find the shortest distance between cities, we label the lengths of the connections as shown in Figure 1.8. Graphs have wide applications in transportation to help find the shortest or fastest route that covers certain points with the least amount of backtracking. An example of this would be the routing of a school bus or a delivery truck.

At this point we will not discuss the storage of a tree or a graph in computer memory. Instead we will ask you to consider this problem: How does one place a nonsequential structure, such as a tree or a graph, in sequential memory locations and accurately represent its structure?

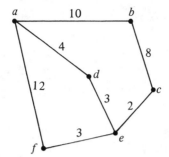

Figure 1.8 A graph whose edges are numbered and nodes (vertices) are lettered

EXERCISES

1. Define the following terms:
   (a) Sequential memory
   (b) Structure
   (c) File
   (d) Game tree

2. Discuss ways in which lists are allowed to grow. How does insertion differ for ordered and unordered lists?

3. If a table (such as the one in Figure 1.5) is stored in sequential memory locations, tell how to locate any value, assuming its row and column number in the table are known.

4. Draw a graph of the Bridges of Konigsberg problem shown in Figure 1.9. This problem prompted Euler (1736) to begin the study of graph theory. The residents of Konigsberg (now Kaliningrad) wished to promenade around town on Sundays, but they had a problem: The town was divided into four parts by a river. How could they cross each of the seven bridges one time only before returning

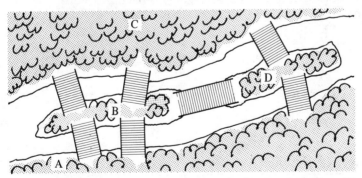

Figure 1.9 The Bridges of Konigsberg connect land masses A, B, C, and D

to their starting point? (*Hint:* Let the land masses be nodes and bridges be edges of the graph.)

5. Draw a tree showing the relationship between countries, states within the United States, and cities within each state. Where does your postal address fit into this structure?

1.2
Storage Versus
Access Problems

Behind the application of most data structures lies a space versus time tradeoff. Typically programmers choose between fast-running programs that use lots of memory and slower programs that use less memory. For example, if we had an alphabetical list of computer users and their job account numbers, we could easily look up a particular user's number. If there were no such person, we would not need to read the entire list since it is alphabetized. However, if we knew a job account number and wanted to find out whose it was, we would have to search the entire list. One solution to this problem would be to have two lists—one ordered alphabetically and one ordered by user number. Thus it could be made easy to retrieve the information, but we would have doubled our storage requirements. If the increase were only from 100 to 200 locations, the extra storage would be negligible. But if the increase were from 10,000 to 20,000, perhaps we should consider whether we wish to sacrifice storage to gain a shorter lookup time.

Another way to make it appear that we have two lists—one in alphabetical order and the other in user number order—is to use links as shown in Figure 1.10. The list is alphabetized, and the links tell the position of the next item *if* the list were in order by user number.

The variable FIRST tells the location of the first user number in the list. Since FIRST = 3, the third user number in the list is the smallest. The link of 121 is 2 which says that 167 (in list position 2) is the next user num-

	Name	User number	Link
1	BAKER J	201	5
2	CRAIG E	167	1
3	FARMER M	121	2
4	JONES A	348	—
5	WALKER T	313	4

3

FIRST

Figure 1.10 A list using links to show order by user number

ber. Following 167 is 201 (in position 1), then 313 (in position 5), and finally 348 (in position 4). The link of 348 is a dash (–) which denotes the last user number. In a computer we might use zero, a negative number, or some special character to represent the end of a list. Links will be discussed in more detail in Chapter 3, but this example emphasizes the space-versus-time tradeoff. Links take up room but give us access to the list in a different order.

The operations of adding or deleting elements from a set of data fall into the category of updating. Updating also includes correcting existing elements. Whenever we add elements we have to consider whether or not there is room for the additional data and if there is room, how to maintain the data's structure. For example, if we have a list of numbers which are in descending order, how do we insert something into its proper place?

Figure 1.11 depicts the original list with location 206 shaded to show that it is not in use. To insert 1945, we must move all the numbers from 1823 to 1607 down one location so that 1945 can go into location 202 and preserve the descending order. Shifting the values down one location may not be difficult to program, but the execution time increases as we have to move more values. If the volume of data is large, we may wish to save time by keeping the original list separate from the updates and making all changes at the same time. For example, a bank waits until the end of the day to process deposits and withdrawals and to compute current balances. It does not update each account whenever a transaction occurs. As we discuss the different structures in detail, keep in mind the updating problem and see how difficult or easy it is with each structure.

A consideration arising from updating a data structure is its dynamic nature: Will the structure remain the same size or will it constantly be changing? Some languages, such as FORTRAN or COBOL, make programmers define the exact size of the arrays and tables. It does not matter

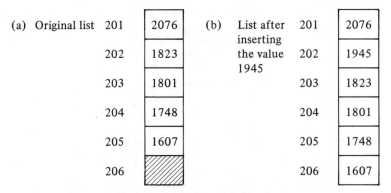

Figure 1.11 A list (a) before and (b) after insertion

if the entire area is used. Other languages, such as ALGOL and PL/I, allow structures to be created dynamically at execution time. This means that during execution there is a supervisory program which gets the required amount of storage and links it to the executing program. Thus a program and its data areas may not be in contiguous memory locations (see Figure 1.12).

On the other hand, programmers can take care of their own dynamic structures. If we are using a system which requires that we request a specific number of locations, we would request some maximum amount of space based on estimates of the original size and growth potential of the data. Within that area we can let the structures grow or shrink, always being careful not to go outside the assigned area.

Whether managed by the computer system or by programmers, dynamic structures usually require more links, tables, and bookkeeping to keep track of the current location of the data. In contrast, a static or unchanging structure may require only a pointer to designate its beginning location and a value to denote its length. Static structures lack the flexibility of dynamic structures.

We will not attempt at this time to solve any of the problems mentioned in this section, but we will discuss them in the following chapters. Keep in mind that we will discuss many different types of data structures. The major structures are lists, trees, graphs, and files. Other structures are variations of these. The choice of a data structure for a particular problem depends on the following factors:

1.   Volume of data involved

2.   Frequency and way in which data will be used

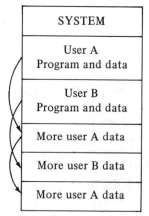

Figure 1.12 Storage and linkage of users' programs and data

3. Dynamic or static nature of the data

4. Amount of storage required by the data structure

5. Time to retrieve an element

6. Ease of programming

If we are given a project whose results are needed immediately, we might choose a structure which is easy to program even though its execution time might be long. At the other extreme, we might choose a complex structure which is more difficult to program but could be accessed in a variety of ways. Actually, there are no strict rules in choosing one particular data structure rather than another. In this book we will present the most commonly used structures, discuss their advantages and disadvantages, and give the reader a feeling for the application of the structures by providing numerous examples.

1.3
A Data Structure
Classification

It may be useful in our study of data structures to remember the framework in which we will work. Figure 1.13 shows how we have diagrammed the interconnected topics discussed in this book. The classification shows how we have related the theoretical and practical aspects of applying data structures.

The emphasis of this book is on practice rather than on theory. Often, however, we rely on theory for the necessary tools to show how various methods of structuring and manipulating data compare. In Figure 1.13 we show a need for graph theory, set theory, combinatorial analysis, and probability theory to analyze data structures and manipulation algorithms. Discrete mathematics is a powerful device that provides performance formulas for analysis of algorithms. Ultimately we use these formulas to select the proper algorithms.

On the practical side of our classification we see that the study of strings, lists, trees, multilinked lists, and files leads to algorithms for manipulation of data. All applications of computers to daily problems require these structures and their algorithms.

As a demonstration let us analyze a problem in programming. Suppose we wish to write a FORTRAN program to store the names of bank customers and their balances. In FORTRAN the only data structure that we can use is the array. An *array* is a special kind of list that we will study fully in Chapter 3.

Our problem is reduced (by FORTRAN's limitation) to working out the proper manipulation algorithms. We need an *insert algorithm* for adding new names to the bank list and a *search algorithm* for finding a given name when requested.

Now suppose we wish to analyze theoretically this practical problem to determine how much   computer time we expect to use each time the program is run. Given that the array is n items in length (contains n names and balances), we ask how long will it take to do an insertion and how long will it take to do a look-up?

In Chapter 3 we show that insertion into an array requires that we move an average of $(n + 1)/2$ items. We arrive at this formula by applying probability theory and discrete mathematics.

Finally, if we know how much time t is required to move a single item in an array, we can expect an average of $t(n + 1)/2$ units of time per insertion. This will establish an estimate for execution time *before* the program is written.

We selected the relationships shown in Figure 1.13 because they are representative of problems and techniques found in daily computing. We have attempted to place this subset of topics in a practical application context. This means that we have sacrificed the theory half of Figure 1.13 in favor of the practical half. The reader is urged to read the papers and books listed in the bibliography for a theoretical perspective.

Let us now give a fuller answer to the question, "What is a data structure?" by referring to Figure 1.13. A *data structure* is an abstract modeled by a graph, set, or combinatorial model. It is also a practical way of organizing strings, lists, trees, and so on, in computer memory.

Data structures are analyzed by theoretical means using discrete mathematics or by practical means measuring the performance of algorithms. Structures are the backbone of programming, file structures, operating systems, and other topics in computer science.

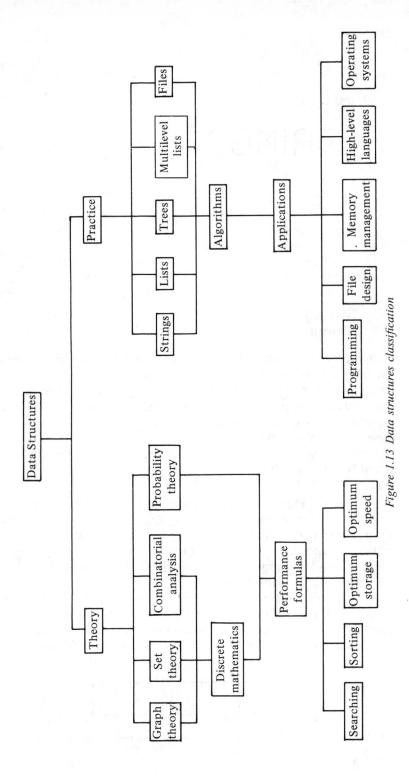

Figure 1.13 Data structures classification

2
STRINGS

2.1
Storing
Strings

Computers were originally designed for mathematical and scientific computations. They worked with numbers, using one memory location as a store for each number. It was soon realized that computers could have applications to data processing. Character data could be coded and stored in memory with one or more characters per word. To simplify our work for the present, we will assume that there is only one character in each memory location. Nor will we be concerned with the internal coding of the characters. Instead we will represent data in a pictorial form as shown in Figure 2.1.

A *string* is a series of characters stored in a contiguous area in memory. Strings may be of any length, including zero length. The memory region illustrated in Figure 2.1 stores a string 11 characters long. A string that contains no characters is called an *empty string* (or *null string*) and has a length of zero. An empty string is not the same as a string of blanks because the latter contains blank characters.

To understand some of the problems involved with the storage of strings, let us look at the string of names in Figure 2.2. How do we tell one name from the next name? Looking at the data we can decide that the first name is Bill Adams, the second A J Cook, and the third Ann Davis. But how

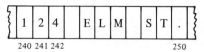

240 241 242   250

Figure 2.1 Storage of characters in memory

14

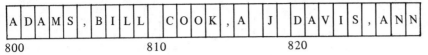

Figure 2.2 A string of names

would a computer separate the names? It cannot proceed on the basis of length because the first name is ten characters, the second eight, and the third nine. Could we instruct the computer to look for blanks? There seem to be blanks between the names but if we say that a blank ends a name, the computer would mistake the J in location 818 for a last name.

One method of separating strings is to insert a special character between the names to denote the end of a name. This could be any character that does *not* appear in a name, such as a dollar sign ($). Our string of names would now appear as shown in Figure 2.3.

An alternative method is to determine the longest substring (a single name) in the list and allot the required number of locations to each name. Names shorter than the span allowed would use blanks to fill up the extra space. Assuming that the longest name is 15 characters, our string would be stored as shown in Figure 2.4. (Notice that we no longer include the dollar signs.) If the first name is in location 800, the second will be in 815, the third in 830, and so on. In general, the nth name will be in location $800 + (n - 1)\,15$.

Comparing the storage methods shown in Figures 2.3 and 2.4, we see that although the method shown in Figure 2.4 uses a lot more space, it is easier to determine the location of a name. In the method shown in Figure 2.3 we must look at each location to see if it contains the dollar sign. A person can scan the entire figure and easily pick out the dollar signs, but a computer must proceed from location to location and compare each character.

A third strategy would be to keep a separate list of *pointers* to the end of each name (see the column labeled END in Figure 2.5). Knowing the end of one name would automatically tell us the beginning of the next name. To locate the first name, we would need a separate pointer which we will call HEAD. In Figure 2.5 we can use the information in HEAD and END to determine that the first name is in locations 800–809, the second in 810–817, and the third in 818–826. To make our information more

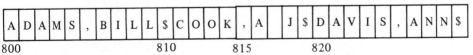

Figure 2.3 A string of names using a dollar sign ($) as a separator

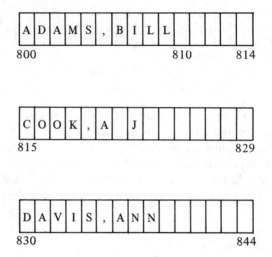

Figure 2.4 String containing substrings of 15 characters

complete, we could include a pointer to the last character in the string. In this example, it would have the value 826.

In addition to the pointers we could include a length field for each name. Storing the lengths in a table would save having to calculate them anew with each reference.

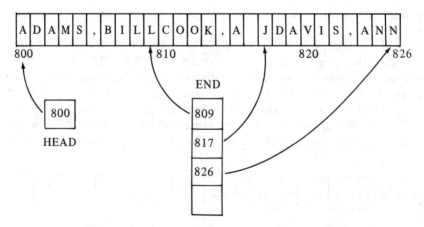

Figure 2.5 Using pointers to mark the end of name strings

EXERCISES

1. Redesign the string structure shown in Figure 2.5 so that the length of each string and the location of the last character are stored in END. Compare the amount of storage and calculation needed to determine the location in storage of each name.

2. Define the following terms:
   (a) String   (c) Field
   (b) Substring   (d) Pointer

3. Draw a flowchart of the algorithm for searching the string of Figure 2.4. Assume Jones, T. W. is the name to be matched against the strings in Figure 2.4.

4. Instead of using pointers to locate the end of each string as shown in Figure 2.5, show how it would appear with pointers to locate the beginning of each string. Do we need a HEAD pointer?

2.2
Operations
on Strings

Working with strings can be tedious if we must keep track of the exact location of each character. Some languages (SNOBOL and PL/I) allow the user to define and name strings. Then the user can refer to the name of the string without worrying about the way it is stored. We suggest that the programming exercises at the end of this section be done in a string manipulation language, if possible. For more information about the string-processing capabilities of PL/I and SNOBOL see Appendix A.

In this section we will refer to strings by a symbolic name rather than by a particular storage location. For example, the phrase

$$TITLE \leftarrow \text{'ONE MISTY NIGHT'}$$

denotes that TITLE is the name of the string ONE MISTY NIGHT. The arrow ($\leftarrow$) means "has the value of," and the single quote marks (') are used to surround the actual characters in the string. The null string could be represented by two single quote marks with no space in between ('').

The most common string operations are concatenation, insertion, deletion, replacement, pattern matching, and indexing. *Concatenation* is the joining together of two or more strings to form a new string. In this book we will represent concatenation with $\|$. Thus if FIRST $\leftarrow$ 'ANN ' and LAST $\leftarrow$ 'MARTIN', FIRST$\|$LAST is 'ANN MARTIN'. Notice that there is a space between the first and last name only because it was included as part of FIRST. If FNAME $\leftarrow$ 'MARY' and LNAME $\leftarrow$ 'COOPER', LNAME$\|$','$\|$FNAME would be the string 'COOPER,MARY'.

Insertion and deletion are actually special cases of replacement. *Replacement* involves searching for a particular sequence of characters, removing them from the string, and inserting other characters in their place. If the empty string is inserted, we call this operation *deletion*. Remember that the empty string is *not* a string of blank characters. Therefore deletion results in a string with a shorter length than the original string. Using set notation, the $\subset$ means "is a subset of" or "is included in." Therefore the statement

$$'2.00' \subset SALARY \leftarrow '2.50'$$

would be interpreted: If the string 2.00 is a substring of SALARY, the 2.00 is to be replaced by 2.50. Thus if SALARY was the string '$2.00', it would be changed to '$2.50'.

Insertion means replacing certain characters with themselves along with some other characters. For example, if SENT $\leftarrow$ 'IF I WISH I MAY GO.', 'WISH' $\subset$ SENT $\leftarrow$ 'WISH,' will insert a comma after the word WISH.

If we want to delete the question mark from LINE where LINE $\leftarrow$ 'HE DID IT?.', we would write '?' $\subset$ LINE $\leftarrow$ '' and the result is LINE $\leftarrow$ 'HE DID IT.'. Notice that LINE now contains 10 characters but it used to contain 11.

In a replacement operation the string is checked from left to right to see if it contains the specified characters. If it does, the characters are replaced. Otherwise nothing happens and the string remains the same. Sometimes we wish to know if a string contains certain characters, but do not wish to replace them with anything. This is called *pattern matching*, and the result should be either yes or no (true or false).

Frequently we may not be looking for a particular substring but for several different substrings. For example, we may wish to determine whether or not a character is alphabetic. The letter could be 'A', 'B', 'C', or any other letter of the alphabet. We will denote "or" with a vertical line (|). Thus to see if CHAR contains one of the letters I, J, K, L, M, or N, we would write

$$'I' \mid 'J' \mid 'K' \mid 'L' \mid 'M' \mid 'N' \subset CHAR$$

If CHAR $\leftarrow$ 'IT' or CHAR $\leftarrow$ '7J', the answer will be true; if CHAR $\leftarrow$ 'OUT', the answer is false.

Another operation on strings is indexing. The *index* gives the position of a specified substring in the string. If the substring is not part of the string, its index would be zero. For example, if PCARD $\leftarrow$ 'C WRITTEN BY CLARK FOSTER', the index of 'C' in PCARD is 1 since it is the first character. If there is more than one occurrence of the substring, the first substring is usually taken. Thus, the index of 'C' in PCARD is 1 and not 14. The index of 'WRITE' in PCARD is zero, since that word is not part of PCARD.

Frequently when working with strings we want to break a string into its components (substrings). Compilers do this operation when scanning a line of a program to pick out key words, such as READ or WRITE, or to determine variable names and constants. We will call this operation *separation*. Let us discuss informally the way compilers make use of separation.

Example   A compiler uses the rules of a language to determine the variables and operators. For example, suppose the rule says that operators are equal signs ($=$) and plus signs ($+$), and variables are letters and/or numbers. Then in the statement

$$X = A1 + B$$

the compiler, which begins scanning from the left, would find the variable X, the operator $=$, the variable A1, the operator $+$, and the variable B. Normally, the compiler would not include the blank following the A1 as part of the variable name. The scanning of A1 would probably proceed in the following way. Is A a letter or a number? It is a letter, so place it in a temporary location, mark it as the beginning of a variable, and go on to the next character in the string. Is 1 a letter or a number? It is a number, so place it next to A, making it part of the variable name. The next character is a blank which we will disregard and go on to the next character. Is the $+$ a letter or a number? It is an operator, so we have found the end of the variable. If the compiler proceeds in this manner when scanning B, it will not recognize the end of the variable until it reaches the end of the line. In some languages (for example, COBOL and SNOBOL) a blank terminates a word, so when the compiler reaches the first blank after a group of characters, it has found the end of a substring.

EXERCISES

1. If A ← '', B ← 'MULE', C ← 'OLD', and D ← 'MY', what is the result of the following?

    (a) A ∥ B

    (b) B ∥ A

    (c) D ∥ C ∥ B

    (d) 'U' ⊂ B ← 'I'

    (e) 'C' ⊂ C

    (f) 'ULE' ⊂ B ← C

    (g) D ∥' '∥B

    (h) B ⊂ B ← (B ∥ 'S')

    (i) index of 'Z' in D

    (j) index of 'D' in C

2. Choose a method for storing strings, describe it, and tell how you would con-

catenate any two strings to form a third. What would happen to the original strings?

3. Choose a method for storing strings, describe it, and tell how you would do a replacement operation. Remember that the number of characters removed is not always the same as the number of characters inserted. What will you do with the original string?

4. In the preceding example how would you determine if the *first* letter of a string is I, J, K, L, M, or N?

5. Using the operations described in this section, develop an algorithm that separates the units of X = A1 + B as in the preceding example.

2.3
Text
Editing

Many computer installations have a text editor to assist in preparing a program or data file for processing. The editor is a program that allows the user to make insertions and deletions to the text, to search for a particular phrase, or to print all or part of the text. To simplify working with the text, the editor divides the text into lines and gives each line a number. Then instead of saying "insert these characters," the user could say "insert this line" or "delete this line." Within each line, however, the editor works with individual characters. Thus the user can reference either an entire line (string of characters) or characters (substring) within the line. In this section we will discuss text editing and the way it utilizes the string structure. (An alternate approach to text editing appears in Section 10.3.)

First, since the text will consist of a collection of lines and each line is a string of characters, we will probably want to keep a record of the location and number of each line, as well as the number of characters in each line. For the moment, let us assume that the text is in memory as pictured in Figure 2.6. The lines are stored in consecutive locations. If we did not have the line table which shows location, number, and length, we would not be able to separate one line from the next. The line table can be constructed at the same time that the text is placed in memory. Problems arise as we start to edit the text.

Suppose, for example, we wish to delete line 120. If we eliminate its entry in the line table, in effect we are removing the line from the text since there is no way to reference locations 216–218. However, we are wasting space unless we can discover a method for reusing those locations.

Next, suppose we wish to change line 110 to read 'I = 1'. For the editor, this involves locating line 110 and replacing the '0' in location 215 with a '1'. But what would we do if we had wanted to change line 110 to 'I =

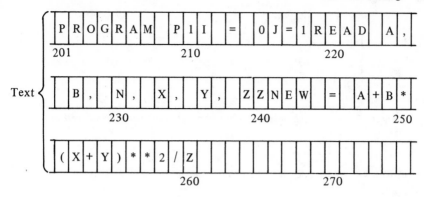

Figure 2.6 Storage of text in memory

35'? This new line contains six characters, while the previous line had only five characters. If we knew that locations 216–218 were not being used, we could expand line 110 and place the five in location 216. Or, if locations 216–218 were being used, we might consider moving the characters in 216–260 down one space (into locations 217–261) so the inserted character could go into 216. Moving characters takes computer time, and the more characters involved in the process, the longer the waiting time for the computer to respond to the user. An alternative to rearranging the strings in memory is to place the new line 110 in an unused area at the end of the text. In Figure 2.6 this area is in locations 261–266, and our line table would now appear as shown in Figure 2.7. Placing line 110 in locations 261–266 would mean that the editor had some way of knowing that those locations were available. Management of memory space is a major problem of data structures, and we will discuss it in a later chapter.

Another topic to consider is the insertion of a line (135) between lines 130 and 140. This requires finding storage locations in which to place the line and adding an entry to the line table. If we wish to keep the line table in order by line number, we will have to move all the entries down one place so that 135 can be inserted. In Chapter 3 we will discover ways to estimate

Line number	Location	Length
100	201	10
110	261	6
130	219	21
140	240	21

Figure 2.7 Line table after deleting line 120 and making line 110 into 'I = 35'

the amount of work required to move characters and will discuss alternate strategies.

EXERCISES

1. List the different problems discussed in Section 2.3 and give examples from the sample shown in Figure 2.6.

2. Obtain the users manual from your computer center and read about the text editor. Which commands perform insertion, deletion, and replacement?

3. Write a program to replace 'ing' with 'e' in a text of words. Use your program on a poem of your choice. What happens to the poem?

4. Design an algorithm for moving a string from one location in memory to another. Assume the string is stored in the way described in Figure 2.6. Will the algorithm work if the string in locations 213–240 is to be moved to locations 220–247? from 308–336 to 298–326?

3
LISTS

3.1
Dense
Lists

On binary computers the smallest unit of information is the *bit* (*binary digit*). To construct an *atom*[1] of data, we combine bits to form a bit string. The bits of an atom may be grouped and interpreted as either characters or numbers. In Chapter 2, where we worked with character strings, we disregarded the bits and concentrated on the characters they represented. Frequently the string structure included pointers to show the location of the characters in the string. Thus our structure consisted of *information bits* (the characters) and *pointer bits*.

Let us consider storing a telephone directory in a computer memory. Because of size limitations probably only a portion of the directory would fit. We will not concern ourselves with that now, but rather look at a data structure (the list) which assists in use of the directory. In general, a *list* is a collection of atoms. Each atom is linked to one or more atoms by a pointer or pointers. In a telephone directory an atom consists of three parts: name, address, and telephone number. The elements into which an atom is divided are called *fields*. If working with files, we call an atom a *record*, which is also a collection of fields. In an actual telephone directory the atoms are printed in line sequence. In the computer we would place the atoms in consecutive storage locations. In a *sequential* or *contiguous* data structure each atom is immediately adjacent to the next atom. A list stored in contiguous locations is called a *dense list* or a *linear list*. A dense list has no need for pointers because we can use an index to locate individual atoms.

---

[1]The terms atom and node will be used interchangeably. Atom is commonly used in programming languages, e.g., LISP; node is borrowed from graph theory.

The *index* is a number corresponding to the relative position of the atom in the list. The index of an atom is computed exactly the same way as the index of a symbol in a string. An atom occupying l storage locations and beginning at location b is illustrated by the dense list in Figure 3.1.

To store the telephone directory, we would decide on a specific order in which to place the fields within each atom. Suppose we put the name first, address second, and phone number third. Then our data would be stored as pictured in Figure 3.2. We could still use the index to locate individual fields within the atom. For example, if the first name starts in beginning location b, the second person's name is in $b + l$, where l is the number of locations required to store each atom. In general, the beginning location of the ith atom (where i is its index) is given by the formula:

$$\text{location} = b + (i - 1)l$$

Within each atom there is a name field of some length, an address field of some length, and a telephone field of some length. We must add these lengths to the location value to access a specific field. For example, if the name occupies four words, the location of the address field is $b + (i - 1)l + 4$. If the address occupies five words, the location of the phone field is $b + (i - 1)l + 9$.

Most programming languages provide a dense list structure so that it is not necessary to calculate the locations of atoms and fields. For example, DIMENSION A(100) is a FORTRAN declaration for a dense list. To ref-

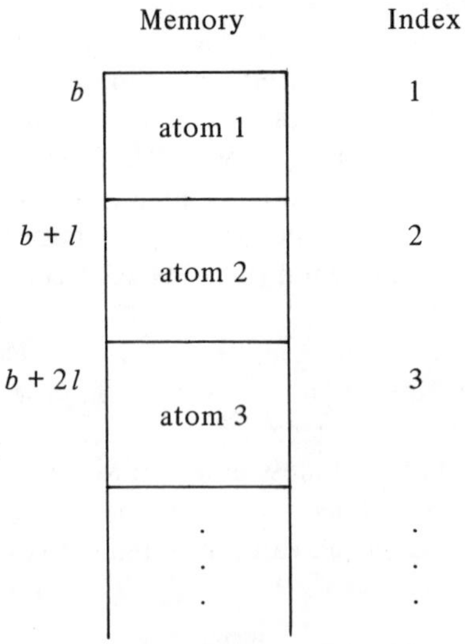

Figure 3.1 Dense list storage of atoms

	Memory	Index
b	name 1	1
	address 1	
	phone 1	
$b + l$	name 2	2
	address 2	
	phone 2	
$b + 2l$	name 3	3
	address 3	
	phone 3	
	.	.
	.	.
	.	.

Figure 3.2 Storage of telephone directory in contiguous locations

erence a particular element of A (100), we use a *subscript,* which is another name for an index. Then A(1) is the first atom, A(2) the second, and A(100) the last.

A *vector* is a dense list in which each element of the vector corresponds to an atom in the list. The *length* of a vector is defined as its total number of elements. For a computer, the definition of a vector or dense list is a natural operation. Knowing the length of a vector means that the required number of memory locations can be set aside, and knowing the beginning location and index means that any element can be referenced. Our telephone directory is not a vector in the strict sense because we would like to be able to reference the individual fields within an atom. Therefore, we should probably classify the directory as an array. In its simplest form an *array* is a collection of vectors in which each vector has the same length. Thus the simplest array (*two-dimensional*) has two dimensions, m and n, where m is the number of vectors in the array and n is the length of each vector. If $n = 1$ (each vector consists of one element), the structure is a vector and is also termed a *one-dimensional array*. A *three-dimensional array* is a collection of two-dimensional arrays, each of which has the same m and n dimensions. We can continue in this manner to define arrays of any dimension.

Normally we think of the telephone directory as it is represented in Figure 3.3; each line contains one person's name, address, and telephone number. However, since one word on a computer is not big enough to hold all that information, we could store it as shown in Figure 3.2. Looking at

Index

.   .

.   .

.   .

10528   Landry, S. G.   512 Foxmoor   233-2050
10529   Louis, A. R.   224 Lippi   235-7305

.   .

.   .

.   .

18611   Morris, A. L.   118 Tennessee   232-7115

.   .

.   .

.   .

Figure 3.3 Segment of a telephone directory

Figure 3.3, we see that any index references an entire line of the directory. If we want only the phone number, we go to the third column of that line. Thus to reference a particular field we need to know two values: line number (index) and column number. These values are usually enclosed in parentheses and separated by a comma. Thus the reference to A. R. Louis's phone number would be (10529,3), since we usually write the line number first and the phone number is in column three.

Logically we picture a two-dimensional array as a rectangle with rows and columns. We reference each element with two values which tell its row and its column number. For example, a 2 × 3 array A (two rows and three columns) would be pictured as shown in Figure 3.4. Each box represents a single element of the array. Altogether there are six (2 × 3) elements. Physically, the array would be stored in a sequential manner. Figure 3.5 contrasts the storage of the 2 × 3 array with the storage of a vector of six elements. It also shows two possible ways of storing the array: by columns as in (b) or by rows as in (c). If an array is stored by columns, we say it is stored in *column-major order* and if by rows, *row-major order.* FORTRAN stores its arrays in column-major order, while PL/I and COBOL store theirs in row-major order.

A language that allows the definition of two, three, or higher multi-dimensional arrays stores them as dense lists. The programmer uses two (or more) subscripts to reference an element, but the computer must cal-

| A(1, 1) | A(1, 2) | A(1, 3) |
| A(2, 1) | A(2, 2) | A(2, 3) |

Figure 3.4 Logical representation of two by three array A

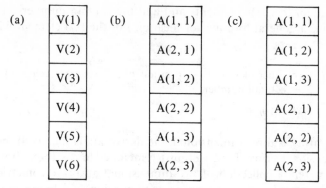

Figure 3.5 Comparison of a vector V and two ways to store a two by three array A

culate the exact location. To do this the computer must know whether the array is stored by column-major or row-major order, and must also know the subscripts and the maximum dimensions of the array. For example, if the array is stored by rows as shown in Figure 3.5 (c), element A(1,2) is in the second position, A(1,3) in the third, and so on. The location of A(i,j) is $3(i - 1) + j$, where 3 is the number of columns in the array. Thus for A(1,1), $3(1 - 1) + 1 = 1$, which means that A(1,1) is in the first location. The element A(2,1) is in the fourth position since $3(2 - 1) + 1 = 4$, and A(2,3) is in the sixth position [$3(2 - 1) + 3 = 6$]. In general, for an array in row-major order whose maximum subscripts are m and n (where m is the number of rows and n is the number of columns), the location l of the (i,j) element relative to the first element is:

$$l = n(i - 1) + j$$

To compute the actual address of the (i,j) element, we would add l to the location of the first element and subtract 1.

The formula for l is derived from the manner in which the array is stored. For a two-dimensional array A whose largest element is A(m,n), there are n elements in each row. If the array is stored by rows, A(1,1), A(1,2), through A(1,n) precede any element in row 2 [A(2,1) for example]. Thus to find the location of an element in row 2 we must go down at least n positions in the list. A(2,1) will be in position $n + 1$; A(2,2) in position $n + 2$; and in general, A(2,i) will be in position $n + i$. To find any element in row 3 we must count down at least $2n$ elements, since there are n elements in the first row and n elements in the second. In general, to find an element A(i,j) (which is in row i, column j), we must skip over the first $i - 1$ rows which contain $(i - 1)n$ elements and add the column numbers of the element. Thus a general formula for location l of the (i,j) element within the array is:

l = (number of rows to skip minus one) $\cdot$ (size of each row)
    + column number

$l = (i - 1)n + j$

   If the array is three-dimensional, the derivation is similar to that of the two-dimensional array. First we must remember that a three-dimensional array is merely a collection of two-dimensional arrays. Geometrically the three-dimensional array is a cubic configuration which is composed of planes. Each plane contains elements in rows and columns (see Figure 3.6). Figure 3.7 illustrates the manner in which a three-dimensional array is stored in memory by rows. This means that the first subscript has the slowest variation—all the elements with a first subscript of 1 come before those with a first subscript of 2. To find an element in the second plane, we would have to go down six storage locations to skip over elements in the first plane. If the largest element in the array is $B(p,m,n)$, this means skipping over $m \cdot n$ elements. The product $m \cdot n$ is the size of the first plane. To locate something in the ith row of that plane, we would skip over $(i - 1)n$ elements since n tells the number of elements in each row of the plane. The complete formula for the location l of element $B(k,i,j)$, where B is stored by rows, is:

$$l = (k - 1)m \cdot n + (i - 1)n + j \tag{3.1}$$

which says that the element is in the kth plane (so we skip over $(k - 1)m \cdot n$ elements), row i (so we go down $i - 1$ rows of n elements each), and column j.

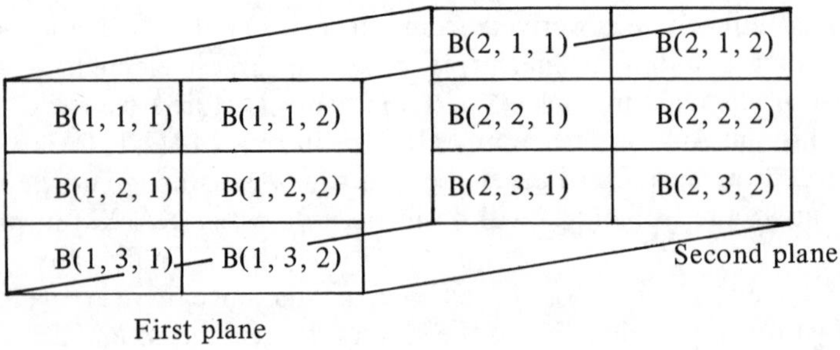

First plane

Figure 3.6 Geometric representation of a three-dimensional array

Location	Element
1	B(1, 1, 1) ⎤
2	B(1, 1, 2) ⎥
3	B(1, 2, 1) ⎥ First plane
4	B(1, 2, 2) ⎥
5	B(1, 3, 1) ⎥
6	B(1, 3, 2) ⎦
7	B(2, 1, 1) ⎤
8	B(2, 1, 2) ⎥
9	B(2, 2, 1) ⎥ Second plane
10	B(2, 2, 2) ⎥
11	B(2, 3, 1) ⎥
12	B(2, 3, 2) ⎦

Figure 3.7 Storing a three-dimensional array by rows

Example Compute the location of B(1,2,1). From the example in Figure 3.7 we see that the answer should be 3. The largest element of B is B(2,3,2), so $p = 2$, $m = 3$, and $n = 2$. Also, $k = 1$, $i = 2$, and $j = 1$.

$$l = (k - 1) m \cdot n + (i - 1)n + j$$
$$= (1 - 1)3 \cdot 2 + (2 - 1)2 + 1$$
$$= 0 \cdot 6 + 1 \cdot 2 + 1$$
$$= 3$$

A dense list, whether it is a vector or an array, contains no pointers to specific elements because an element's location can be computed relative to the beginning of the list. We must remember only the appropriate formula and the location of the first element. A structure that contains pointers wastes memory because pointers are not useful data. The function of a pointer is to assist in handling information. Therefore, to utilize memory efficiently, it is desirable to minimize the size and number of pointer fields.

A measure of a structure's memory utilization is its density. *Density* is the ratio of the number of information bits to the total number of bits:

$$\text{density} = \frac{\text{number of information bits}}{\text{total number of bits}}$$

A dense list has density 1.0. The total number of bits exactly equals the number of information bits; there are no pointers. A dense list structure is the best utilization of memory. Why then do we need other structures?

A dense list is useful for data that does not change frequently. Suppose we want to add two new names to the telephone directory. If the names are Aaron and Zybicki, we would probably have little trouble since these names conveniently fall near the beginning and the end of the list. Problems will arise, however, because we wish to maintain order in the directory.

For example, suppose we wish to include the new entry, Lee, R. T., 550 Palm Ave., 235-1020, in our computer memory pictured in Figure 3.3. As you can see, this entry must be inserted between 10528 and 10529. The only way to place the new entry in the dense list is to move every entry from 10529 to the last entry into positions 10530 on down. This would leave 10529 vacant for the new entry.

Alternately, suppose that A. L. Morris moves out of town. The memory location occupied by index 18611 should now become available space. How are we to delete this entry? The simple solution is to move all the items below 18611 up one position so that the atom with index 18612 will now have an index of 18611. Often, however, the entry is merely marked deleted, and the actual movement takes place when many similar requests are fulfilled. One way to mark or flag the entry would be either to change the name to all blanks or to make the telephone number 000-0000. Some lists have a special bit reserved with each atom to denote whether or not the atom is valid.

If we are going to move atoms to insert and delete entries, let us estimate the average number of moves made. Suppose we have a list with n entries and wish to delete the atom with index k. We would have to move $n - k$ entries to fill the k vacant spot. If $n = 8$ and $k = 5$ as shown in Figure 3.8,

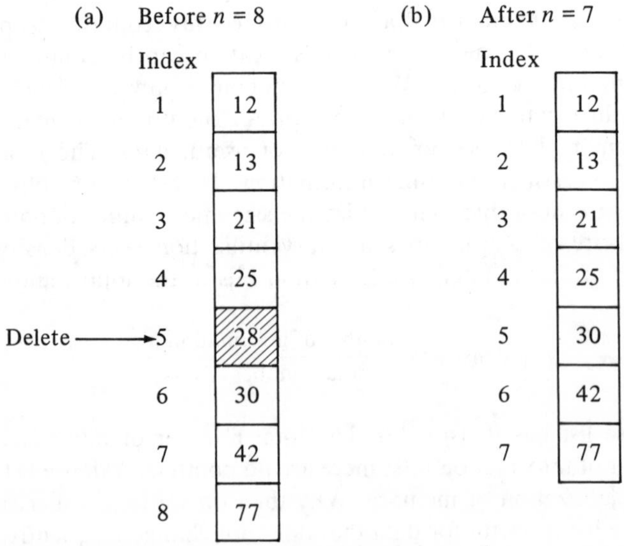

Figure 3.8 Deletion of atom 5 from a list

three atoms (indexes 6, 7, and 8) are moved. Also, as a result of the move, the value of n has decreased by one.

If we wish to insert an atom at position k in a list of n elements, $n - k + 1$ moves are necessary. For example, to insert the value 24 into the list in Figure 3.9, the atoms with indexes 4 through 8 must be moved into positions 5 through 9. Then 24 is inserted and has index 4. As with the deletion operation, we assume movement takes place at the end of the list. After an insertion, the value of n increases by one. This means that an insertion may cause an *overflow* if the list exceeds the available space. We will discuss overflow later.

The average number of moves made during an insertion or deletion depends not only on the number of items to move but also on the probability that the insertion or deletion will take place at a particular location. If the operation occurs near the end of the list, fewer elements need to be moved than if the operation occurs near the beginning. However, if most insertions or deletions occur near the beginning, the average will be close to n (n is the total number of elements in the list). In general, the average number of moves during an insertion (m_i) is given by the equation:

$$\text{Insertion: } m_i = \sum_{k=1}^{n} (n - k + 1) \cdot p_k$$

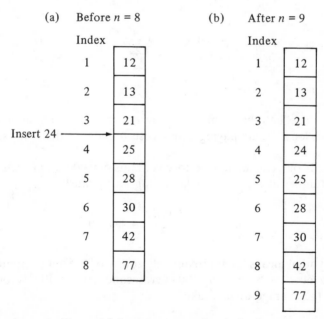

Figure 3.9 Insertion into index 4 of a list

where p_k is the probability of inserting an atom into location k.

The average number of moves during a deletion (m_d) is given by the equation:

$$\text{Deletion: } m_d = \sum_{k=1}^{n} (n - k) \cdot p_k$$

where p_k is the probability of deleting the kth atom. The probability of accessing any atom in an insertion or deletion operation depends on many factors, such as the data in the list, the reason for updating an item, and so on. Unless we know otherwise, we may reasonably assume that every atom is equally likely to be accessed. That is, the probability of accessing any atom out of a total of n is $1/n$ ($p_k = 1/n$ for all k). Then we may compute m_i and m_d:

$$m_i = \sum_{k=1}^{n} (n - k + 1)\frac{1}{n} = \frac{1}{n} \sum_{k=1}^{n} (n - k + 1)$$

$$= \frac{1}{n}\left[\sum_{k=1}^{n} (n + 1) - \sum_{k=1}^{n} k \right]$$

$$= \frac{n(n + 1)}{n} - \frac{1}{n} \cdot \frac{n(n + 1)}{2} = n + 1 - \frac{n + 1}{2} = \frac{n + 1}{2}$$

$$m_d = \sum_{k=1}^{n} (n - k)\frac{1}{n} = \frac{1}{n} \sum_{k=1}^{n} n - \frac{1}{n} \sum_{k=1}^{n} k = n - \frac{n(n + 1)}{2n}$$

$$= n - \frac{n + 1}{2} = \frac{n - 1}{2}$$

On the average, half the list must be moved during an insertion or deletion. If the list is long, we are paying a high cost to update a dense list structure.

Example   If our telephone directory contains 500,000 atoms, what is the average number of moves to make during an update?

$$m_d \approx m_i \approx \frac{500,000}{2} = 250,000$$

(The $\approx$ symbol means "is approximately equal to.") If our computer is fast enough to move one atom every 100 microseconds (100×10^{-6} second), how long will the average update take?

$$\text{move time} \approx (100 \times 10^{-6} \text{ sec.}) \cdot (250,000) = 25 \text{ sec.}$$

If the typical update operation involves 1% of the atoms in the directory, how much computer time is required to perform the update?

$$\text{update time} = (.01)(500,000)(25 \text{ sec.}) \approx 35 \text{ hours}$$

The previous example shows how costly a dense list structure may be even though it utilizes memory efficiently. In Section 3.2 we will see how the use of pointers can eliminate the necessity to move information around in memory.

EXERCISES

1. If a list contains 32 atoms, how many bits are needed to point to any one of the atoms? In other words, how many bits long must the index be? (*Hint:* A vector of length 128 needs an index of seven bits.) How many bits are needed for the index of a list whose length is 8192; of length 10,000?

2. Define the following terms:
   (a) List   (d) Index   (f) Array
   (b) Dense list   (e) Vector   (g) Subscript
   (c) Density

3. Derive a formula for the location (index) of an element of a two-dimensional array C stored in column-major order. The maximum subscripts of C are C(4, 5). Sketch a picture of the order in which the elements of C are placed in memory.

4. Derive a formula for the location of an element of a three-dimensional array X stored in column-major order. The maximum subscripts of X are $X(s_1, s_2, s_3)$. Explain the components of the formula.

5. In general, the correspondence between the subscripts $(j_1, j_2, \ldots, j_n)$ of an n-dimensional array stored in row-major order is given by the following formula. (The maximum subscripts of the array are $A(d_1, d_2, \ldots, d_n)$.)

$$\text{location} = \sum_{r=1}^{n-1} (j_r - 1) \prod_{s=r}^{n-1} d_{s+1} + j_n$$

First, assume $n = 3$ and show that this formula produces the one in the text (3.1) if p is substituted for d_1, m for d_2, n for d_3, and so on. Then explain in general terms the components of the formula.

$$\textit{Note:} \prod_{s=r}^{n-1} d_{s+1} = d_{r+1} \cdot d_{r+2} \cdot d_{r+3} \cdots d_n \quad \text{(pi product)}$$

6. Derive a formula for the location (index) of the element of an array stored in row-major order whose subscripts may be positive, negative, or zero. The declaration of the array is $A[l_1:u_1, l_2:u_2, l_3:u_3, \ldots, l_n:u_n]$, where l_i is the lowest value of the ith subscript, and u_i is the largest value of the ith subscript.

For example, A[2:3, −3:0] defines an array with eight elements A[2, −3] through A[3, 0] (see Exercise 5).

7. What are the assumptions involved in computing the average number of moves made to update a dense list? Discuss ways to reduce the overhead of insertion and deletion by keeping an auxiliary dense list to store the update atoms.

8. Calculate the location of A(3, 6, 4) of an array in row-major order whose maximum subscript is A(10, 20, 5). What would its position be if the maximum subscripts were not known?

9. What problems are encountered in looking up a person's name whose telephone number is known? What if the number is not in the directory?

10. Write a computer program which will input the values of n, d_1, d_2, . . . , d_n and will compute the location of any element $A(j_1, j_2, \ldots, j_n)$. Use the formula in Exercise 5.

3.2
Linked
Lists

Although the dense list is a very simple structure, it does have some disadvantages. It is difficult to make insertions or deletions if the list must be kept in order. Another problem arises if we try to change the size or shape of the list. Suppose, for example, we have a list that occupies 200 locations. This means that somewhere in memory there are 200 contiguous locations which we have set aside for the list. What if we wish to double the size of the list? In most cases we cannot use the 200 locations which follow the list, because they probably are reserved for other data. We cannot use just any 200 locations because our list must be contiguous. In some programming languages (FORTRAN and COBOL) expanding a list means recompiling the program to allocate the exact number of requested locations. Other languages (ALGOL, APL, and PL/I) allow the programmer to change the size of lists or arrays during execution. The processor of the language reserves a large block of memory for defining or redefining data structures as requested by the programmer.

To make a list more flexible and easier to update, we can include a pointer (link) with each atom in the list. In a *linked list* each atom contains a pointer which tells the location of the next atom; the pointer eliminates the need to store the atoms of a list in a contiguous memory region. To illustrate how pointers are used to logically connect the elements in a list, we will consider a portion of the telephone directory. We will begin with a large block of memory and will assume that each atom occupies 13 locations (five each for name and address, two for phone number, and one for pointer). Initially the atoms and pointers are in the same order (see Figure

3.10). Basically our structure is a dense list with a pointer field included. The hyphen (-) in the last pointer field represents the end of the list. It is called the *nil pointer* because it points to nil or nothing. In the computer we would use a negative number, zero, or anything that is not a valid pointer. The first atom in the list is special and we will discuss it shortly.

First, let us add a name to the directory. We can place it at the end of the list (beginning in location 2078) and change pointers so it is in the correct alphabetical position. For example, suppose the entry is Lang, Al, 311 Moss, 236-1111. To decide where the name should go, we begin with the first name which is Abel. Since Lang does not come before Abel, we look at Abel's pointer to see which name comes next. The next name is in the next set of memory locations 2013–2025. Since Lang does not come before Baker, we use Baker's pointer to go on to Carter. Lang does not come before Carter, but on going to the next name we find that Lang does belong before Minte. This means that Lang's pointer should be 2039. Now we must change Carter's pointer so that it leads to Lang. The updated pointers and inserted name appear in Figure 3.11. Notice that the list no longer appears in alphabetical order as it does in Figure 3.10. However, the pointers keep the order intact.

Let us now delete Al Minte from the list. We must first locate his name and find the atom which points to him. Currently, Al Lang's pointer (2039) references Al Minte, and Al Minte's pointer is 2052. To delete Minte, we must change Lang's pointer to 2052; this is demonstrated in Figure 3.12. Even though Minte's name appears in the list, there is no pointer to it and locations 2039–2051 are available for an insertion. We now need to mark these locations so they may be used later. We could keep a list of free locations or we could make the phone number 000-0000. We will discuss ways to recover unused memory locations in Chapter 9.

The last atom in a linked list has a nil pointer to show that no atom follows it, so it is frequently called the *tail.* The first atom is the *head* of the list and is pointed to by a separate atom called the HEADER. The HEADER may contain additional information about the list, such as name,

Location	Information			Pointer
2000	ABEL, J. G.	110 OAKLEAF	236-4010	2013
2013	BAKER, SUE	409 SUNSET	784-1182	2026
2026	CARTER, L. H.	17 BERNAY	785-1365	2039
2039	MINTE, AL	204 PINE	236-7295	2052
2052	PONT, M. R.	1 MARKET	480-1027	2065
2065	SANDS, T. H.	671 FIRST	784-8240	–

Figure 3.10 Telephone directory with pointers

Location	Information			Pointer
2000	ABEL, J. G.	110 OAKLEAF	236-4010	2013
2013	BAKER, SUE	409 SUNSET	784-1182	2026
2026	CARTER, L. H.	17 BERNAY	785-1365	2078
2039	MINTE, AL	204 PINE	236-7295	2052
2052	PONT, M. R.	1 MARKET	480-1027	2065
2065	SANDS, T. H.	671 FIRST	784-8240	–
2078	LANG, AL	311 MOSS	236-1111	2039

Figure 3.11 Telephone directory after inserting Lang

creation date, or length. The lists in Figures 3.10 through 3.12 should contain the following HEADER.

	Title	Pointer
HEADER	Telephone Directory	2000

If insertions or deletions occur at the head of the list, we will have to change the HEADER pointer. If the entire list is deleted, the HEADER will be retained. Its pointer field will be nil, but as long as the HEADER is there the list is still available for use.

Let us describe how pointers generally change during an insertion or deletion. We assume that $atom_i$ has $pointer_i$ and is logically followed by $atom_{i+1}$ with $pointer_{i+1}$. In other words, $pointer_i$ tells the location of $atom_{i+1}$. To insert $atom_{new}$ between $atom_i$ and $atom_{i+1}$, we must do the following. The HEADER atom locates the beginning of the linked list. We follow the pointers until $atom_i$ is reached. At this point the INSERT algorithm below is performed.

INSERT: $atom_{new}$: $pointer_{new} \leftarrow pointer_i$

$pointer_i \leftarrow$ location of $atom_{new}$

Location	Information			Pointer	
2000	ABEL, J. G.	110 OAKLEAF	236-4010	2013	
2013	BAKER, SUE	409 SUNSET	784-1182	2026	
2026	CARTER, L. H.	17 BERNAY	785-1365	2078	
2039	~~MINTE, AL~~	~~204 PINE~~	~~236-7295~~	~~2052~~	Available
2052	PONT, M. R.	1 MARKET	480-1027	2065	space
2065	SANDS, T. H.	671 FIRST	784-8240	–	
2078	LANG, AL	311 MOSS	236-1111	2052	

Figure 3.12 Telephone directory after deleting Minte

(a)   Before

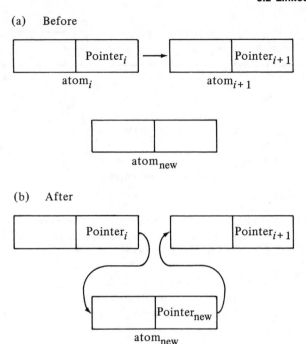

(b)   After

Figure 3.13 Insertion of atom$_{new}$ between atom$_i$ and atom$_{i+1}$

Figure 3.13 illustrates the effects of the INSERT algorithm.

Deletions are handled in a similar manner. To delete atom$_i$ we locate atom$_i$ and its predecessor atom$_{i-1}$ and perform the DELETE algorithm.

$$\text{DELETE: atom}_i: \text{pointer}_{i-1} \leftarrow \text{pointer}_i$$

Figure 3.14 illustrates the effects of the DELETE algorithm. The dotted line represents the locations freed by the deletion.

The insertion and deletion algorithms do not include specific steps for finding the desired atom. These steps are performed by the FIND algorithm.

FIND X 1. Let X be the atom to locate.

2. POINTER is initially set to the value contained in HEADER.

3. Repeat while POINTER not equal to NIL:
    (a) If X equals the atom located by POINTER, exit from FIND and return the value of POINTER.
    (b) Otherwise, replace POINTER by the pointer value contained in the tested atom.

(a)   Before

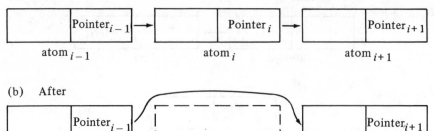

(b)   After

Figure 3.14 Deletion of atom$_i$

4.   POINTER equals NIL implies we have reached the end of the list without finding the desired atom X. Exit from FIND and return NIL as the value of POINTER.

A linked list requires more storage and more complex algorithms than a dense list. For example, if the linked list representation of the telephone directory requires five words for the name, five for the address, two for the phone number, and one for the pointer, we can compute the density as:

$$\text{density} = \frac{5 + 5 + 2}{5 + 5 + 2 + 1} = .923$$

The density of the dense list is 1.0, so the linked list uses more storage. However, update operations do not require us to move any atoms. At most we need to change two pointers.

We have not yet considered the amount of time required to search a list for an item that should be deleted, or to locate the place where an item should be inserted. On the average, assuming that the probability of updating any atom is equally likely, we should expect to read through half the list. Whether we use a dense list or a linked list structure, we will have to include a search as part of the update operation. The real advantage of a linked list is that we need not move the atoms around the way we must with a dense list. (Searching is discussed in Chapter 8.)

EXERCISES

1. Why are linked lists needed and used in spite of their cost in memory utilization?

2. What is the purpose of the HEADER atom? What happens if there is no HEADER and the list is empty?

3. How do we determine the number of bits needed in the pointer field of an atom?

4. Given a telephone directory as described in the text, write an algorithm (flow-chart) which will determine the location of a particular name in the directory. If the name does not appear, print a message to that effect. On the average, how many names will have to be read before we find the one we are looking for?

5. Given a telephone directory as described in the text and a telephone number, write an algorithm (flowchart) which will produce the name of the person belonging to that number. If there is no such number in the directory, write a message to that effect. How does this algorithm differ from the one in Exercise 4?

6. Assuming that it is equally likely to access any atom in a linked list, show that on the average we must examine $n/2$ atoms before finding the one we are seeking. (The total number of atoms is n.)

7. Write a program which will store and update a small telephone directory in memory in the form of a linked list. Print the original directory. Then make some insertions and deletions and print the final directory. Use any format for input and output you desire.

3.3
Multilinked
Lists

Often a single pointer with each atom is not enough. For example, in the telephone directory the pointers ordered the names alphabetically. How would we tackle the problem of finding a person's name if given only the number? Searching would not be an easy task. We would have to read every entry in the directory just to discover that the number is not listed. Lest we run the telephone directory into the ground, let us discuss a similar problem in a different field. The First National Bank of Boulder Creek has numerous accounts. To keep the customers happy the bank does business using the customer's name. However, the bookkeeping department has to deal with the Federal Reserve Bank and works entirely with account numbers. Therefore they need a way to provide easy access to the accounts—either by account number or by customer name. A solution to this problem is to use a *multilinked list,* a list in which each atom has two or more pointers. Let us see how pointers with each atom can provide the type of data structure this bank needs.

Initially let us suppose that the accounts have been alphabetized and stored in memory. To simplify matters, we will refer to the atoms by index rather than by memory location and will make the account numbers four digits. A sample listing of the accounts appears in Figure 3.15. We will first discuss the two pointer fields: alpha pointers and account pointers.

The alpha pointers will show the alphabetical listing of customers. Initially, each alpha pointer is one more than the index of the atom, since

Index	Name	Alpha pointer	Account	Account pointer
1	ADAMS, D. A.		9089	
2	BAKER, J. R.		1195	
3	CARR, D. M.		1034	
4	DAVIS, J. H.		3782	
5	MILLER, I. M.		6217	

Figure 3.15 Initial listing of customer accounts

the names are in alphabetical order. After several insertions or deletions this may no longer be true. The account pointers are more difficult to define, except in this short example where we could do it by inspection. If the list were longer, it would be almost impossible to do by hand. However, since each account has an index to tell its location, we can use the index and account numbers to determine the account pointers.

We will first order the accounts numerically, keeping the index with each account number. The result is shown in Figure 3.16. From it we can determine the account pointers. Each account should be linked to the one following it, as represented by the arrows. Account 9089 has no successor, so its pointer will be nil. Figure 3.17 shows the complete listing of customer accounts with alpha and account pointers. The two HEADERS show the first element in each ordering.

Insertions and deletions require more effort with the multilinked list than with the singly linked list because the former has more pointers to change (see Exercises 1 and 2 at the end of this section). The multilinked list also requires more memory for pointers. However, pointers provide an alternative to having two copies of the lists, each in a different order. And we can work with the accounts in either alphabetical or numerical order.

The multilinked list is also used to keep track of an atom's predecessor as well as its successor. This means that we would have a *forward pointer*

Index	Account
3	1034
2	1195
4	3782
5	6217
1	9089
–	

Figure 3.16 Accounts with index listed in ascending order

Alpha header	1		Account header	3	

Index	Name	Alpha pointer	Account	Account pointer
1	ADAMS, D. A.	2	9089	–
2	BAKER, J. R.	3	1195	4
3	CARR, D. M.	4	1034	2
4	DAVIS, J. H.	5	3782	5
5	MILLER, I. M.	–	6217	1

Figure 3.17 Final listing of customer accounts

to show the atom which follows and a *backward pointer* to show the predecessor. This type of list is called a *doubly linked list.* Forward and backward pointers are extremely useful in an update operation. During an insertion (pictured in Figure 3.13) we determined the pointer for the new atom by deciding that it should precede $atom_{i+1}$. We also had to locate $atom_i$, which pointed to $atom_{i+1}$ (but now must point to the inserted atom). In a deletion (Figure 3.14) we also had to determine the location of the atom preceding the one to be deleted. If we had used backward pointers and had found the atom to delete, we would have known its predecessor.

Figure 3.18 shows the representation of a doubly linked list. In general, the forward pointer of $atom_{i-1}$ is the same as the backward pointer of $atom_{i+1}$; that is, they both point to $atom_i$. The first atom has a nil backward pointer and the last atom has a nil forward pointer. The HEADER points to the first atom and the TAIL points to the last.

Throughout our discussion all the lists have been *linear* with a beginning (first) element and an end (last) element. An alternate kind of list, whether it has single or multiple links, is the *circular list* or *ring.* In this structure the last element points to the first, and there is no nil pointer (see Figure 3.19). Often a circular list is used to implement a work area or buffer for input and output. We store data in the first area (or first few areas) and can continue storing data until we are back at the beginning of the list. Concurrently, while data is being placed in the area, it can be removed from the beginning. Thus the circular nature of the ring allows the same memory area to be reused. Of course we must be careful not to let the ring overflow by writing new data over old data before it can be used.

To help visualize the nature of the circular list, consider an automatic bottling machine. The empty bottles approach the machine on a linear conveyor belt. As they pass into the filling machine, they enter a circular conveyor belt. While moving around this ring the bottles are filled, hopefully before they get back to the starting point. After they are filled the

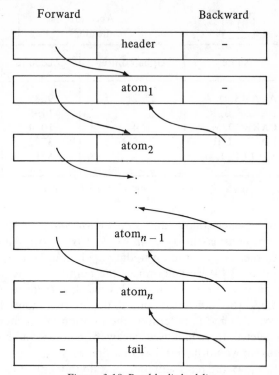

Figure 3.18 Doubly linked list

bottles are removed from the circular ring and placed on another linear conveyor belt which proceeds to the capping machine. Empty bottles cannot enter the filling machine faster than filled ones can be removed. Filled bottles cannot be removed faster from the machine than empty ones can enter. The problems and advantages of a circular bottling machine correspond in an analogous fashion to those of circular list structures in a computer.

EXERCISES

1. Write an algorithm (flowchart) to insert atoms into a multilinked list, such as the bank's customer accounts.

2. Write an algorithm (flowchart) to delete atoms from the multilinked bank customer account list.

3. How does the algorithm for insertion and deletion of atoms from a ring differ from the algorithm for insertion and deletion of atoms from a linked list?

4. If the customer's name requires 240 bits, the account number 30 bits, and the

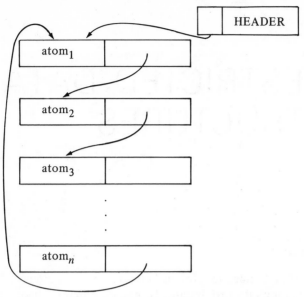

Figure 3.19 Circular list (ring)

pointers 16 bits each, compute the density of the multilinked list structure of the First National Bank pictured in Figure 3.17. What is the density for a list of 100 accounts? of 500 accounts?

5. *Backtracking* is the operation of scanning a list in reverse (finding successive backward pointers). Explain the difference between backtracking using a dense list, a singly linked list with forward pointers, and a doubly linked list.

4
RESTRICTED DATA STRUCTURES

4.1
Queues

The dense list and linked list structures discussed in Chapter 3 require time and programming effort to update. To update a dense list of length n requires both searching and moving approximately $n/2$ items, while a linked list requires only search time. (Remember that these averages assume equally likely access for any atom.) Regardless of the list's structure, it is time-consuming to scan the list.

How can we decrease the amount of scanning required? To do so we must be willing to give up something in exchange for time and/or memory. If we are willing to access only the first and last atoms of a list, our structure is either a queue or a deque. A *queue* is a list that allows insertion of atoms at one end and deletion of atoms at the opposite end. A *deque* (double-ended queue) allows insertion and deletion of atoms at both ends of the list. A deque is a more general structure than a queue. Since a deque has limited usage in computer science, we will discuss it later.

A queue is a first-in, first-out (FIFO) structure needed for many applications of computer science. Fortunately, examples from everyday experience help us to understand queues. Every time you get in a line for service at a grocery store, bank, and so on, you are actually entering a queue. You gradually move toward the head of the queue as those in front of you finish their business and leave. Newcomers enter the line behind you, at the tail of the queue.

Most computer operating systems form queues at many places throughout the system. An example would be an output queue. Normally, all the output produced in a single job resides on a disk until a printer is available. The entire collection of jobs waiting to be printed forms an output queue.

Assuming a nonpriority system and only one printer, the first job that finishes outputting information is the first one printed. Depending upon the speed of the printer and the amount of printing, the size of the queue grows or contracts. At times there may be no jobs on the queue; other times there may be so many jobs that the Central Processing Unit (CPU) must suspend operations.

How does the operating system implement the queue? There are many possible methods, several of which we will examine. One method is to reserve a block of memory that is big enough to hold the largest expected queue and to require the system to signal a queue overflow. The essential information that the queue must contain is a job identifier and a location of the job's output, although the queue may have other information, such as the number of lines of output. Initially the first jobs are placed at the beginning of the memory block. When the printer is free, the job removed from the queue is at the head of the list. Instead of moving all entries forward to close up the space left by the first one, we advance the HEAD pointer. The TAIL pointer shows the location of the last entry in the queue and any additions must follow it. Figure 4.1 (a) shows the original queue; 4.1 (b) illustrates the result of removing job X167 from the queue; and 4.1 (c) shows the addition of two new jobs to the queue. In Figure 4.1 (d) the first three entries of the memory block are vacant but will not be used because the queue is gradually moving to the end of the area. If nothing is done, it will appear that the queue has overflowed when the reserved memory area is not nearly full. A solution to this problem would be to move all the entries to the head of the list whenever an attempt is made to store something beyond the designated area. Figure 4.2 illustrates an example of this solution.

An alternate solution that eliminates moving the queue around would be to make the queue memory area into a circular list. If an entry would cause an overflow, place it at the beginning of the area. Thus the end of the queue "comes before" the beginning if we examine the memory addresses involved. Logically, though, the end follows the beginning.[1] (See Figure 4.3.) With this scheme we still need to worry about overflow, which would occur if the TAIL moved down and covered up the HEAD.

In either solution the update operations are similar. Basically they are given by the following algorithms. (The name QUEUE refers to the entire storage area of the queue; QUEUE[i] is the ith atom.)

INSERT   Increment TAIL pointer to next location: TAIL ← TAIL + 1;
                 Insert new entry into location: QUEUE[TAIL] ← new entry;

---

[1]Typically, such bookkeeping is simplified by the use of modular arithmetic.

(a) Original queue

	Index	Job	Location
1 (HEAD)	1	X167	34201
	2	BJ20	20684
	3	ZP11	77413
3 (TAIL)	4		
	5		
	6		

(b) One deletion

	Index	Job	Location
2 (HEAD)	1		
	2	BJ20	20684
	3	ZP11	77413
3 (TAIL)	4		
	5		
	6		

(c) Two insertions

	Index	Job	Location
2 (HEAD)	1		
	2	BJ20	20684
	3	ZP11	77413
5 (TAIL)	4	XY30	42713
	5	PQR8	11402
	6		

(d) Two deletions

	Index	Job	Location
4 (HEAD)	1		
	2		
	3		
5 (TAIL)	4	XY30	42713
	5	PQR8	11402
	6		

Figure 4.1 Output queue as a dense list

DELETE   Remove QUEUE[HEAD];
               Increment HEAD pointer: HEAD ← HEAD + 1;

These INSERT and DELETE algorithms are not complete because they do not consider either overflow or *underflow* (trying to remove an atom from an empty structure). We therefore give the revised algorithms. (They assume that the largest index is N.)

Algorithm 4.1 *Update a Queue*
Elements are moved to the beginning of the list if overflow occurs.
Initially HEAD ← nil and TAIL ← nil.

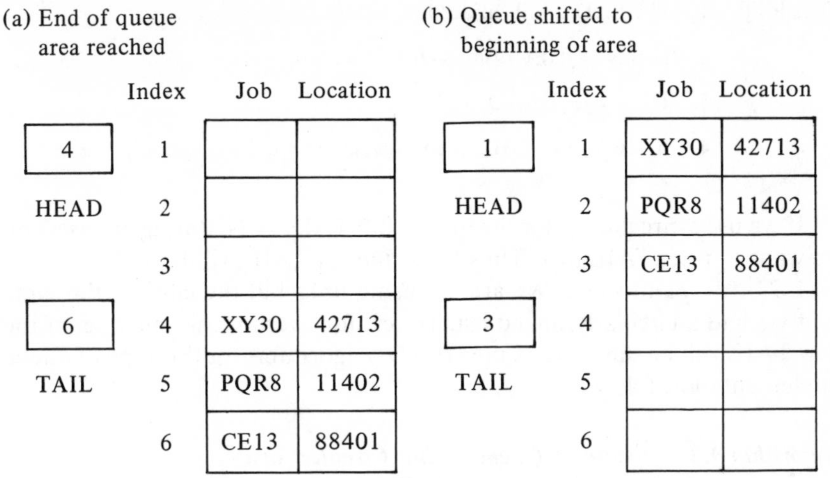

(a) End of queue
    area reached

Index	Job	Location
4 (HEAD) 1		
2		
3		
6 (TAIL) 4	XY30	42713
5	PQR8	11402
6	CE13	88401

(b) Queue shifted to
    beginning of area

Index	Job	Location
1 (HEAD) 1	XY30	42713
2	PQR8	11402
3 (TAIL) 3	CE13	88401
4		
5		
6		

Figure 4.2 Moving queue to prevent overflow

INSERT   1. Do only one of the following cases:
   (a) If TAIL − HEAD + 1 = N, queue is full and insertion would cause overflow so exit;
   (b) If HEAD is nil, set HEAD ← 1, TAIL ← 0;
   (c) If TAIL = N, move QUEUE[HEAD] through QUEUE[TAIL] to locations QUEUE[1] through QUEUE[TAIL − HEAD + 1] and set HEAD ← 1, TAIL ← N − HEAD + 1;

2. TAIL ← TAIL + 1;

3. QUEUE[TAIL] ← new entry;

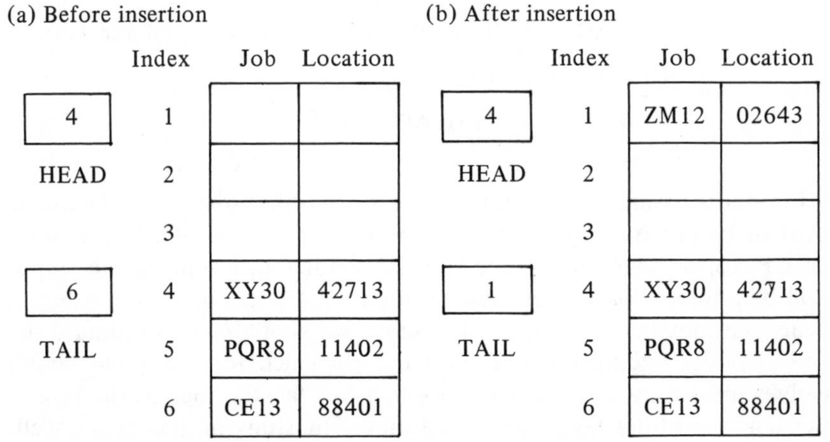

(a) Before insertion

Index	Job	Location
4 (HEAD) 1		
2		
3		
6 (TAIL) 4	XY30	42713
5	PQR8	11402
6	CE13	88401

(b) After insertion

Index	Job	Location
4 (HEAD) 1	ZM12	02643
2		
3		
1 (TAIL) 4	XY30	42713
5	PQR8	11402
6	CE13	88401

Figure 4.3 Using a circular list to prevent overflow

DELETE   1.   if HEAD is nil, underflow would occur so exit;

2.   remove QUEUE[HEAD];

3.   HEAD ← HEAD + 1;

4.   if HEAD > TAIL then HEAD ← nil, TAIL ← nil;

If we use a circular list for the queue and TAIL = N, during an insertion we want to reset TAIL to 1. Thus the values of TAIL will be 1, 2, 3, . . . , N, 1, 2, . . . , and so on. We are not using links but the effect is the same as if we had a circularly linked list. To test for overflow, we must see if the new TAIL will be the same as the HEAD. Algorithms for this type of queue implementation follow.

Algorithm 4.2   *Update of Queue Using Circular List*
Initially TAIL ← nil and HEAD ← nil.

INSERT   1.   if TAIL − HEAD + 1 = 0 or N, queue is full and insertion would cause overflow so exit;

2.   if HEAD is nil, set HEAD ← 1, TAIL ← 0;

3.   if TAIL = N, set TAIL ← 0;

4.   TAIL ← TAIL + 1;

5.   QUEUE[TAIL] ← new entry;

DELETE   1.   if HEAD is nil, underflow would occur so exit;

2.   remove QUEUE[HEAD];

3.   if HEAD = TAIL, set HEAD ← nil, TAIL ← nil and exit;

4.   HEAD ← HEAD + 1;

5.   if HEAD > N, set HEAD ← 1;

In our discussion of the output queue we said that sometimes the queue might be empty and at other times the queue might be full. In the latter case CPU operations would have to be suspended until some of the output could be printed. It is not desirable to stop the CPU just because the output queue may not be big enough. Therefore we should try to estimate the "best possible" size for the output queue. The calculation of queue length involves measuring and estimating quite a few factors, such as the rate of insertion, rate of deletion, and service time. The study of queues is a well-established part of statistics, and therefore we will not attempt to derive any of the following results.* If the average deletion rate μ is greater than the average insertion rate λ, the length of the queue will reach equilibrium. If the average insertion rate were greater than the average deletion rate, the queue would gradually grow longer and longer and would not stabilize. Assuming also that the service time is short for the majority of users and long for only a few, then the average queue length l is given by the formula:

$$l = \frac{\lambda}{\mu - \lambda}$$

Remember that this is only an average. Sometimes the queue will be longer and sometimes it will be shorter.

If we can tolerate an overflow only z percent of the time, how much space must be set aside for the queue? The length k is given by the formula:

$$k = \frac{\log z/100}{\log \rho} = \frac{\ln z/100}{\ln \rho}$$

and is derived by looking at the distribution of queue lengths. In the formula z is a percentage; dividing z by 100 converts it to a decimal. The symbol ρ is the *traffic intensity* and is defined as λ/μ. In calculating k and l, very likely we will not obtain an integer answer. Therefore to be safe, we should always convert the result to the next largest integer. For example, 1.3 should be converted to 2.

Example A queue is expected to grow at the rate of 5 atoms/millisecond and to shrink at the rate of 8 atoms/millisecond. How much space should be needed for a queue which will overflow only 1 percent of the time?

The solution is obtained by substitution of the numbers in the formulas. The average length l is:

$$l = \frac{5}{8 - 5} = 1.667 \approx 2$$

However, the length so that overflow will occur only 1 percent of the time is:

$$k = \frac{\log \dfrac{1}{100}}{\log \dfrac{5}{8}} \approx 10$$

*The interested student may wish to take a course in queuing theory or operations research. For derivation of queue length see Norman T. J. Bailey, *The Elements of Stochastic Processes* (New York: John Wiley & Sons, 1964), pp. 136–143.

which is quite a bit larger than the average length. These lengths assume a dense list representation of a queue. If pointers are included, the amount of storage locations required would be greater. Suppose, for example, the density is 1/3. The amount of space needed for a sparse list is 10 ÷ 1/3 = 30 locations.

EXERCISES

1. How much memory is required to prevent overflow from ever happening to a queue?

2. Use Algorithm 4.1 and show (in diagrams) the items on the queue and the current values of HEAD and TAIL after each of the following updates. The code i is for an insert, d is for a delete. Assume N = 6.

Job	Location	Code
AB11	43109	i
EF32	10741	i
MN01	82705	i
XR43	24722	i
ZR08	46210	i
AB11	43109	d
EF32	10741	d
BC39	21742	i
XT14	71348	i
LM75	24631	i

3. Using the following data, follow the instructions in Exercise 2.

Job	Location	Code
PR73	42765	d
XA41	21708	i
BR11	89034	i
XA41	21708	d
BR11	89034	d

4. Use the data in Exercise 2 but Algorithm 4.2 to update the queue.

5. If λ = 4 atoms/second and μ = 7 atoms/second, compute the average queue length l and the queue length k so that overflow will occur approximately 5% of the time.

6. Write subroutines to perform insertions and deletions from a queue. Design your own input format, output format, and the type of information that should go on the queue.

7. Design update algorithms for a queue that is stored in a linked list structure. How are overflow and underflow handled?

8. Design update algorithms for a queue stored in a doubly linked list structure. How are overflow and underflow handled?

4.2
Stacks

A *stack* is a list that restricts insertions and deletions to one end, which is called the *top* of the list. The opposite end is called the *base* which does not allow any update operations. This means that we need only a HEAD pointer instead of a HEAD and a TAIL as with a queue. However, in a stack we can access only the top atom. To access the nth atom we must delete the first $n - 1$ atoms. Thus the stack may seem quite restrictive and almost useless, when in fact it is a very useful structure in computer science.

For example, a stack assists a compiler in the correct interpretation of arithmetic expressions. To get an idea of the operations involved, let us suppose that an expression contains only operands which are one character long and the operators $+, -, \times, \div$ (no parentheses will be allowed). The rules for evaluation state that normally evaluation proceeds from left to right but that multiplication and division will be done before addition and subtraction. Thus $A + B \times C$ will be interpreted as $A + (B \times C)$ and $X \div Y \times Z$ as $(X/Y)Z$. It may be easy for us to follow the rules and evaluate expressions, but the computer's algorithm must work so that it has to scan only one character at a time. With this restriction in mind, we will rely on two stacks to save operands and operators which will not be needed until later. For example, in the expression $A + B \times C$ we must save the $A +$ until after $B \times C$ has been computed. Then we can take the result and add A. In one stack we will place operands, in another stack the operators.

Before stating the algorithm we will go through the expression $A + B \times C - D$ and show how it is evaluated.

In the following discussion the arrow ($\downarrow$) will show the character being scanned. The first two steps are to place A on the operand stack and plus ($+$) on the operator stack.

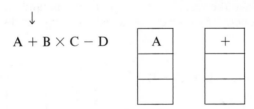

The next character is an operand, so it goes on the operand stack. Notice that B goes on the top of the stack and A is now second on the stack.

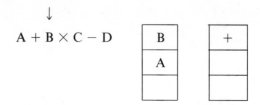

The next character is an operator, so we must compare it to the top of the operator stack. A multiplication ($\times$) operation is done before an addition ($+$) operation, so we say that it has higher precedence. An operator of higher precedence is placed on the stack.

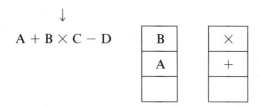

The C is an operand so it goes at the top of the stack pushing B and A down.

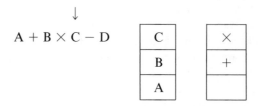

The next character is minus ($-$), which has lower precedence than multiplication ($\times$) at the top of the operator stack. This is a signal that an operation can be performed. The operation involves taking the top operator ($\times$) with the top two operands (C and B) to evaluate B $\times$ C. We will call the result R_1. We now place the result on the top of the operand stack. Notice that B, C, and the operator ($\times$) were removed from the stacks.

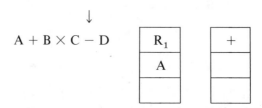

In addition, note that A and plus ($+$) have moved up. Since the operator stack has changed, we must compare minus $(-)$ and the top operator $(+)$. These operators have the same precedence, so we perform another operation which is $A + R_1$. Let us call the result R_2. As before, it is placed on the operand stack.

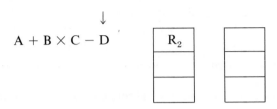

$$A + B \times C - D$$

The operator stack is now empty, so we may place minus $(-)$ on it and continue. The next character is D which goes on the operand stack.

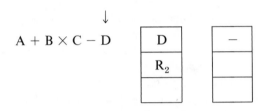

$$A + B \times C - D$$

D is the last character in the expression, so we can evaluate all the remaining items on the stacks, always taking one operator with the top two operands on the stack. In this case we compute R_3 as $R_2 - D$. Thus our evaluation has been

$$R_1 = B \times C$$
$$R_2 = A + R_1$$
$$R_3 = R_2 - D$$

The general algorithm for expression evaluation is Algorithm 4.3. Remember that it assumes the expression has been correctly formed, that the expression does not begin with a plus $(+)$ or minus $(-)$ sign, and that there are no parentheses included. We are attempting to illustrate the use of the stack, not the details of expression evaluation.

Algorithm 4.3   *Evaluation of an Arithmetic Expression*

1. Until the end of the expression is reached, get a character and perform only one of the cases 1 (a) through 1 (d):
    (a) If character is an operand, push it onto the operand stack.
    (b) If character is an operator and operator stack is empty, place it on operator stack.

(c) If character is an operator and operator stack is not empty and character's precedence is greater than the precedence of the top operator on the operator stack, place character on operator stack.

(d) Otherwise, remove top operator from stack and top two operands. Perform the operation *s* op *f*, where *s* is the second operand removed and *f* is the first operand removed, and op is the operator. Place the result back on the top of the operand stack.

2. Repeat 1 (d) until both stacks are empty. If one stack is empty before the other, an error has occurred because the expression was not correctly formed.

Frequently we picture a stack as though it were built on top of a spring. Adding an atom to the top puts on more weight and pushes everything down. Removing an atom releases weight and the spring pushes everything up. The top atom is always at the same level, while the bottom of the stack may go up and down. In our implementation of a stack there will be no movement of the elements; instead we will use a pointer to locate the top. The vocabulary of stack operations, however, does reflect movement. The insertion of an atom to a stack is called *putting* or *pushing;* deletion of an atom is called *popping* or *pulling.*

In the implementation of a stack we may decide to reserve a block of memory so that the stack can grow and contract within that area. This is very similar to the implementation of a queue except that there is only a head pointer which we will call TOP, instead of the HEAD and TAIL pointers of a queue. Also notice one major difference: The TOP of the stack points to the last atom in the stack area. For better visual effect we might want to turn the stack upside down. Figure 4.4 illustrates the stack after insertion of A, B, and C, deletion of C, insertion of E and F, and finally removal of F, E, and B. Notice that although B, E, and F appear in positions 2, 3, and 4, they are removed in the opposite order from the stack. First F will be popped, then E, then B. The stack is often called a *push-down stack* or *push-down store* because the insertion of an atom causes other atoms to go further down on the stack. It is also a last-in, first-out structure (LIFO).

The algorithms for putting an element on the stack (insertion) and popping an element from the stack (deletion) are given in Algorithm 4.4. They assume that the stack has room for *n* elements and that initially TOP is nil. The name STACK [*i*] refers to the *i*th element on the stack.

Algorithm 4.4   *Update a Dense List Representation of a Stack*

PUSH
(INSERT)   1. if TOP is nil, set TOP ← 0;

2. TOP ← TOP + 1;

3. if TOP > N overflow, else STACK[TOP] ← new atom;

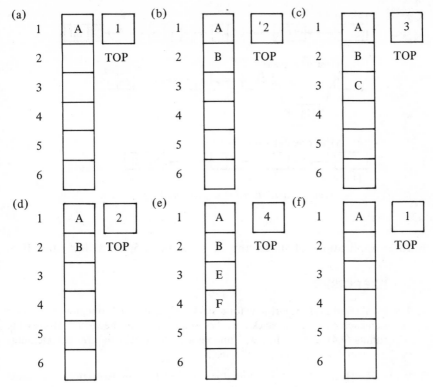

Figure 4.4 Implementation of a stack in a dense list

POP
(DELETE)   1. if TOP is nil, underflow so exit;

2. remove STACK[TOP];

3. TOP ← TOP − 1;

4. if TOP is 0, set TOP ← nil;

To prevent stack overflow, we can use a linked list, as pictured in Figure 4.5, to implement the stack structure and rely on a storage management algorithm to supply us with additional space whenever an element is added. This method has the advantage that our stack will occupy only the amount of space required at any one time. When an atom is popped from the stack, we could return the unused space to the storage manager. Thus we may save space, but require more time to call the storage manager.

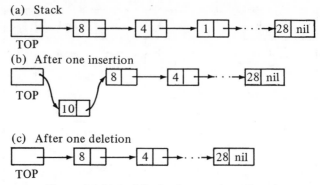

Figure 4.5 Linked list implementation of stack

Further applications of stacks appear in Sections 5.3, 7.2, 10.6, and 10.8.

EXERCISES

1. The PUSH and POP Algorithms for a stack (Algorithm 4.4) operate on a vector in which each entry in the stack occupies one position in the vector. Modify the Algorithms (4.4) so that they will update a stack which requires ten elements of the vector for each entry in the stack.

2. Write PUSH and POP Algorithms for a linked list representation of a stack.

3. Trace through Algorithm 4.3 with the following expression:

$$X - A + B \div C \times Y \times P$$

4. Modify Algorithm 4.3 so that it will work with parenthesized expressions. If you pick the correct precedences for the left and right parentheses, the algorithm requires only minor changes.

5. In an operating system which is better and why is it better: an output queue or an output stack?

4.3
Deques

A deque is a generalization of a queue because it allows insertions and deletions at both ends. An alternate way to picture a deque is as two stacks joined together at the base. If there is a definite boundary between the stacks or if we can locate the last element of each stack, the deque provides a means for the stacks to share the same memory area. Each stack would have the potential to be as long as the maximum size allotted for the deque, yet we would need only one memory area for both stacks. Problems arise if both stacks are concurrently large, because they might overflow the area.

To implement a deque we will use a dense list structure and will reserve a fixed amount of space. Since the deque can grow or shrink at both ends, we will need two pointers. Often we label the ends of a deque left and right or top and bottom, but to avoid any positioning of the deque, we will use END1 and END2. If the deque represents two stacks, END1 and END2 locate the tops of those stacks. To minimize the likelihood of the deque to overflow at either end, we should keep the atoms near the center of the list. Figure 4.6 illustrates a deque to which atoms are inserted and deleted. The numbers on the atoms refer to the order in which the atoms enter the deque. In step 4.6(e) there is no room to add any more atoms at END2. At this point, we can shift the deque toward the center of the area. Depending upon the application, we may want to move the elements one position or enough positions so that there are an equal number of empty positions at each end of the deque. This movement is very similar to the implementation of the queue in which we moved the queue to the beginning of the area whenever we reached the end. As with queues and stacks, underflow can occur if we try to delete elements from an empty deque.

Because a deque allows insertions and deletions at both ends, we can use it as either a superqueue or superstack. In a queue, normally the first atom in is the first atom out. If we wanted to give a high priority to an atom, we could place it at the head instead of the tail of the queue. In a strict sense insertions cannot be made at the beginning of a queue, but they can be made in the beginning of a deque. In a stack the ordering is first one in, last one out. If the stack grows to a maximum size and overflow occurs, we could delete the atom at the bottom because it has been on the stack the longest. A deque in which output (deletions) can occur at only one end is called an *output-restricted deque*. A deque in which input (insertions) can occur at only one end is called an *input-restricted deque*.

An alternate way to represent a deque is to use either a singly or doubly linked list. Thus when we need to add an atom, we request additional storage from a routine that keeps track of available memory space. When atoms are deleted, we return the free space to the memory management routine. To save memory space we are using more time. Do not forget that links take added space.

Deques are the least restrictive structures discussed in this chapter; at present they are also the least useful in computer programming.

EXERCISES

1. Design an algorithm to insert an atom to END1 of a deque. Be sure to test for overflow. Will this algorithm work for END2?

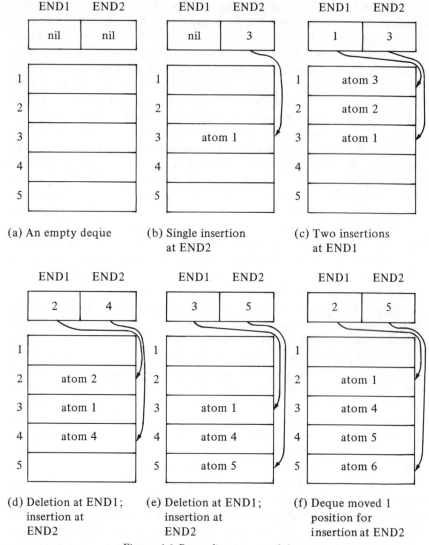

Figure 4.6 Dense list storage of deque

2. Design an algorithm to delete an atom from END1 of a deque. Be sure to test for underflow. Will this algorithm work for END2?

3. If a deque occupies k spaces out of a total of n in the dense list, how many positions should there be at the top and bottom of the area so that the deque will be in the center of the list (approximately)?

4. Write algorithms to update a singly linked deque at either end.

5. Describe a doubly linked deque; write algorithms to update it at either end.

5
GRAPHS AND TREES

5.1
Definitions

In Chapters 1 through 4 we approach the study of data structures from an applications and implementation viewpoint. Chapter 5 shifts emphasis momentarily to the study of structure as modeled by graphs. We must therefore introduce terminology and definitions that will describe data structures in a more general sense.

Once the principles of graphs are understood, the definitions of trees, files, and formal structures become easier to grasp. Moreover, graph theoretical terminology is commonly encountered in computer science, and you should become familiar with it.

Perhaps the most significant reason for studying graph theory as a topic in data structures is that it gives an abstract model of structure. An abstract model is useful in discussing data structures without concern for implementation details. In addition we often discover similar structures in many applications. Therefore we will be less concerned for the moment about implementation and will continue with an abstract orientation provided by graph theory.

Graphs and trees are different from the linear structures we have already studied. We could list the atoms, but that would not tell us anything about the interconnections of the atoms. One of the best ways to represent a graph is with a diagram, because it pictures both the atoms and the relationships among the atoms.

A *nondirected graph,* such as the one shown in Figure 5.1, is a set of two types of objects: nodes and edges. A *node* is an element or atom of the graph; an *edge* joins two nodes. In the diagram in Figure 5.1 the nodes are the lettered circles and the edges are the lines. An edge has no direction;

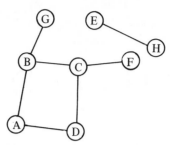

Figure 5.1 Nondirected graph

that is, an edge between C and D is the same as the edge between D and C: It goes both ways.

If we name the nodes n_1, n_2, n_3, . . . , n_k, a *path* from n_i to n_j is a set of nodes n_i, n_{i+1}, . . . , n_{j-1}, n_j and edges such that there is an edge between successive pairs of nodes (n_i and n_{i+1}, n_{i+1} and n_{i+2}, . . . n_{j-1} and n_j). In Figure 5.1 there is a path from A to F. In fact, we could choose either path A-B-C-F or A-D-C-F. In this case we say that the graph contains an *alternate path* since there is more than one path from one node to another. There is no path from H to F or from H to any other node except E. We say that this graph is disconnected. A *connected graph* has a path between any two nodes; a *disconnected graph* has at least two nodes with no path between them.

In Figure 5.1 there is a path which begins at node A, goes through nodes B, C, and D, and returns to node A. This path represents a *cycle:* a set of nodes n_i, n_{i+1}, . . . , n_j and edges for which there is an edge between successive pairs of nodes; all nodes are distinct except for the first and last, n_i and n_j, which are the same.

Applications of nondirected graphs include road maps, communications networks, and many other systems in which the components are connected by some means. Cycles in a map, network, or other type of graph indicate that there is more than one path from one place to another. Thus we can consider ways to find either the shortest path or cheapest path. In the case of a road map, the cheapest path may be the fastest path, which is not always the shortest one. Another common problem is to devise a graph that will provide the "cheapest" network joining all the nodes. The cheapest graph should not contain any cycles, since a cycle represents a duplication of paths and part of the cycle could be erased. We will discuss this problem later.

We first need to consider *directed graphs,* or graphs in which the direction of the edge is important; an edge from A to B is *not* the same as an edge from B to A. Figure 5.2 represents a directed graph (*digraph*); the arrows show the direction of the edges. The definitions of cycle and path

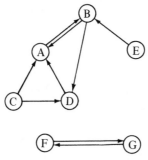

Figure 5.2 A directed graph

are the same for both digraphs and undirected graphs, but we must remember that an edge has direction. Thus in Figure 5.2 there is a path from
E to D, but no path from D to E. The path B–D–A–B is a cycle, but there
is no cycle containing the nodes D, C, and A. Ignoring directions, we could
say that nodes D, C, and A form a loop or cycle, but considering direction
all we have are two alternate paths from C to A. A digraph is *connected*
if we ignore direction of the edges and the resulting undirected graph is
connected. Thus the graph in Figure 5.2 is not connected, but the subgraph
containing nodes A, B, C, D, and E is connected. A *subgraph* contains a
subset of nodes of the original graph together with a subset of the edges
connecting those nodes.

In a directed graph we can talk about a successor node and the successor
set of a node. A node n_i is the *successor* of node n_j if there is a path (not
necessarily an edge) from n_j to n_i; conversely, n_j is the *predecessor* of n_i.
The *successor set* of a node contains all the nodes which are its successors.
In Figure 5.2, D, B, and A form the successor set of E; C is the successor of
no node since there is no edge pointing to it.

A tree is a special case of a graph. An *undirected tree* is an undirected
graph which is connected and contains no cycles. A *directed tree* is a directed
graph which has one node (called the *root*) whose successor set consists of
all other nodes, and the graph contains no cycles and no alternate paths.
An undirected tree has the special feature that any node can be the root;
in a directed tree there is only one root. In Figure 5.3, (a) shows an undirected graph, (b) the same graph with C as the root, and (c) the same
graph with E as the root. Contrary to nature, tree data structures are normally illustrated with the root at the top. Figure 5.4 illustrates a directed
tree which has an arrow representing the direction of an edge. A directed
tree can have only one root even though the root may not appear at the
top. In Figure 5.4, diagrams (a) and (b) represent the same tree.

A *subtree* is a subgraph of a tree with the property that the subgraph is
itself a tree. In Figure 5.4 the subgraphs containing nodes A, E, and F, and

(a) Original graph

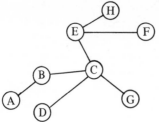

(b) Graph (tree) with root C

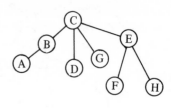
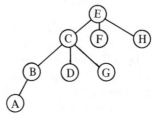

(c) Graph (tree) with root E

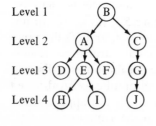

Figure 5.3 Undirected tree

nodes A, D, E, H, and I form subtrees. A subgraph is formed from nodes E, H, I, C, and G, but it is not a subtree because it is not connected.

In a directed tree we can count the number of edges pointing to a node (*indegree*) and the number of edges leaving a node (*outdegree*). The root has indegree of zero; the nodes with outdegree equal to zero are called *terminal nodes*. In Figure 5.4 the terminal nodes are D, H, I, F, and J. The level of a tree is a measure of the height or length of the longest path. The *level* of the root is 1; the level of every other node is one more than the level of its immediate predecessor. Thus nodes A and C in Figure 5.4 are at level

(a) Directed tree with root B

(b) Directed tree with root B not at top

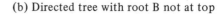

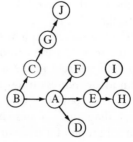

Level 1

Level 2

Level 3

Level 4

Figure 5.4 Directed tree

2; nodes H, I, and J at level 4. Normally when drawing trees we place the root at the top and nodes at the same level on the same horizontal line.

Because a tree as a data structure is similar in structure to a living tree, much of the terminology is common to both. Edges are often called *branches;* a collection of disjoint trees is a *forest;* and terminal nodes are *leaves.* Instead of predecessor and successor we may speak of *ancestor* and *descendant* or father and son in keeping with the vocabulary of family trees. The collection of sons descended from a particular father is sometimes called a *filial set.*

Trees have a wide variety of uses in computer science and other fields. Trees are used for sorting, evaluating expressions, making decisions, diagramming sentences, or representing a variety of hierarchical structures. A tree is not a linear structure, so we must exercise care in storing it in memory. If the tree varies in shape, we must choose a method that provides easy updating. Since trees are special types of graphs, we will discuss their storage and manipulation before proceeding with graphs.

EXERCISES

1. Describe an algorithm to convert nondirected graphs to directed graphs and an algorithm to convert directed graphs to nondirected graphs. If you start with an arbitrary graph and apply one algorithm and then the other, do you get back the original graph?

2. In the illustrated nondirected graph, list all the paths from B to E and all the cycles in the graph. Is the graph connected?

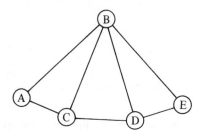

3. List the nodes and edges of each subgraph of the digraph below. Is the digraph connected? If there are any cycles or alternate paths, give examples.

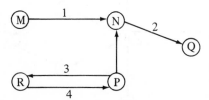

4. Redraw the following graph as a tree with root Y. List the nodes at each level.

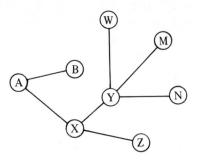

5. List all subtrees of the directed tree below. Give nodes and edges in each. How many nodes are in the largest subtree? How many nodes are in the smallest subtree?

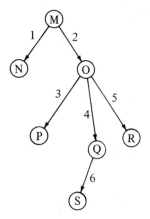

6. Give the indegree and outdegree of each node of the tree in Exercise 5.

7. Show how any forest can be connected into a single tree by the addition of a single node. How many edges need to be added? Can you do it without adding an extra node?

8. List the successor set of node B in the following digraph.

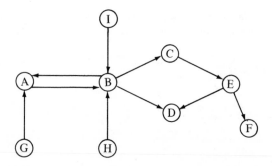

5.2
Storing and
Representing Trees

We can store a tree by using a multilinked list and by including a pointer for each of the node's branches. The only difficulty with this method is that frequently trees are not regular, e.g., not all the nodes have the same number of branches. For example, Figure 5.5 shows a tree and a representation as a multilinked list. Since the maximum outdegree (number of branches) is three, each atom has three pointers. Most of the nodes have outdegree less than three, so most of the pointers are null and we are wasting space. We can solve this problem by letting each node have a different number of links. To do this we store in each atom a number that tells the number of links. Terminal nodes have no links.

Another method to solve the problem of pointers is to store every tree in a canonical fashion which requires at most two pointers at each node. Such a tree, with outdegree at most two, is called a *binary tree*. The problem is to start with an arbitrary tree, store it as a binary tree, and then recover the structure of the original tree. We will see later that binary trees have many other advantages, so this problem is well-worth solving.

Suppose we start with the tree shown in Figure 5.6 (a). One binary tree representation is shown in Figure 5.6 (b), another is shown in Figure 5.6 (c). Beginning with the root node A in the directed tree (a), we find its immediate successors B, C, and D. One of these, typically the leftmost, is put on the left branch of the binary representation. The right branch of A in the binary representation is reserved for a node at the same level as A in the directed tree (there are none in this case). The same rules apply to each node. Consider, for example, node B in Figure 5.6 (b). Its left branch points to node E and its right branch to C, because E is a successor of B in the directed tree and C is at the same level as B in the directed tree. Both B

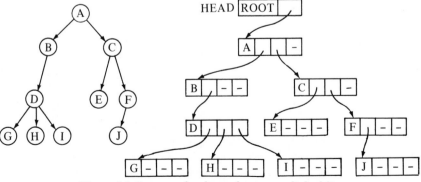

Figure 5.5 Storage of a directed tree as a linked list

(a) Directed tree   (b) One binary tree   (c) Another binary tree
                                  representation   representation

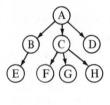
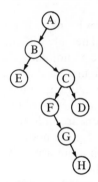
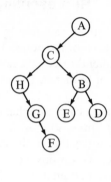

Figure 5.6 Directed tree and binary tree representations

and C are immediate successors of A in the directed tree. Similarly, D is on the right branch of C in the binary tree and is at the same level as C and B in the directed tree. Nodes F, G, and H are all at the same level and are the immediate successors of C in the directed tree.

Figure 5.6 (c) illustrates a binary tree created by placing C on the left branch of A instead of B. This shows that there are many binary tree representations of a given directed tree. To avoid confusion we will adhere to the method illustrated in Figure 5.6 (b).

Consider the inverse problem: Given a binary tree, find the directed tree corresponding to it. First we locate the root node [L in Figure 5.7 (a)] and make it the root node in the directed tree. The immediate successors of L in the directed tree are obtained from the left branch of L in the binary tree (M) together with any nodes which can be reached from M by always

(a) Binary tree   (b) Corresponding
                                directed tree

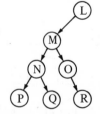
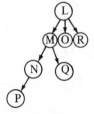

Figure 5.7 Binary tree and corresponding directed tree

following the right branch in the binary tree (O and R). Since O and R have no left successor in the binary tree, they have no successors in the directed tree. The successors of M in the directed tree are determined in the same fashion. They are N and Q, since N is on the left branch of M and Q is on the right branch of N.

In Figure 5.7 (a) the root L has only a left branch. What if the root had a left branch and a right branch as shown in Figure 5.8 (a)? Any node on a right branch is at the same level as its immediate predecessor. Thus A, C, E, and G are at the same level. Since A is the root node of the binary tree, C, E, and G must also be root nodes. A tree has only one root, therefore C, E, and G are roots for three distinct trees. Thus the binary tree in Figure 5.8 (a) defines the forest shown in Figure 5.8 (b). Even though the tree with root G has only a single node, it is still a tree.

Since every node of a binary tree has at most two branches, we can use a multilinked list with two links: one for the right branch and one for the left branch. The binary tree in Figure 5.7 would be stored as shown in Figure 5.9. The node name appears in the center of the atom.

Because each node of a binary tree has only two pointers, we can implement the multilinked list in a dense list array structure. We use three columns: one for node name, one for left pointer, and one for right pointer. If the tree were not a binary tree, we could still use the same sort of organization as long as there were enough columns to allow for the maximum number of branches at each node. However, that storage structure would probably waste space because there would be many null pointers. Figure 5.10 illustrates a binary tree and one way it could be stored in a dense list. The tree has a header called ROOT that points to the root of the tree. In

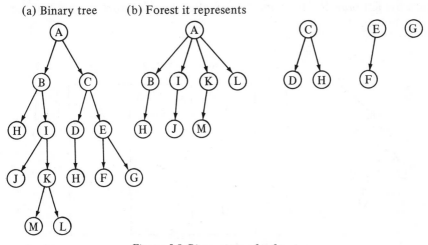

Figure 5.8 Binary tree of a forest

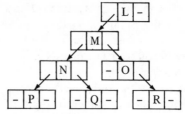

Figure 5.9 Binary tree of Figure 5.7 stored in multilinked list

searching the tree we start with ROOT and follow right and/or left pointers until we reach a leaf. Certain questions naturally arise. Which pointer (left or right) is traced first? Is the order of the nodes important in the dense list?

In the previous examples, the size and shape of a tree were known and the problem was to accurately record that information. In other applications we encounter trees which grow and change shape with time. As an example of growth and change factors, we will construct an algorithm that uses a tree to order a set of numbers from smallest to largest.

Let us assume that we have a list of distinct numbers in a random order. Using these numbers, we construct a binary tree in the following fashion: The first number in the list becomes the root node of the tree. The next number in the list goes on the left branch if it is smaller than the root and on the right branch if larger. We take subsequent numbers in the list and compare them with the root node. If the number is smaller, it goes on the left branch; if it is larger, it goes on the right branch. If this process traces down a branch which has already been allocated to a previous number in the list, make the same comparison with the nodes at lower levels. That is, take the left branch if the number is smaller than the current node and the right branch if it is larger.

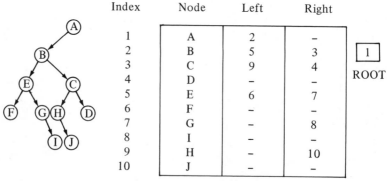

Figure 5.10 Binary tree stored as dense list

(a) Defining root

(b) Adding 240 and 572

(c) Adding 280

(d) Adding 108

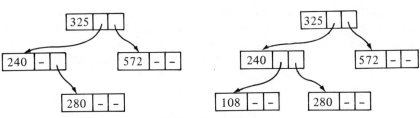

Figure 5.11 Creating a binary sort tree

Consider the set of numbers {325, 240, 572, 280, 108, 436, 720, 620}. We begin by making 325 the root node as indicated in Figure 5.11 (a). Since 240 is smaller than 325, it goes on the left branch [Figure 5.11 (b)], and of

(a)   (b)

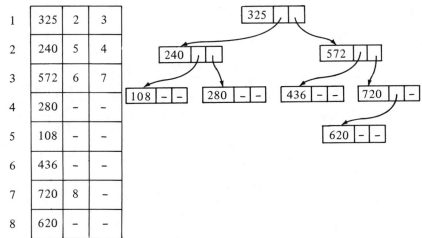

Index	Value	Left	Right
1	325	2	3
2	240	5	4
3	572	6	7
4	280	–	–
5	108	–	–
6	436	–	–
7	720	8	–
8	620	–	–

Figure 5.12 Completed binary sort tree

course 572 goes on the right branch. Now how is 280 handled? Since 280 is smaller than 325, we proceed down the left branch to 240. We now compare 280 with 240 and put 280 on the right branch of 240.

Finish the list of numbers, making sure that the tree is equivalent to the one shown in Figure 5.12. Two representations of the tree are given: one in a linked list diagram, the other in a dense list representation of a linked list.

The purpose of this algorithm is to order (sort) a set of numbers. Does the set of numbers shown in Figure 5.12 appear ordered yet? To complete the algorithm, we must specify how the branches of the tree are traced to give the correct order to the set of numbers. This tracing process is referred to as *scanning* the tree and will be discussed in the Section 5.3. An alternate to the binary sort tree is the B-tree, described in Section 10.10.

EXERCISES

1. Convert the following directed tree into a binary tree. How many levels does the binary tree have? the directed tree?

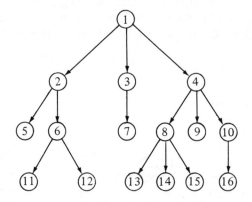

2. Convert the following binary tree into a directed tree or forest.

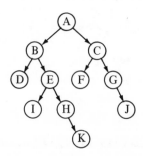

3. Given a binary tree stored in a dense list (see Figure 5.10 for an example), how can we determine the terminal nodes? Is there a way to find the root node? If the binary tree defines a forest, can we find the roots?

4. Suppose we are given a diagram of a binary tree. Design a method for inputting the tree and constructing its dense list representation. For example, you might decide that an input of X, W, Z means that node X has W as its left successor and Z as its right successor.

5. Design an algorithm to create a sort tree from a list of numbers in which there may be repetitions (that is, not all the numbers are distinct).

6. Design an algorithm to print the nodes of a sort tree, such as the tree shown in Figure 5.12, in descending order (from largest to smallest).

5.3
Operations on Trees

Scanning a tree is necessary when searching for a particular node on the tree or determining where an insertion should occur. A tree scan is more complicated than a list scan because a tree is not a linear structure. One of the easiest ways to search a list is to begin with the first element and continue from first to second on through the list to the last element. The ordering of a tree's nodes is not as easy. At every node in a binary tree we usually have the choice of taking either the left branch or the right branch. In the tree scan we must be methodical and yet trace all the branches without visiting any node twice and without omitting any node. The fundamental part of a binary tree structure is a node with two branches (left and right). Every portion of the tree looks like that below, except in places where one or both branches may not point to another node. In those cases the branches are not usually drawn. Considering this fundamental part of the structure, we see that there are three places to begin the search: at the root node (N), the left branch (L), or the right branch (R). Listing all possible combinations of L, N, and R, we find there are six different scanning orders: LNR, LRN, NLR, NRL, RNL, and RLN. L and R point to subtrees that have the general form shown below and which also must be scanned. In the following discussion we will select three of the six possible scan orders and apply them recursively to each node of the tree, usually beginning with the root.

An *NLR-recursive scan* of a binary tree considers first the root, then the left subtree, and finally the right subtree. In each subtree, the scan follows the same NLR rule: node, left subtree, right subtree. To understand the implementation of this rule, consider the sample tree in Figure 5.13. Begin with node A, and then work with the left subtree, which consists of nodes B, D, E, and H. Looking at only the left subtree we scan its root node B, left subtree (node D), and right subtree (nodes E and H). Since D is a terminal node, we have completed scanning the left subtree of B and can now scan the right subtree. In NLR order we first examine E (root node of right subtree of B) and then H. So far, we have considered nodes A, B, D, E, and H in the NLR-order scan and proceed to the right subtree. Processing it with the same NLR-recursive scan rule produces the ordering C, F, G, I, and J. Thus the complete scan is A, B, D, E, H, C, F, G, I, J.

An *LNR-recursive scan* considers the left subtree, node, and then right subtree. Using the tree in Figure 5.13, the LNR-recursive order scan produces the ordering D, B, H, E, A, F, C, I, G, J. The *LRN-recursive scan* considers first the left subtree, then the right subtree, and finally the node. Using the same tree (Figure 5.13), the LRN-recursive scan yields D, H, E, B, F, I, J, G, C, A.

Which of the scans would we use to print the nodes of the sort tree in Figure 5.12 in ascending order? Recalling the way the tree was constructed, a value less than the root went on the left branch, and a value larger than the root on the right. Thus in the sort tree all nodes on the left subtree are smaller than the root and all nodes on the right subtree are larger than the root. Using an LNR-recursive scan we can construct the list of numbers, ordering from smallest to largest.

Since trees have pointers from nodes to their successors, it is easy to travel "down" the tree from node to node until reaching a terminal node. Then the question becomes: How do we get back "up" the tree to go down another branch? We can look at the diagram of a tree and easily determine

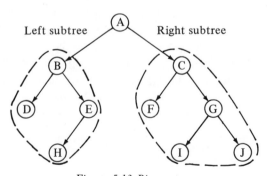

Figure 5.13 Binary tree

a root's predecessor, as well as its successors. But if the tree is given as a multilinked list, how can this be implemented without inserting backward pointers? We can, of course, use a stack and store the path that goes down the tree.

For example, to traverse (scan) a binary tree in an NLR order, begin with the root node. If the root node has a right subtree, place the right branch pointer on the stack to save the right node for processing later. Scan the root node. If the root has a left branch, follow it and process the left node as if it were the root. If there is no left branch, pop the top pointer from the stack and process the node to which it points as if it were the root. The effect is to proceed down succeeding left branches until encountering a terminal node. Then back up to the node's predecessor and process the predecessor's right subtree. When finished with the right subtree, back up one more level by removing another node from the stack and process its right subtree. After backtracking all the way to the root node and processing its right subtree, we have finished the scan. Algorithm 5.1 presents this scanning method.

Algorithm 5.1 *Scanning a Binary Tree in NLR-recursive Order*
    with Use of a Stack

Algorithm 5.1 assumes that there is a pointer to the root of the tree. The variable P is a pointer to the location of the node currently considered by the scan.

SCAN (P)   1.   Let L and R be the left and right pointers, respectively, of the node at location given by pointer P.
            2.   Repeat the following until the stack underflows. (Underflow halts the algorithm.)
               (a)   Output the node at location P.
               (b)   If R is not nil, push R onto the stack.
               (c)   If L is not nil, set P ← L, otherwise set P ← top element popped from stack.
               (d)   Call SCAN (P) recursively.

Example   We will use Algorithm 5.1 to scan the tree shown in Figure 5.13. Initially the data stack is empty and P points to the root node A. Each time SCAN is entered, the L and R pointers are assigned from the left and right pointer fields of the node at P.

In step 2 (a) we output P → A (node A). In step 2 (b) we test R which points to node C, find that it is not nil, so push it onto the stack. Continuing to step 2 (c) we see that L (pointing to B) is not nil, so we set P equal to L. Finally, step 2 (d) recursively calls the SCAN algorithm with P pointing to node B.

Upon second entry into SCAN we output B, push R of B onto the stack, and assign P to point to node D. A third entry is made with P set to node D.

At this point the stack contains: BASE, ↑C, and ↑E, where ↑C means a pointer to node C and ↑E means a pointer to node E. BASE indicates the base of the stack.

The third execution of SCAN produces D as output and finds that R and L are nil, so calls SCAN with P → popped pointer which is ↑E. Subsequently, nodes E, H, C, F, G, and I are output with every right node R pushed along the way. When J is reached, the stack underflows as we attempt to pop a pointer, and the SCAN stops.

An alternate way to backtrack during a tree scan is to construct the tree with additional pointers. These pointers are called *threads* because they tie the nodes together thus assisting in the scan. The threads occupy places which normally would be nil pointers. The size of a threaded tree is the same as that of a nonthreaded tree, and scanning requires no stack. Figure 5.14 illustrates the tree in Figure 5.13 with NLR-recursive threads included. The dotted lines represent the threads. The right thread of a node points to the node's immediate successor in the NLR scan; the left thread of a node points to the node's immediate predecessor. If we chose to use an LNR or an LRN scan, the threads would be different because the predecessors and successors are not the same as in NLR ordering. An NLR scan proceeds down the left branch until it reaches a node with a left thread. Then the scan follows the node's right thread because it points to the node's successor in NLR order. The algorithm used to scan a threaded tree is given in Algorithm 5.2. It assumes that P is a pointer.

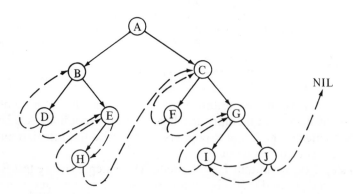

Figure 5.14 Tree with NLR-recursive order threads

Algorithm 5.2   *Scan of a Threaded Tree in NLR-recursive Order*

1. Let P be a pointer. Set P ← location of the root node.

2. Repeat the following until P is nil:
    (a) Output the node pointed to by P.
    (b) If the node's left branch is a thread, set P ← node's right branch, other-
         wise, set P ← node's left branch pointer.

In Figure 5.14 J node's right thread points to no node because J is the
last node in the NLR order. If implemented on a computer, this thread
would be nil. Figure 5.15 shows a way the threaded tree in Figure 5.14
could be stored as a dense list. The threads are negative indexes to denote
that they are threads. Thus in step 2 (b) of Algorithm 5.2, we should make
sure that P is always positive.

To make efficient use of a threaded tree, it is important to create the
threads as we create the tree. If, for example, we had inserted threads in
our sort tree, when the tree was completed, we could have scanned it in
LNR order and outputted the nodes in sorted order. Of course, we would
have to be certain that the threads reflected the LNR ordering also. Remember that scanning the tree is a method for visiting each node of the
tree once in an orderly fashion. It does not always provide the best way to
search for a particular node. Trees have a variety of uses in computer science, and we will continue to explore them in this book.

Index	Node	Left	Right
1	A	2	3
2	B	4	5
3	C	6	7
4	D	-2	-5
5	E	8	-8
6	F	-3	-7
7	G	9	10
8	H	-5	-3
9	I	-7	-10
10	J	-9	-

Figure 5.15 Dense list storage of threaded tree

EXERCISES

1. List the nodes of the following tree in NLR-recursive, LNR-recursive, and LRN-recursive order.

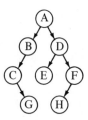

2. Write an algorithm to scan a tree using the LNR-recursive rule.

3. Convert the following tree into a binary tree. Then list the nodes in NLR order and LNR order. What is the difference between these two orderings applied to the original tree?

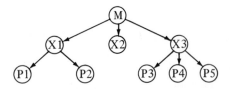

4. Write an algorithm to do an LRN-recursive scan of a binary tree.

5. Can the rules for NLR-, LNR-, and LRN-recursive order scan be modified for a tree each of whose nodes has at most three branches? If so, choose one of the orderings and write the appropriate rule.

6. Draw the LNR-order threads for the tree in Figure 5.13. How does your diagram differ from the one in Figure 5.14? With which node does the scan begin? How can we locate it easily?

7. Write an algorithm to scan a threaded tree with LNR-order threads.

8. If a binary tree has *n* nodes and is stored as a dense list, how many left and right pointers will there be? Of the left and right pointers, how many will not be nil?

9. What major problem occurs in tree scanning that is partially overcome by threading the tree? How do threads change the definition of a tree?

10. Design an algorithm to create a sort tree inserting LNR-order threads as it is created.

5.4 Manipulating Graphs

Since we have already discussed basic concepts of graphs, we can turn our attention to some applications. The study of graphs is a complete topic in itself, so we will mention only a few applications in this book.

A common example of a graph is a road map; the nodes are cities or intersections and the edges are roads or streets. A graph (or digraph) in which the nodes have weights is a *weighted graph* (or *weighted digraph*). On a road map the weights might be speed limits, average traveling times, or lengths of roads. On most graphs we label the nodes for easy identification. If nodes have more than one edge joining them, it is convenient to label the edges as well.

Recall that a path is a collection of nodes a_i, a_{i+1}, . . . a_j such that there is an edge between successive pairs of nodes. In a *simple path* all nodes are unique. The shortest path between two points is necessarily a simple path. For example, in Figure 5.16 path a_3, a_4, a_5, a_3, a_6, a_7 contains a cycle and therefore is not a simple path. However, it can be reduced to the simple path a_3, a_6, a_7 by removing the cycle. Some of the oldest problems in graph theory are concerned with finding a simple path containing every node of the graph. Such a path is called a *Hamiltonian path*. It is named after Sir William Rowan Hamilton who first introduced the problem in the form of a puzzle (see Exercise 1 at the end of this section). In a more practical form this puzzle occurs frequently enough so that considerable computer time is spent searching for solutions. A recent application involves a computer search to determine a Hamiltonian path which passes through every state capital of the United States and minimizes the total amount of travel. Although computers are ideally suited to this type of search, the amount of computation involved can be enormous, even with a modest number of

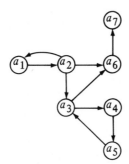

Figure 5.16 A digraph

nodes. Because the number of edges can increase rapidly, it is worthwhile to study storage of graphs before investigating applications.

A graph is completely determined by a list of pairs of nodes, where a pair indicates an edge between the nodes. Thus (A, B) indicates an edge between nodes A and B; the order is not important for a nondirected graph, so (A, B) is the same as (B, A). To specify a digraph, use pairs of nodes but add the rule that (X, Y) means an edge from X to Y, but not necessarily an edge from Y to X.

One straightforward way to store a graph is by storing a list of the nodes and a list of the node pairs which determine the edges. Since this method requires a lot of memory, we will use conventions to save space and to facilitate work with the graph. Instead of listing node pairs like (A, B), (A, D), (A, F), we will shorten them to (A: B, D, F). This notation says that there are three edges which begin at A and end at B, D, and F, respectively.

Figure 5.17 illustrates a graph and its tabular representation using this notation. The table says that there are edges from the first entry in a row to each of the other entries in the row. The introduction of pointers allows us to condense the table into a list structure. In Figure 5.18 we see a possible implementation. All the structure of the original graph is contained in these lists, but it is becoming more obscure. The INITIAL and TERMINAL tables list the initial and terminal nodes of each edge in the graph. For example, rows B,3 and C,7 of the INITIAL table tell us that there are four $(7 - 3 = 4)$ edges which begin at B and end at nodes A, C, D, and E. The pointer associated with B (a 3) locates the first of these four nodes in consecutive locations in the TERMINAL table. The last entry in the INITIAL table serves the purpose of determining the number of edges which begin at G. Notice that Figures 5.17 and 5.18 list every edge twice. It is possible to eliminate this redundancy, but manipulation of the graph becomes more difficult.

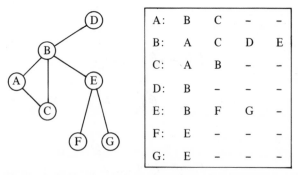

A:	B	C	–	–
B:	A	C	D	E
C:	A	B	–	–
D:	B	–	–	–
E:	B	F	G	–
F:	E	–	–	–
G:	E	–	–	–

Figure 5.17 Nondirected graph and tabular representation

Node	Pointer	Index	
A	1	1	B
B	3	2	C
C	7	3	A
D	9	4	C
E	10	5	D
F	13	6	E
G	14	7	A
–	15	8	B
		9	B
	INITIAL	10	B
		11	F
		12	G
		13	E
		14	E

TERMINAL

Figure 5.18 Graph representation using pointers and list structures

Another method for storing a graph involves the construction of an *incidence matrix* (sometimes called a *connection matrix*). To form the matrix, list the nodes along the left side and across the top of the matrix. If there are *n* nodes in the graph, then there will be *n* rows and *n* columns in the incidence matrix or a total of n^2 elements. Place the number 1 in position *i,j* of the matrix (row *i*, column *j*) if there is an edge between node *i* and node *j*. If there is no edge between nodes *i* and *j*, place zero (0) in the matrix. Figure 5.19 illustrates a graph and its corresponding incidence matrix. For a nondirected graph the incidence matrix is *symmetric*, that is, entry *i,j* is the same as entry *j,i* for all values of *i* and *j*. For a directed graph the incidence matrix would not necessarily be symmetric. However, in defining

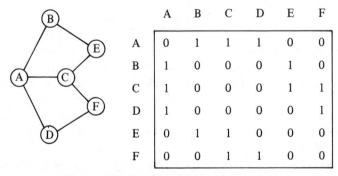

Figure 5.19 Graph and its incidence matrix

the incidence matrix for a digraph we must be careful to denote direction. Thus the number 1 in position i,j means that there is an edge from i to j. If the edges are weighted, we could record the weights in the incidence matrix instead of using number 1; in the case of multiple edges between nodes, we could record the number of edges in the incidence matrix.

An interesting feature of the incidence matrix is that the number of paths of length two, three, four, and so on, can be calculated in a straight-forward manner. The original matrix M identifies those nodes which are joined by a path of length one (an edge). Nodes joined by a path of length two (2 edges) are identified by the matrix M^2 (that is, M $\times$ M). Paths of length three are in M^3 (M $\times$ M $\times$ M), and so forth. For example, consider the digraph in Figure 5.20. Listing all paths of length exactly two, we obtain $(v_1\ v_1\ v_2)$, $(v_1\ v_1\ v_1)$, $(v_1\ v_2\ v_3)$, $(v_3\ v_1\ v_2)$, $(v_3\ v_1\ v_1)$, and $(v_2\ v_3\ v_1)$. The square of the incidence matrix yields:

$$
M^2 = \begin{array}{c|ccc}
 & v_1 & v_2 & v_3 \\
\hline
v_1 & 1 & 1 & 1 \\
v_2 & 1 & 0 & 0 \\
v_3 & 1 & 1 & 0 \\
\end{array}
$$

Thus M^2 shows that it is possible to get from v_3 to v_2 by a path of length two, but not from v_2 to v_3 by such a path. Notice, however, that M^2 does not say what the path is; it just says that the path exists.

Multiplying M^2 by M to produce M^3 we can determine those nodes connected by a path of length three. This yields:

$$
M^3 = \begin{array}{c|ccc}
 & v_1 & v_2 & v_3 \\
\hline
v_1 & 2 & 1 & 1 \\
v_2 & 1 & 1 & 0 \\
v_3 & 1 & 1 & 1 \\
\end{array}
$$

Even though our original matrix contained only zeroes and ones, we see that successive multiplications of the matrix by itself can introduce integers other than zero or one. This number indicates how many paths there are between two nodes. In this example we discover that there are two paths of length three between v_1 and itself. Saying this a different way, there are two cycles at v_1. Examining the graph we see that they are $(v_1\ v_1\ v_1\ v_1)$ and $(v_1\ v_2\ v_3\ v_1)$.

The preceding discussion suggests that there is no best way to store a graph. Often the application helps decide the way the graph should

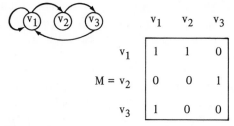

Figure 5.20 Digraph and its incidence matrix

be represented. The most concise method is not necessarily the best. If one desires information about the various paths among nodes, the incidence matrix is very useful even though it takes more memory than other techniques.

Let us now consider a problem that frequently occurs in transportation or communication networks. Given a *network* (weighted, connected graph), find a way to connect all the nodes so that the total weight is minimized. This means that the resulting structure has no cycles and therefore is a tree. Such a tree is called a *minimal spanning tree* because it connects (spans) all the nodes of the graph. The branches of the tree are edges in the original network. For example, Figure 5.21 shows a network and its minimal spanning tree. The weights are the lengths of the edges.

Algorithm 5.3 is used to construct the minimal spanning tree of a network. It assumes that the weights of the edges are known.

Algorithm 5.3   Minimal Spanning Tree of a Network

1. Select any node and place it on the tree.

2. Do the following until the tree contains all the nodes:
   (a) From the nodes not in the tree select a node which has an edge of minimal weight and joins the node to one already in the tree.
   (b) Include this node and edge in the spanning tree.

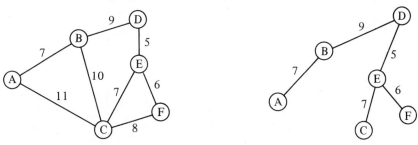

Figure 5.21 Network and its minimal spanning tree

Implementing Algorithm 5.3 we could use the incidence matrix to store the weights: A nonzero quantity is the weight of an edge between two nodes, and a zero means there is no connecting edge. Initially finding the minimal weight in step 2 (a) means that we look at just one row of the matrix—the row corresponding to the node selected in step 1. Later executions of step 2 (a) require that we examine more rows of the matrix. For example, refer to Figure 5.22 and notice that if we select node C first, the next node to add to the tree is E. Having selected C and E for the tree, we look at both their rows and find that the likely candidates for the next node are A, B, D, and F. The node with minimal weight (D) is added.

Finding the shortest path from one node to another is also a common problem in graph theory (see Chapter 10). It involves scanning a tree in such a way that all nodes of interest are considered and that no node is considered twice.

Like the algorithm for tree scan, a graph scan uses a stack to keep track of possible paths to try, but it also includes a flag with each node to tell whether or not the node has been previously scanned. Since graphs can have cycles, the VISIT flag will keep us from getting into an infinite loop. Algorithm 5.4 assumes that it is given a digraph and a particular node. It will then scan the graph visiting each node only once. (Algorithm 5.4 can easily be modified to work for nondirected graphs as well as directed graphs.) The notation VISIT[N] refers to the value of VISIT for node N; each node has its own VISIT flag. If VISIT[N] = 1, the node has not been visited; if VISIT[N] = -1, the node has been visited.

Algorithm 5.4   *Scanning a Graph*

1. Initially set VISIT[J] ← 1 for every J in the graph. This indicates that no nodes have been visited.

2. Input N as the first node to be scanned (starting node).

	A	B	C	D	E	F
A	0	7	11	0	0	0
B	7	0	10	9	0	0
C	11	10	0	0	7	8
D	0	9	0	0	5	0
E	0	0	7	5	0	6
F	0	0	8	0	6	0

Figure 5.22 Incidence matrix for graph in Figure 5.21

3. Repeat the following until the stack underflows:
   (a) Repeat until VISIT[N] = +1: Set N to the node pulled from the top of the stack.
   (b) Place all nodes pointed to by N on the stack.
   (c) Output node N.
   (d) Set VISIT[N] ← −1. This marks N as visited.

Applying Algorithm 5.4 to the digraph in Figure 5.23 yields one possible ordering: A, B, D, C, E. Will the graph scan algorithm (5.4) give only one possible solution? Not necessarily. The order depends upon the order in which the nodes are placed on the stack. For example, starting at node A, step 3 (b) says to put B and C on the stack. If we put B on first and then C, we do not obtain the same scan order as if C went on the stack before B.

The graph scan algorithm applies to any data structure. The maximum length of the stack must be such that the largest branch can be backtracked, and each node in the backtrack can store its pointers.

EXERCISES

1. The figure below represents the graph introduced as a puzzle by Sir William Rowan Hamilton in 1859. Each node was named after a different city and the object was to find a simple path which visited each city only once. Begin at node 1 and list the nodes and edges for such a path.

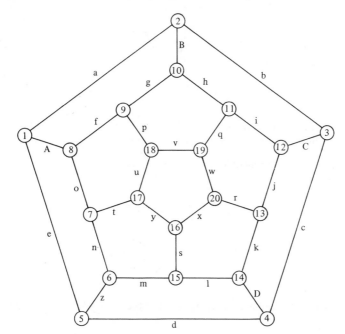

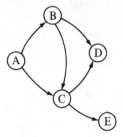

Figure 5.23 Directed graph to scan

2. Compare the methods for storing graphs. Which one requires the most room in memory? Which one the least? Can you devise other methods for storing graphs?

3. Give both the tabular method (as illustrated in Figure 5.17) and the list-pointer method (Figure 5.18) for the digraph below.

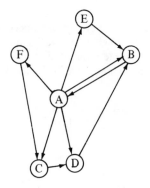

4. If a graph contains *n* nodes, what is its maximum number of edges? What is the maximum number of edges for a digraph with *n* nodes?

5. Given the following incidence matrix, draw its corresponding graph. Compute M^2 and M^3 for the graph.

$$M = \begin{bmatrix} 1 & 0 & 0 \\ 1 & 0 & 1 \\ 1 & 1 & 0 \end{bmatrix}$$

6. Determine the minimal spanning tree for the network at the top of page 85.

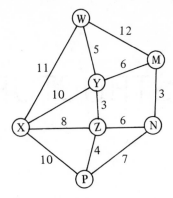

7. Scan the digraph in Exercise 3 starting at node F.

8. Write a computer program to perform the graph scan algorithm. What is the best way to store the graph? Can you improve the algorithm?

9. How do cycles show up in the incidence matrix for a graph? Be sure to consider the original matrix M and its powers M^2, M^3, and so on.

10. Is it possible to use threads to aid in the scanning of a graph? What are some of the problems involved?

11. Suggest alternate devices for scanning a graph so that all nodes will be scanned and infinite loops will be avoided.

6
FILE STRUCTURES

6.1
Some Hardware Considerations

In this section we will discuss basic hardware considerations which are pertinent to the applications in the remainder of the book. If you already know about peripheral devices and how they work, you may wish to skip this section.

In many cases computer hardware imposes restrictions on the types of data structures which can be implemented efficiently. For example, complex structures, such as trees and graphs, are not easily manipulated if stored on magnetic tape. The volume of data, its frequency of access, the access keys, and amount of updates are also important in the choice of the appropriate storage medium.

Most computer systems contain two types of storage: main storage and auxiliary storage. The central processing unit can access main storage (main memory) directly but must access auxiliary storage indirectly. Anything placed in auxiliary storage must first be transferred into main memory for processing. Typically, main memory is constructed of ferrite cores or semiconductor circuits and holds less than a million characters.

Auxiliary (secondary) memory usually takes the form of rotating or moving magnetic material (disk, drum, or tape). It is slower and less expensive than main memory, but can store a much larger volume of data.

Since the data in auxiliary storage cannot be addressed directly by hardware, it is necessary to keep extensive directories giving the location of various items. These directories are used frequently by the operating system and consequently must be organized efficiently. Part of the structure of these directories is dependent upon design features of the auxiliary memory. Addressing data on different devices is particularly important. Before investigating the structure of the directories, we will discuss the two most common forms of auxiliary storage: magnetic tape and disk.

MAGNETIC TAPE

Magnetic tape is often used to handle large volumes of information. It is a much faster technique than punched cards and relatively inexpensive. Standard magnetic tape is a strip of plastic $\frac{1}{2}$ inch wide, coated with a magnetic oxide material. A standard reel of tape 2400 feet long can hold the equivalent of 400,000 punched cards. The device that reads or writes information on the tape is called a tape drive (see Figure 6.1).

The tape drive records data when the tape passes over an electromagnetic device called a read/write head. The head writes characters by mag-

Figure 6.1 Tape drive (courtesy of IBM)

netizing small areas on the oxide coating of the tape. Each character is a specific pattern of dots extending across the width of the tape. For example, in a seven-track tape the pattern of dots requires seven positions. Each position is called a track. Figure 6.2 illustrates these patterns for seven- and nine-track tapes. A zero on a seven-track tape is represented by dots in tracks 3 and 5; a zero on a nine-track tape is represented by dots in tracks 2, 3, 4, 5, and 6.

To write a group of characters (a record) on the tape, the tape drive must accelerate the tape from a stopped position to its operating speed, write the characters, and then stop the tape. As the acceleration and deceleration take place, some tape passes by the read/write head and so remains blank. Thus there is a space between each record on the tape. This space is called the inter-record gap (IRG) and is normally 3/4 of an inch long.

(a) Seven-track tape

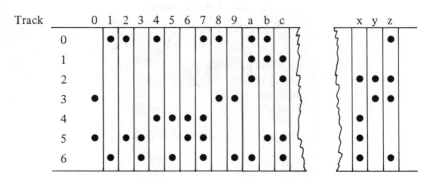

(b) Nine-track tape

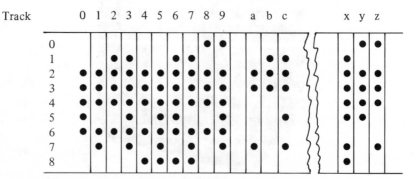

Figure 6.2 Character representation on magnetic tape

The number of characters per inch which can be stored on a tape determines the tape's density. Common tape densities are 800, 1600, and 2400 bpi (bits per inch). On a tape with density of 800 bpi, 80 characters occupy 1/10 of an inch. If information is written in 80 character records and the IRG is 3/4 of an inch, most of the tape will be blank (see Figure 6.3).

To make more efficient use of tape, records are often stored in memory until there is a large group (or block) which can be written to tape at one time. The IRG of a blocked tape is referred to as the interblock gap (IBG). Some higher level languages (COBOL, for example) have routines which automatically block the records when written and deblock them when used. Users think they are writing one record at a time; actually the tape appears as shown in Figure 6.4.

The more records fitted in a block, the denser will be the data; that is, the tape contains more information and less blank areas. However, to create a large-size block, there must be enough room in memory to accumulate the data. Remember, starting and stopping the tape makes gaps. All the data in a block must be written at the same time.

The amount of information written on a tape at a single time is called a *physical record*. Thus a block and a physical record are the same concept. Each individual record in a block is termed a *logical record*. In Figure 6.3 there is 1 logical record/block; in Figure 6.4 there are 10 logical records/block. For example, suppose the telephone directory is stored on tape. Logically, a record contains a name, address, and phone number, but for better efficiency there might be 10 names, addresses, and phone numbers/block.

Since blocks are placed on the tape one after another, we say that tape is a linear or sequential access device. Any additions to the tape can go only at the end; otherwise the new data would erase the old data. This sequential nature also makes it difficult to delete a record or to search for a particular record. In fact, working with a tape is identical to working with a dense list structure. Because of these problems, other types of secondary storage have been developed.

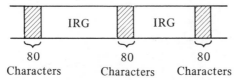

80 Characters   80 Characters   80 Characters

Figure 6.3 800 bpi tape with 80 character records

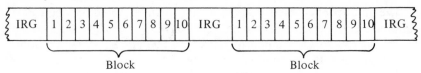

Figure 6.4 Tape with ten 80-character records/block

Rotating memory devices, such as magnetic drums and disks, are similar to tape in some ways, but allow direct access to any record without processing all preceding records. A disk is similar to a thin, metal phonograph record, covered with a magnetizable substance, much like the oxide on a magnetic tape. Several disks may be mounted together on a vertical shaft to comprise a disk pack. A pack may contain six disks with a total of ten surfaces for holding information. The surfaces are magnetized along concentric tracks (not in a spiral as on a phonograph record), usually about 200 tracks/surface, or 2000 tracks/pack (see Figure 6.5).

In a movable head disk device the read/write heads are located on arms that move in and out over the disk to reach a specified track, while the disks rotate beneath the heads (see Figure 6.6). The heads ride on a cushion of air and do not actually touch the surface of the disk. All the disk's arms move simultaneously, and all the heads are positioned over the same track, but on different surfaces. These vertical tracks constitute a cylinder. Even though only one head can read or write (not both) at a time, the other heads are ready to access other data on the cylinder.

Data is placed on each track in records. Records on a track are numbered sequentially from a location called the home address (track address). Records are separated by gaps, such as the gaps on tape, and overflow is handled by placing records on the next lower track of a cylinder.

To access a record in either a read or write operation, three steps are involved:

1. Seek: Move the read/write heads to a position over the proper track.

Tracks 000–200

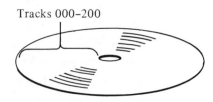

Figure 6.5 Diagram of tracks on a disk

Read/Write Heads

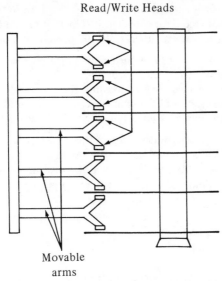

Movable
arms

Figure 6.6 Diagram of disk read/write heads

2. Search: Activate the appropriate head and locate the desired record on the track by counting from the home address.

3. I/O: Read or write the record.

Often the operating system or disk hardware mechanisms take care of these steps, so the programmer is not aware of them. However, two different time delays are involved: rotational delay (looking for the home address) and seek delay (movement of the read/write heads). These delays are on the order of 10^{-2} second, while main memory access time is on the order of 10^{-7} second. Hence, disk systems access data at a much slower rate than main memory.

These access times may sound minute and the differences may seem insignificant. However, if these operations are repeated thousands of times, differences become important. In the next sections we will discuss file structures and efficient ways to organize data on auxiliary memory devices.

EXERCISES

1. Why are main and auxiliary memory needed?

2. What causes gaps on magnetic tape?

3. If a record is 100 characters long and an IRG is $\frac{3}{4}$ inch long, how much of the tape will be blank if records are blocked 10/block? if blocked 20/block? Perform these calculations for tapes with density 800 bpi and density 1600 bpi.

4. A random search of a tape for a particular record requires that nearly half the tape be read. A disk search requires on the average that half a track rotate beneath the read/write head before locating the home address. Why do these operations require one half of a scan? (*Hint:* This is an average computed by assuming that each record is equally likely to be accessed.)

5. The average number of cylinders crossed during a seek operation is 67 ($\frac{1}{3}$ times 200). How is this average computed? (*Hint:* Assume that each cylinder is equally likely to be accessed. Also, the average of the distribution of the absolute difference of two random numbers ($k = |i - j|$) is $\frac{1}{3}$.)

6.2
Files

From a graph theory or data structure point of view, files are nothing more than data structures that reside physically on secondary storage devices, such as disk or tape. File structures may be thought of as special data structures with an emphasis on retrieval efficiency. Since secondary storage devices are slower than main memory, a high penalty is paid for every access to information stored in a file. The objective, then, is to design a data structure for secondary storage devices that minimizes operating overhead. Such a design is based on the following considerations:

1. Volume of information.

2. Frequency of retrieval.

3. Frequency of update.

4. Number of access key fields per record.

The file designer must evaluate these considerations before deciding which structure to employ. After selecting a structure, algorithms for carrying out the needed operations must be programmed. These algorithms allow the user to store, maintain, and retrieve a set of data.

Historically, files have been studied separately from data structures. As a result, there is a distinct vocabulary for files, even though concepts in the two areas may be the same. Table 6.1 lists corresponding terms for data structures and files.

A *field* is a unit of information. A *record* is a collection of related fields treated as a unit. A *file* (or *data set*) is a collection of related records. For example, the entire collection of an insurance company's data would be a

**Table 6.1   Corresponding Vocabulary for
Files and Data Structures**

Files	Data Structures
Field	Field
Record	Atom or node
Key	Identifier field
Address	Pointer or address
File	Data structure (list, string, tree, graph)
Library	Collection of data structures

file. The policy number, premium rate, and expiration date are examples
of fields. Information pertaining to a single policy is a record. To facilitate
handling of data, records are formatted so that each field occupies a particular location within the record. In addition, field lengths are kept constant. For example, Figure 6.7 illustrates a record format for an insurance
company. The record designer must decide not only what to include in a
record but also the length of each field. If the name field is limited to 30
characters, there must be a rule for handling a name with more than 30
characters. For ease in reference, the name and address fields might be
divided into subfields of last name, first name, middle initial, street, city,
state, and zip code. If we divide into subfields, we must decide the exact
location of each subfield. Thus if we are searching for policy holders in
Texas, we do not have to scan the entire 50-character address field looking
for TX.

Records are also classified by length. There are *fixed-length records*
and *variable-length records*. Fixed-length means all file records are the same
length and variable-length means all file records are not the same length.
However there are minimum and maximum lengths. For example, a registrar's transcript records contain a complete list of students' courses and
grades. Using fixed-length records is wasteful, since all students do not take
the same number of courses, resulting in a good percentage of blank record,
especially for freshmen and sophomores. If the records are variable length,
then each record contains the same basic information for each student
(name, student number, class, major, etc.) and only completed courses.

Policy number	Name	Address	Coverage codes	Premium	Expiration date	Last use
1 10	11 40	41 90	91 100	101 105	106 111	112 117

Figure 6.7 Record format for insurance file

A *key* is one or more characters of a record used to identify the record or to control its use. Typically, a key is one of the record's fields. When the file is sorted, the key determines the order in which the records are arranged. Files may have single keys or multiple keys. A *single key file* has 1 key per record. A *multiple key file* has more than 1 key per record, but all records have the same number of keys. In a single key file, retrieval and update are solved relatively easily by careful selection of file structure. For multiple key files, file organization becomes a challenging problem.

Example A registrar's file would normally contain a single key—student's social security number—since there would be no chance of two students having the same number. However, an insurance company file might need two keys: the policy holder's name and account number. The account number is of primary importance to the company, but the name is more significant to the policy holder.

EXERCISES

1. List the four most important parameters to consider in file structure design.

2. Give an example of the following structures:
   (a) Large file
   (b) Frequently updated file
   (c) Multiple key file
   (d) Frequently accessed file

3. Define the following terms and give examples:
   (a) Variable-length record
   (b) Key
   (c) Record format

6.3
File Storage
and Retrieval

The storage of a file and the subsequent retrieval of its records go hand in hand. The storage method determines the manner and speed of accessing the data. Basically, there are two types of access modes: sequential and random. In a *sequential access file,* records must be processed in the order in which they were written on the file. For example, a tape file is a sequential file because of the nature of magnetic tape. Disk files can be either sequential or random access. In a *random access file,* records can be retrieved in any order either because the position of a record is known or it can be determined from a key. Many file organizations are of the random access type, and we will discuss the basic ones in this section. First, however, let us consider the simplest organization, that is, the sequential.

A sequential file is a good system for handling a large volume of data that rarely changes and is processed as an entire unit. A company's payroll for salaried employees is a good example. Every payday the entire file is read and checks are printed. If raises were granted, new employees hired, or old employees retired, a file update is necessary. If the file's record order is not important, new records can be added to the end. But how can changes or deletions be handled? If the changed record is the same size as the previous record, it may be possible to write the new record over the old. On a tape file, writing new records over old records may not work unless the tape drive is adjusted properly. (Remember that tape drives start and stop. A slight differential in the operating speed could place the inter-record gap in the wrong place, making it impossible to access other records on the tape. See Figure 6.8.) In Figure 6.8 the dotted lines show misalignment of data, so part of data$_2$ is taken up by IRG. If the file's records are blocked, a change to a single record means the entire block must be rewritten.

Frequently a sequential file is updated by making a new copy. With tapes, it means writing a second tape, copying the unchanged records from the original file, deleting (not writing) specified records, and inserting new records where required (see Exercise 6). The old tape can be kept as a backup or reused for another file. With disk files, the operations are similar. After the updated copy is created, the previous disk space is available to other users. Thus disk management and memory management requirements are similar.

If the sequential file is ordered according to a key field, updating necessitates creating a new file. Typically, all records to be updated are placed on a separate file and are ordered in the same way as the original master file. Then the master file and update file are merged to form a new master file. Keeping both the master and update files in order facilitates the merger.

(a) Before writing

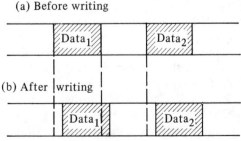

(b) After writing

Figure 6.8 Misalignment of data during a rewrite

Example   Merger of master file and update file to create a new master sequential file. The file contains a warehouse inventory, including part number, number on hand, and reorder point. The file is arranged according to part number. Each record of the update file contains a code that tells whether the record is an addition to the inventory (1), a change to the inventory (2), or a deletion (3).

OLD MASTER FILE			UPDATE FILE			
Part Number	On Hand	Reorder Point	Part Number	On Hand	Reorder Point	Code
1076	460	200	1091	120	85	1
1088	240	100	1098	45	20	1
1093	25	50	1104			3
1104	362	300	1152	950	500	2
1152	891	500				
1683	208	120				

To create the new master file, we must read both the old master and update files, reading one record at a time from each file and comparing the records. Initially, the master file part numbers are less than the first update record (1091). This means that all records from the master file can be copied directly to the new file until a part number equal to or greater than 1091 appears. When 1093 is read from the old master, we know that 1091 must be an addition to the new master file. After adding 1091, we go on to the next update record (1098) and continue copying old master records until we can correctly insert 1098. The next record is 1104, which we delete. We continue to process in this manner to the ends of both files.

Example   The regional office of a medical insurance company wants to design a file containing information on its current policies. Each record will consist of policy number, policy holder's name, type of coverage, premium, expiration date, type of last claim, and settlement. The purpose of the file organization is to provide easy access for hospitals. On entering a hospital, a telephone call will verify the patient's insurance coverage and obviate the usual hospital written forms.

All these considerations mean that once created the file will be large, retrieval must be rapid (while the hospital waits on the phone), and updates will occur less often than retrievals. The search of a sequential file for a particular record usually requires scanning half the file. (This fact is demonstrated in Chapter 8.) Therefore, the best way to organize the file is to use one of the random access methods. As you read about the various access methods, keep this problem in mind and determine the best method for the insurance file.

DIRECT ACCESS

One random access method is *direct* access. With this type of organization there is a special relationship between a record's key and the key's actual address. Each key has a corresponding unique address, so that only one seek and one read are necessary to retrieve the record. Of course the key-address relationship is dependent on the data in the file and the storage device chosen for the file. As a very simple example, suppose that each record in a file occupies one track and that the records are numbered 0001, 0002, and so on. Assume further that the disk has 10 tracks per cylinder. To make efficient use of the disk's head movement, records from 1 to 10 are on the same cylinder, 11 to 20 on the next cylinder, and so on. Thus given record number n, we divide by 10 to compute the cylinder number (relative to the beginning cylinder allocated to the file) and use the remainder of the division to specify which disk surface or head the record is on. For example, if the file begins on cylinder 25 and ends on cylinder 40, record 0043 is on cylinder 28, head 3.

$$\text{Cylinder} = \text{beginning cylinder} + \frac{\text{record}}{10} - 1$$
$$= 25 + \frac{43}{10} - 1$$
$$= \underline{28}$$

$$\text{Head} = \text{remainder of } \frac{\text{record}}{10}$$
$$= \text{remainder of } \frac{43}{10}$$
$$= \underline{3}$$

RANDOMIZING (Hashing)

Normally record keys are not well-numbered, so more complicated schemes are necessary. One such scheme is called *randomizing* or *hashing*. (Hashing is discussed in more detail in Section 8.3.) It is generally used if the entire range of keys is large compared to the actual number of records in the file. For example, in a company that uses a six-digit employee number, there are a million possible numbers, 000000 through 999999. Instead of reserving space for a million records, a computation is performed on the employee number to convert it to a range of 0 through 9999. Assuming there are only 8000 employees in the company, our scheme looks good. To store a record, we take the key, perform the computation, and obtain an address. We then store the record at that location. This scheme is called a *key-to-address* transformation or more commonly, hashing. When accessing a record, we perform the same computation and determine where the record should be stored.

For example, to convert an employee number in the range 0 through 999999 to a number in the range 0 through 9999, we could either drop the last two digits, drop the first two digits, or use a more complicated scheme. However, no matter what we do there is always the likelihood that two keys will produce the same result. In this event the records are called *synonyms*. We also say that a *collision* has occurred. Thus there are two aspects to hashing: the key-to-address transformation and collision handling. Several of the more common key-to-address transformations are the following:

1. Division: The key is divided by an integer (often a prime) slightly smaller or equal to the number of distinct addresses available. The remainder of the division is used as the address.

2. Midsquare: The key is squared and the digits in the middle are retained for the address.

3. Folding: The key is divided into several parts, each of which has no more digits than the desired address. Then the parts are operated on in some way. Folding offers a variety of randomizing techniques, depending upon the operation chosen. For example, the parts could be added together.

4. Random: The key is used as input to a random number generator. The output of the generator will be the address.

Ideally the computation performed on a key would yield unique addresses for different keys and scatter the records uniformly throughout the address space. Because of this, the term *scatter storage* is applied to the technique, as well as randomizing, hashing, or key-to-address transformation. Surprisingly, one of the best hashing techniques is also the simplest, that is, the division technique.

The second consideration in hashing or scatter storage is handling collisions. One of the simplest schemes involves storing the record in the first free area after the computed address. However, this tends to cluster records with the same hashed key. With files, clustering of records leads to the definition of buckets. A *bucket* is a unit of storage that can hold several records. On a disk a bucket might be a track or a cylinder. As the file is created, records whose keys hash to the same address are stored sequentially in the same bucket. If the bucket is full, overflow occurs. When accessing a record we compute the address of a file bucket and perform a linear search (discussed in Chapter 8) within the bucket for the record. This is called the open hash technique.

If overflow occurs in the open hash technique (the appropriate file bucket is full), we have to decide where to put the record. We can, of course, use a nearby bucket, or a bucket specifically designated for overflow records.

The *loading factor* is a measure of the density of the file storage area. It is the ratio of the number of records to the total number of record slots in the primary file area, assuming that collision records are placed in the overflow file area. If each bucket has room for k records and there are b buckets in the primary storage area, the loading factor l is:

$$l = \frac{n}{bk}$$

where n is the number of records in the file. In general, the percentage of overflow records increases with a higher loading factor and decreases with larger bucket size. A low loading factor means a large number of vacant spaces in the primary storage area, but good retrieval time. Larger loading factors require a larger number of accesses to retrieve a record, but save total memory. For a particular file we must consider storage costs versus frequency of retrievals in deciding what the loading factor should be.

INDEX (Dictionary)

To avoid the computation of a record's location, we can keep an index (dictionary) of all key values and corresponding addresses. Retrieving a record involves scanning the index for the record's key, getting the key's address, and reading the record. Retrieval time is shortened because only one access is made to the secondary storage device. The index requires space and search time, but searching the index may be cheaper than searching records stored in secondary memory.

Updates to the file involve updating the index. If a record is deleted from an auxiliary storage device, it need not be altered as long as its entry is deleted from the index. If there are many deletions, we would want to recover the space belonging to the deleted records and make it available for reuse. If a record is added to the file, its physical location in relation to other file records is not important. The important aspect is the inclusion of the record address and its key in the index.

If the file is large, the index can become a problem. The size of the index depends on the number of records in the file. As index length increases, search time also increases. We can solve this problem by using a sequential organization for the file with an index to certain key points in the file.

INDEXED SEQUENTIAL

The indexed sequential file requires the file records to be ordered according to a key. Rather than scan the entire file for a particular record, we consult a partial index which indicates approximately where to start and how far to continue scanning before deciding that the record is not in the file. The partial index is set up when the file is created, according to the way records are grouped into blocks. There is one entry in the index for each block. It contains the location of the block and either the lowest or highest key (depending upon the ordering) in the block. If the file is large, even the partial index may be unmanageable. In this case we can define a higher-level index which does the same thing for the partial index that the partial index does for the file.

For a simple example, consider the parts inventory file. The records are referenced by part number and the numbers are in increasing order. The file is stored on cylinders 21 through 25 and occupies 10 surfaces on each cylinder. The high-level index gives the location (cylinder number) of the lower-level indexes. The part number represents the largest part number stored on that cylinder.

High-level Cylinder Index

Cylinder	Part Number
21	0829
22	1450
23	2079
24	3635
25	4721

Each cylinder has its own low-level track index, which gives the surface number and highest part number stored on that surface. For example, the track index of cylinder 23 might look like the following.

Low-level Track Index for
Cylinder 23

Surface	Part Number
1	1512
2	1582
3	1640
4	1690
5	1725
6	1776
7	1834
8	1899
9	1963
10	2079

The cylinder index helps direct us to the correct track. For example, any part with a number between 1451 and 2079 will be on cylinder 23, if it is in the file. The cylinder index tells us that no part numbers above 4721 exist in the file. To retrieve information on part number 1703, we must first search the cylinder index to determine the correct cylinder (23), and then search the track index of cylinder 23 to locate surface 5. Then cylinder 23, surface 5 must be read and each record's key compared with 1703. One of two things will happen: Record 1703 will be found and its information will be copied into main memory for processing, or a key larger than 1703 will be read implying that there is no part number 1703.

Remember that an indexed sequential file is a sequential file and its records can be processed sequentially. On the other hand, partial indexes permit relatively fast random access. Thus it is a flexible file organization. However, insertions and deletions may necessitate updating indexes and may create overflow areas, which slow down access to individual records.

TREE

The tree organization is used frequently to define file directories and to determine access rights and privileges. Most large computer systems allow users to define their own disk files. Each user can declare the file sharable or nonsharable, read-only, write-only, read-and-write, and so on. Some systems allow users to specify those who have access to a file and their corresponding access rights. For example, some users may have read-only privileges, others read-and-write. Protecting the files from incorrect access is an important problem in large file or data-base systems which do permit sharing of data.

A tree is a good way to represent the file directory. The nodes of the tree can contain the access information and location of the file. Thus the operating system can check the directory to see if a user has access to a particular file, and can then locate the file. To illustrate the tree organization of the directory, we will assume there are two basic types of files: system files and user-created files. The *system files* are compilers, assemblers, and various other utility programs which anyone can use (on a read-only basis). The *user files* are those created by the users. System files are normally referenced by name, user files by name and/or user number. Figure 6.9 gives an example of the tree directory.

In Figure 6.9 user files are classed under the number of the user who created the file. If user M4613 wanted to access the CEN file, the name CEN would have to be used. Most systems look first in a user's set of files before seeing if the request is for a system file. Thus the system would proceed down the user file branch to user number M4613 and then would retrieve the CEN file. If the same user requested PROC, the system would not find it under M4613 and would go back to the directory root and search the system file branch. If M4613 requested *B4810.PROC, the system would

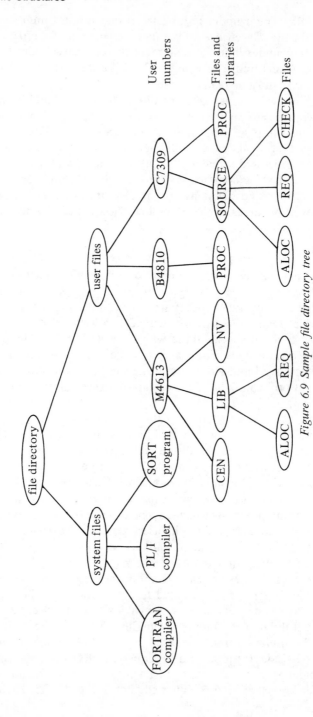

Figure 6.9 Sample file directory tree

look under user B4810 for PROC. The B4810. preceding the name PROC qualifies PROC and says that it is in a special part of the file tree. The asterisk (*) is used in our example to denote that B4810 is a user number. Users can also establish libraries (collections of files) and reference a particular file in the form: library-name.file-name.

Thus user C7309 would access REQ with the phrase SOURCE.REQ. The name REQ would not be good enough because the system would look for a name on the same level as SOURCE. The methods of qualifying and user number identification make it possible for two users to use the same file names; yet the system keeps them separate because of the directory.

An advantage of the tree organization is that deletions and insertions can be made without affecting the rest of the structure. For example, if new users create files, we add their numbers and file names to the user file subtree. If users erase all their files, we simply remove their branches of the tree. As with all tree structures insertions and deletions require extra memory space for needed pointers, but the technique permits fast access.

Figure 6.9 is only a diagram of the tree structure; Figure 6.10 gives an implementation of the tree directory. Each node of the tree contains two pointers: One references the next node at the same level in the tree and the other locates the node's successors. Although not included in the diagram, terminal nodes would contain information about the file and its protection.

EXERCISES

1. Define the following terms:
   (a) Sequential file   (d) Synonym   (f) Loading factor
   (b) Direct access   (e) Bucket   (g) Index
   (c) Hashing

2. Give one advantage and one disadvantage of each of the following file structures: sequential, indexed, indexed sequential, and tree.

3. Why is hashing difficult to apply to a multiple key file?

4. A hashing function is to be applied to a file with a capacity of $k = 10$ records/bucket. How many buckets are needed to store $n = 1000$ records and at the same time maintain a loading factor of $l = .85$?

5. Devise an update algorithm for inserting a new record in the indexed sequential file shown in the text. What are the problems encountered?

6. Devise an algorithm to update a sequential file stored on tape. Assume that tape 1 contains records to be inserted and/or deleted; tape 2 contains the master file to be updated. The output of the update should go on tape 3.

7. How are bucket overflows handled in a file system employing buckets?

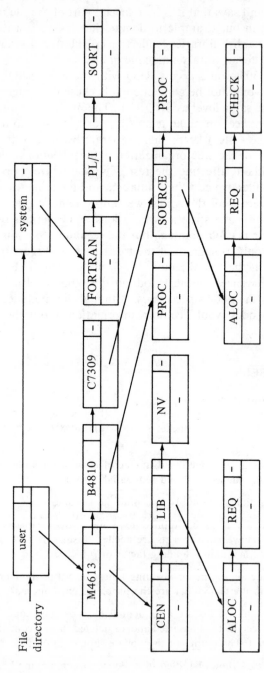

Figure 6.10 Storage of file directory tree

6.4
Attribute-based
Files

We have been treating records identified uniquely by their key fields. If one or more keys are used, we assume that one and only one record is identified by the keys. In many applications, however, uniqueness is not possible. Indeed, often in a file retrieval system it is desirable to fetch many records with exactly the same key fields. Such a file is called an *attribute-based file.*

For example, census data is an attribute-based file with an abundance of key fields. Examples include income bracket, state, county, census tract, sex, and so on. Suppose that a regional census wants to organize a file system based on state, sex, and income bracket. The keys of interest are shown in Figure 6.11; the states are California, Idaho, Nevada, and Oregon; the income brackets are upper (U), middle (M), and low (L). The object is to count or retrieve all records with certain attributes, such as CA-M-U (meaning males in California in the upper-income bracket). The problem is to devise a file organization that facilitates this type of processing.

INVERTED FILE STRUCTURE

An inverted file structure contains one index for each key. Each index gives the address of all records having a particular value of the key. For example, for the regional census file described above, we would need three indexes. An example of the indexes and the file are shown in Figure 6.12. An inverted file organization has the advantage that the values of the key attributes do not have to be duplicated throughout the file. They appear once in the index, and other information is kept in the file. However, it takes a considerable amount of effort to create the indexes, and it is not easy to update them.

To reference all records with keys CA-F-M (California-female-middle-income bracket) we consult the indexes. The records with state CA are

Attribute	State	Sex	Income bracket
Values	CA	M	U
	ID	F	M
	NV		L
	OR		

Figure 6.11 Attributes and values for regional census file

State		Sex		Income bracket	
CA	1, 3, 4, 6	M	2, 3, 7, 8, 11	U	1, 3, 7
ID	2, 9	F	1, 4, 5, 6, 9, 10	M	2, 4, 5, 6, 10
NV	5, 8, 10			L	8, 9, 11
OR	7, 11				

	Name	Tract	No. dep.	Auto
1	HUTTON, A.	362	4	17
2	MATHEWSON, J.	487	2	18
3	DUGGAN, P.	609	4	17
4	MCINTOSH, J.	365	1	15
5	BROWN, I.	284	2	16
6	TOPSY, L.	642	1	15
7	LOUIS, P.	211	1	17
8	WHITE, P.	304	2	14
9	BERGS, C.	416	5	12
10	CLARK, A.	207	4	16
11	SANDS, M.	316	3	11

Figure 6.12 Sample inverted file

{1, 3, 4, 6}, sex F are {1, 4, 5, 6, 9, 10}, and middle-income bracket are {2, 4, 5, 6, 10}. The records with CA-F-M are {4, 6}, which is the intersection of the three sets.

The inverted file structure makes reference of records by one or more keys possible. However, the size of the indexes requires a considerable amount of space, and the more keys in the file the more space needed. Also, some indexes may not convey a lot of information. For example, an index with few key values (such as sex) will not discriminate among records sufficiently to be of use. It is better to store this type of information as a field in each record. Another file organization that cuts down the size of the indexes is the multilist file.

MULTILIST

Multilist files are similar to inverted files in that there is one index for each key. However, the index points to only one record with a particular value of the key. That record must contain a pointer to another record with the same key, and so on, until all records with the same key are linked together. Thus the indexes are small, but the records must contain a pointer field for each key. This type of organization is not good for retrieval of multi-attribute records, such as CA-M-U in the census data example. Following the pointers takes too long, especially since the pointers are part of the file.

   Examples of multilist files appear in Section 3.3 if we imagine that the multilinked lists are stored on a disk (in particular see Figure 3.17).

EXERCISES

1. What is the essential difference between a multilist file and an attribute-based file?

2. Draw a graph corresponding to the file of Figure 6.12.

3. Write a program to perform updates on either an inverted file or an attribute-based file.

7
SORTING

7.1
Simple
Sorts

Scatter storage and the techniques of multilinked lists might give the impression that the arrangement of data is not important. Indeed, the physical order of data within memory is not important, but for effective use of the data, it must be placed in logical order before it is of real value. Moreover, searching techniques (Chapter 8) are greatly facilitated if data is kept in some sort of order. As with most problems involving large data bases, sorting is best done by computer, using the more efficient sorting algorithms.

Perhaps the simplest algorithm is the *bubble sort*. It compares successive pairs of elements in the list and interchanges two elements if necessary. The list is scanned repeatedly until no further exchanges are required: then the list is in order. Figure 7.1 shows how an item is "bubbled" to the top of the list. Comparisons begin at the bottom and work up. If there are n items in the list, the first pass requires $n - 1$ comparisons. Notice that after the first pass, the smallest number is at the top of the list. After the second pass (which requires only $n - 2$ comparisons) the first two numbers are in their correct places.

Another sorting technique that is easy to understand is the *selection sort*. Given a list of n elements, compare the first entry to the second, third, fourth, and so on. Any time that a value larger than the first value is found, swap it with the first entry. After going through the list once, the largest value will be at the head of the list. Then compare the second element with the third, fourth, fifth, and so on. Again, swap elements so that the largest of the remaining $n - 1$ values winds up second in the list. Continue in this manner until finally the $(n - 1)$st element is compared with the nth, and the larger of the two is put in the $(n - 1)$st position. At this point the list

Initial list	After first compare	After second compare	After third compare	After first pass	After second pass
19	19	19	19	01	01
01	01	01	01	19	11
26	26	26	26	11	19
43	43	43	43	26	21
92	92	92	92	43 · · ·	26
87	87	87	87	92	43
21	21	21	11	87	92
38	38	11	21	21	87
55	11	38	38	38	38
11	55	55	55	55	55

Figure 7.1 Partial result of bubble sort

is in order from high to low. A minor change in the algorithm would produce an ascending order.

These two algorithms are straightforward approaches to sorting and are easy to program. They are fine for short lists or for lists that do not need reordering often. However, these algorithms are too slow when frequent use is desired or when large amounts of data are involved.

To determine the "best" algorithm, we must establish standards. We will use two common measures: storage requirements and average number of comparisons. We are posing two questions: What algorithms require the least amount of comparisons (on the average)? What algorithms require the least amount of storage?

Concerning the question of comparisons, what is the minimal number of comparisons possible? If a list is in order, it still requires a minimal number of comparisons to discover that fact. But if the list is in reverse order, we might expect that more comparisons will be required. The number of comparisons needed to order an unordered list is called the *sort effort*. The minimum sort effort is (see Knuth, Volume 3):

$$n \log n$$

where n is the length of the list. For example, if the list contains 100 entries, then the minimum sort effort is approximately:

$$100 \log 100 = 100 \cdot 2 = \underline{200}$$

This is a theoretical limit. Most algorithms require more comparisons. In the final analysis, the "best" algorithm is the one that runs fastest on a particular machine. It has been empirically determined that quickersort (discussed in Section 7.2) is the fastest sorting technique on most machines.

Before examining specific examples, let us mention that sorting techniques fall into certain classes. Algorithms may be classified as *internal* or *external,* depending on whether the data being examined will fit in main memory or will require secondary storage. Usually external sorting depends on the electromechanical capabilities of the secondary storage device. and incorporates an internal sorting algorithm as part of a programmed user's program.

Algorithms may also be classified as comparative sorts or distributive sorts. *Comparative sorts* operate by comparing and exchanging two keys at a time, such as the bubble sort. *Distributive sorts* separate keys into subsets so that all items in one subset are greater than all those in the other subset. Radix sort, quickersort, and merge sort are examples of distributive sorts. The minimum sort effort of $n \log_2 n$ applies only to comparative sorts.

EXERCISES

1. Perform a selection sort on the list in Figure 7.1.

2. What is the minimal sort effort for a list of 1000 items?

3. Give examples of distributive and comparative sorts.

4. Define the following terms:
   (a) internal sort
   (b) external sort

7.2
More Sorting
Algorithms

The following algorithms are presented by example. The sorting effort is given without derivation and should be compared with the theoretical limit of $n \log_2 n$.

RADIX

The radix sort is the principle employed in mechanical card-sorting machines, which were developed years before electronic computers. To sort numbers the algorithm requires the establishment of ten queues, one for each of the digits zero through nine. The algorithm examines the numbers one digit at a time, starting with the least significant (rightmost) digit. The steps in the radix algorithm are:

1. Examine the least significant digits and move each number to the appropriate queue.

2. Reconstruct the list by concatenating the elements in the queues in order from zero through nine.

3. Repeat steps 1 and 2 on the second digit, third digit, and so on, until all digits have been examined, and the list is in order.

The number of passes through the list equals the number of digits in the largest key. In Figure 7.2 the sort requires two passes because the largest number contains two digits.

It may seem that the radix algorithm examines the digits in the wrong order. It starts with the rightmost digit and works to the left. Use the numbers in the example and work from the leftmost digit to the right and see where the algorithm fails.

In general, for n keys, q queues, and k digits in each number, the storage S and the number of compares C are computed by averaging over uniformly occurring values:

$$S = (n + 1)q$$
$$C = n \log_q k$$

Initial list	Pass 1 queues	First reconstruction	Pass 2 queues	Final reconstruction
19	0 70	70	0 01	01
01	1 21,11,21,01	01	1 19,11	11
26	2 92	21	2 26,21,21	19
43	3 43	11	3 38,36	21
92	4 54,64	21	4 43	21
87	5 55	92	5 55,54	26
21	6 36,26	43	6 64	36
38	7 77,87	64	7 77,70	38
11	8 38	54	8 87	43
55	9 19	55	9 92	54
21		26		55
64		36		64
54		87		70
70		77		77
36		38		87
77		19		92

Figure 7.2 Steps in radix sort for decimal keys

Thus in the example of Figure 7.2:

$$S = (16 + 1)10 = 170$$
$$C = 16 \log_{10} 2 \approx 5.0$$

A *binary radix* sort is sometimes preferred for binary machines, in which case the numbers are encoded into binary values and there are only two queues involved. For a binary radix sort of the numbers in Figure 7.2, we compute:

$$S = (16 + 1)2 = 34$$
$$C = 16 \log_2 7 \approx 47$$

Thus an obvious tradeoff between storage and time is possible by changing the base of the numbers.

BUBBLE

Bubble sort is discussed in Section 7.1. The maximum number of comparisons occurs when the items are in reverse order. Thus for a list of length n, the maximum is:

$$C_{\max} = (n - 1) + (n - 2) + (n - 3) + \cdot \cdot \cdot + 2 + 1 = \frac{n(n - 1)}{2}$$

The minimum number of comparisons occurs when the list is already ordered and:

$$C_{\min} = n - 1$$

On the average we would expect an element to be compared with about half the elements in the list before finding its correct place. The total number of comparisons on the average is:

$$C = \frac{1 + 2 + \cdot \cdot \cdot + n - 1}{2} = \frac{n(n - 1)}{4}$$

MERGE

Merging involves combining two or more lists so that the combined list is also in order. It does *not* mean combine the elements and then order them. (A merge algorithm is given after the discussion of the two-way merge sort.) Merging is competitive with other internal sorts in terms of speed, but requires twice the amount of storage to merge the numbers from one pass to another. The steps in the two-way merge sort are:

1. Compare pairs of items and put each pair in order.

2. Merge pairs of pairs so that the resulting quadruples are in order.

3. Merge pairs of quadruples and continue in this manner until no more merges can occur.

The number of passes in the sort is approximately $\log_2 n$, where n is the number of elements in the list. Figure 7.3 (page 114) shows the two-way merge sort of a list of 16 numbers. It requires four passes to order the list. Notice that storage of the values alternates between the original array and a spare array.

The algorithm in Figure 7.4 (page 115) shows steps needed to merge two lists, A[1]–A[N] and B[1]–B[M], to form a third list C[1]–C[N + M]. It is assumed that the original lists are arranged in ascending order.

TREE SORT

In tree sort an array of values is either given as a tree or is treated as a tree structure with the values in random order at the nodes. Tree sort is a different approach from the sort tree discussed in Section 5.2, which ordered the elements as the tree grew. The steps in the tree sort algorithm are:

1. Starting with the root, number the nodes so that nodes at the same level are numbered consecutively.

2. Repeat steps 3 through 6 until all nodes are pruned from the tree. The order in which the values are pruned gives the correct order of the elements.

3. Start at the lowest level (furthest from the root) and compare each terminal node with its predecessor. If the terminal node is smaller, swap it with its parent node.

4. Repeat step 5 until reaching the root of the tree. At this point the root contains the smallest element in the tree.

5. Move up to the next level and compare each node with its parent; exchange values when necessary.

6. Swap the root node's value with the value of the last node in the tree. Prune or remove the last node from the tree, save the value, and decrease the number of nodes by one.

Figure 7.5 traces the execution of the tree sort algorithm until the smallest element on the tree is found and pruned. Figure 7.5 (a) depicts

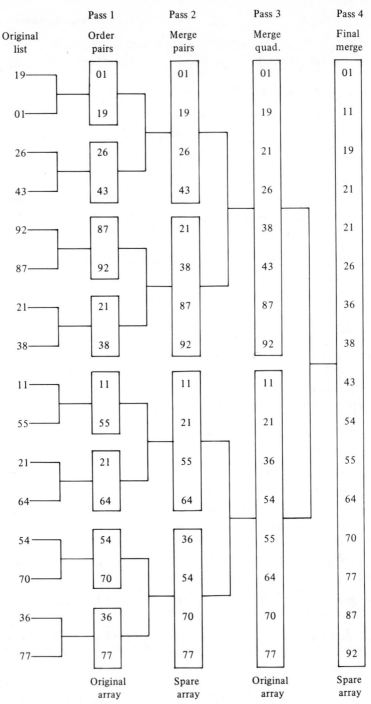

Figure 7.3 Merge sort of 16 numbers in four passes

MERGE: 1.   Initially set I ← 1, J ← 1, K ← 1.

     2.   Do the following until I > N or J > M.
          If A[I] ≤ B[J]

             then set C[K] ← A[I]
                   K ← K + 1
                   I ← I + 1
             else set C[K] ← B[J]
                   K ← K + 1
                   J ← J + 1

     3.   If I > N copy B[J] through B[M] into
                       C[K] through C[N + M]
           else copy A[I] through A[N] into
                       C[K] through C[N + M].

Figure 7.4 Algorithm to merge arrays A and B into array C

the original tree and the numbering of the nodes. In 7.5 (b) two exchanges have been made at the lowest level, and both 60 and 22 have moved up to positions 4 and 5, respectively. On the second level [7.5 c] only one exchange is possible, but at the first level there are also two comparisons. We begin comparisons from the right, so 12 is swapped with 59, leaving 12 as the new root. Then 12 is compared with 10 and the two values are swapped. These movements are represented by swap lines A and B. Notice that 12 has moved from its position at node 3 to node 1 to node 2. The final step involves exchanging the root node's value with that of the last node and pruning the last node. The pruned value could now be placed on a queue so that when all nodes have been pruned, the queue will contain the values in their sorted order.

An arbitrary dense list can be interpreted as a tree structure by making the kth element the parent of elements $2k$ and $2k + 1$. Thus the tree sort algorithm can be used on a list without actually converting the list into a tree structure. The subscripts of the list become the pointers for the tree.

The number of comparisons in this technique is approximately:

$$C = 1.4(n + 1)\log_2 n + (1 + \gamma)n$$

where $\gamma = .57721$. For the example in Figure 7.5, $n = 11$, and C is approximately 75:

$$
\begin{aligned}
C &= 1.4(11 + 1)\log_2 11 + (1.57721)11 \\
&= 1.4(12)(3.45943) + 17.34931 \\
&= 58.118424 + 17.34931 \\
&= 75.46773
\end{aligned}
$$

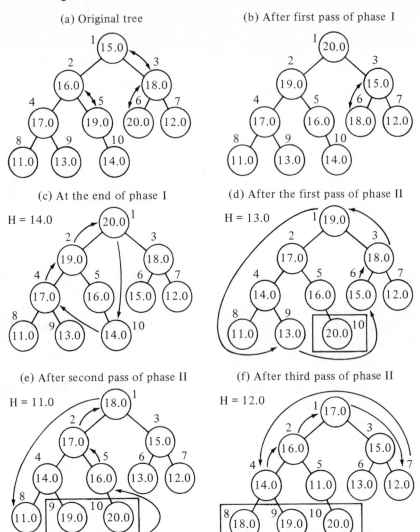

(a) Original tree

(b) After first pass of phase I

(c) At the end of phase I

(d) After the first pass of phase II

(e) After second pass of phase II

(f) After third pass of phase II

Figure 7.5 Partial execution of tree sort algorithm: finds two smallest values

QUICKERSORT

In the bubble sort algorithm the distance that an element moves after a comparison is either zero or one position. Thus if an item is at the wrong end of the list, it will take many comparisons and moves to locate it to the correct place. In the selection sort one item may move quite a few spaces, but at the expense of possibly relocating another element at the wrong end of the list. The purpose of quickersort is to cover a lot of distance in one move in the correct direction.

Basically quickersort selects the middle element of the list and divides the remainder of the list into two parts—one part containing all values less than the middle element, and the other part containing all values greater than the middle element. These two parts may or may not be the same size, and values equal to the middle element may go in either part. The next step is to store one of the sublists on a stack and then work on the other sublist in the same manner. Thus we are constantly working on smaller and smaller sublists. When left with a sublist of length two (anything less than ten is just as efficient), order the elements and process one of the sublists from the stack. When the stack is empty, the entire list is in order. To ensure that this process is not magical, let us study the following numerical example. Then we will go into the details of the algorithm.

Suppose we are given the values:

$$20 \quad 73 \quad 42 \quad 11 \quad 80 \quad 39 \quad \textcircled{72} \quad 30 \quad 100 \quad 46 \quad 88 \quad 32 \quad 21$$

The "middle" of the list is 72, the seventh number, which we circle. Next we begin at the left end looking for a value greater than 72 and at the right end looking for a value less than 72.

$$20 \quad 73 \quad 42 \quad 11 \quad 80 \quad 39 \quad \textcircled{72} \quad 30 \quad 100 \quad 46 \quad 88 \quad 32 \quad 21$$
$$\uparrow \qquad\qquad\qquad\qquad\qquad\qquad\qquad\qquad\qquad\qquad \uparrow$$

The arrows point to numbers which satisfy this rule. Now we exchange these values and continue our search for two more numbers.

$$20 \quad 21 \quad 42 \quad 11 \quad 80 \quad 39 \quad \textcircled{72} \quad 30 \quad 100 \quad 46 \quad 88 \quad 32 \quad 73$$
$$\uparrow \qquad\qquad\qquad\qquad\qquad\qquad\qquad\qquad\qquad \uparrow$$

We swap these and continue, but do not consider 72.

$$20 \quad 21 \quad 42 \quad 11 \quad 32 \quad 39 \quad \textcircled{72} \quad 30 \quad 100 \quad 46 \quad 88 \quad 80 \quad 73$$
$$\uparrow \quad \uparrow$$

After swapping 100 and 46 we realize that we cannot continue and have divided our list into two parts. We have to move our "middle" element into its correct position between 46 and 100.

$$\underbrace{20 \quad 21 \quad 42 \quad 11 \quad 32 \quad 39 \quad 30 \quad 46}_{\text{sublist}_1} \quad \textcircled{72} \quad \underbrace{100 \quad 88 \quad 80 \quad 73}_{\text{sublist}_2}$$

Since sublist$_1$ is longer than sublist$_2$ we will apply the same algorithm to it, leaving 72 in its correct position and temporarily leaving sublist$_2$ as is. Picking 32 as the "middle" of sublist$_1$ we are able to form two new sublists.

$$\underbrace{20 \quad 21 \quad 30 \quad 11}_{\text{sublist}_3} \quad \textcircled{32} \quad \underbrace{39 \quad 42 \quad 46}_{\text{sublist}_4} \quad \textcircled{72} \quad \underbrace{100 \quad 88 \quad 80 \quad 73}_{\text{sublist}_2}$$

We could continue working on each sublist, but since there are so few numbers in each, we might as well point out a few things. First of all, 32 and 72 are in their correct positions, according to the final ordering. All sublists are in their correct positions, relatively speaking. That is, all numbers in sublist$_3$ are less than 32; all numbers in sublist$_4$ are between 32 and 72; and all numbers in sublist$_2$ are greater than 72. Thus if we order each sublist, we will obtain the desired result.

$$11 \quad 20 \quad 21 \quad 30 \quad 32 \quad 39 \quad 42 \quad 46 \quad 72 \quad 73 \quad 80 \quad 88 \quad 100$$

Perhaps one of the most subtle tricks in the quickersort algorithm involves handling the middle element. In the example, 72 started out in the seventh position and was inserted in the ninth position between 46 and 100. An insertion of this type means moving elements and moving requires time. To eliminate moving a lot of elements, temporarily remove the middle element, place it in an area outside the list, fill its spot with the first element in the list, and begin processing with the second element. After splitting the list into two parts, place the middle element back into the list and put an appropriate value in the first position. Our example would have started in the following way: The first element replaces 72 and 72 is set apart from the list.

$$\boxed{20} \quad 73 \quad 42 \quad 11 \quad 80 \quad 39 \quad 20 \quad 30 \quad 100 \quad 46 \quad 88 \quad 32 \quad 21 \quad \textcircled{72}$$

After making all swaps the list is now in the following arrangement.

$$\boxed{20} \; | \quad 21 \quad 42 \quad 11 \quad 32 \quad 39 \quad 20 \quad 30 \quad 46 \quad 100 \quad 88 \quad 80 \quad 73$$
$$\uparrow \qquad \uparrow$$

Now 46 is at the end of the left sublist. Since 46 is less than 72, we move 46 to position one and let 72 occupy the place of 46. We still have two sublists—one with numbers less than 72 and one with numbers greater than 72.

$$46 \quad 21 \quad 42 \quad 11 \quad 32 \quad 39 \quad 20 \quad 30 \quad \underbrace{\qquad\qquad\qquad\qquad\qquad}_{\text{sublist}_1} 72 \quad \underbrace{100 \quad 88 \quad 80 \quad 73}_{\text{sublist}_2}$$

If we find a number that belongs in the right sublist but do not find a number to swap with it, we place the middle value in front of that number, after removing the number previously stored there and placing it in position one. For example, suppose we begin with the following list.

$$45 \quad 73 \quad 12 \quad 80 \quad 100 \quad 62 \quad 48 \quad 60 \quad 46 \quad 71 \quad 89$$
$$33 \quad 92 \quad 87 \quad 36 \quad 61 \quad 50$$

We remove 46, the middle element, and put 45 in its place. The first position is marked to show that it is not under consideration.

$$\boxed{45} \quad 73 \quad 12 \quad 80 \quad 100 \quad 62 \quad 48 \quad 60 \quad 45 \quad 71 \quad 89 \quad 33$$
$$\uparrow$$
$$92 \quad 87 \quad 36 \quad 61 \quad 50 \quad \textcircled{46}$$
$$\uparrow$$

After swapping 73 and 36, we go on to swap 80 and 33, and then 100 and 45. Now we discover that 62 should go on the right sublist, but that there is nothing to swap with it.

$$\boxed{45} \quad 36 \quad 12 \quad 33 \quad 45 \quad 62 \quad 48 \quad 60 \quad 100 \quad 71 \quad 89$$
$$\uparrow$$
$$80 \quad 92 \quad 87 \quad 73 \quad 61 \quad 50 \quad \textcircled{46}$$

Therefore 62 becomes the beginning of the right sublist, if we put 46 in the position occupied by 45 and place 45 in the unused first position.

$$\underbrace{45 \quad 36 \quad 12 \quad 33}_{\text{sublist}_1} \quad \textcircled{46}$$
$$\underbrace{62 \quad 48 \quad 60 \quad 100 \quad 71 \quad 89 \quad 80 \quad 92 \quad 87 \quad 73 \quad 61 \quad 50}_{\text{sublist}_2}$$

Thus we have separated the original list into two sublists and can continue with the algorithm. Since we can work with only one sublist at a time, we save one sublist's left and right pointers and work with the other sublist. In this example, we stack the left sublist pointers (1 and 4) and work with the right sublist. Pointers for sublist$_2$ are 6 and 17 for the left and right ends, respectively. After processing sublist$_2$, using 89 as the middle, we have the following.

$$45 \quad 36 \quad 12 \quad 33 \quad \textcircled{46}$$
$$\underbrace{\hspace{4cm}}_{\text{sublist}_1}$$

stack

$$73 \quad 48 \quad 60 \quad 50 \quad 71 \quad 62 \quad 80 \quad 61 \quad 87 \quad \textcircled{89} \quad 92 \quad 100 \quad \boxed{1,4}$$
$$\underbrace{\hspace{6.5cm}}_{\text{sublist}_3} \qquad \underbrace{\hspace{2cm}}_{\text{sublist}_4}$$

As before, we stack the left sublist pointers (6 and 14) and work with the right sublist. Since there are only two elements in sublist$_4$, we order them and remove a sublist from the stack.

$$45 \quad 36 \quad 12 \quad 33 \quad \textcircled{46}$$
$$\underbrace{\hspace{4cm}}_{\text{sublist}_1}$$

stack

$$73 \quad 48 \quad 60 \quad 50 \quad 71 \quad 62 \quad 80 \quad 61 \quad 87 \quad \textcircled{89} \quad \textcircled{92} \quad \textcircled{100} \quad \boxed{\begin{matrix} 6,14 \\ 1,4 \end{matrix}}$$
$$\underbrace{\hspace{7cm}}_{\text{sublist}_3}$$

After processing sublist$_3$ we now find that all circled elements are in their correct locations and are no longer considered in the sorting. We stack the pointers for sublist$_5$ and are ready to work on sublist$_6$.

$$45 \quad 36 \quad 12 \quad 33 \quad \textcircled{46} \quad 62 \quad 48 \quad 60 \quad 50 \quad 61 \quad \textcircled{71}$$
$$\underbrace{\hspace{4cm}}_{\text{sublist}_1} \qquad \underbrace{\hspace{4cm}}_{\text{sublist}_5}$$

stack

$$80 \quad 73 \quad 87 \quad \textcircled{89} \quad \textcircled{92} \quad \textcircled{100} \quad \boxed{\begin{matrix} 6,10 \\ 1,4 \end{matrix}}$$
$$\underbrace{\hspace{3cm}}_{\text{sublist}_6}$$

By now you should be able to continue this example on your own and verify that the quickersort algorithm does produce an ordered list.

The expected number of comparisons for quickersort is:

$$C = 2n \ln n$$

where there are n elements in the list. However, quickersort also requires a stack for $\log_2 n$ pointers.

SUMMARY

The proper sort algorithm to choose for a given situation depends upon many factors. Frequently sorting speed may not be the overriding consideration. If the sort will be used infrequently, then perhaps ease of programming is most important in choosing an algorithm. The amount of storage required and the average number of comparisons for various algorithms appear in Figure 7.6.

EXERCISES

1. Write a sort algorithm for one (or more) of the sorting techniques in the section.

2. Write a program for one (or more) of the sorting techniques in the section. Run it with different sets of data and compute the average number of comparisons. Compare your program's average with the theoretical average.

3. Alter the algorithm in Figure 7.4 so that it can be used in a two-way merge sort. Remember that the data to be merged is stored in the same array.

4. What are some of the considerations involved when sorting names or other alphanumeric data? Write a program to sort a list of names. Use any sort algorithm desired.

5. Complete the execution of the tree sort algorithm on the tree in Figure 7.5.

6. Compare tree sort and quickersort when the original list (7, 5, 4, 3, 2, 1) is in reverse order.

7. Plot the number of comparisons for C versus the size of the list n for all sorting algorithms, and n in the range of 100 to 1000.

Sort	Storage	Comparison
Radix	$(n + 1)q$	$n \log_q k$
Bubble	n	$\dfrac{n(n-1)}{4}$
Selection	n	$\dfrac{n(n-1)}{2}$
Merge	$2n$	$n \log_2 n$
Treesort	n + pointers	$2.4n \, (\log_2 n)$
Quickersort	n + stack	$2n \ln n$

Figure 7.6 Summary of internal sorting algorithms

7.3
External
Sorting

Interest in external sorting has declined since the mid-1960s with increased use of random access devices. Before that time external sorting involved the use of tapes and was a combination of internal sort and string merges. The four general string merge techniques are:

1. Balanced or von Neumann

2. Cascade

3. Polyphase

4. Oscillating

The balanced merge and cascade merge are not as efficient as the polyphase and oscillating merge in most cases. They are explained only briefly here.

BALANCED

Given t tape units, the internal sort routine produces an equal number of ordered strings of the same length on half the tape units.

For example, suppose there are $t = 4$ tape units. Initially one of the t tapes contains the unordered string. The internal sort routine will produce $s = 6$ substrings on two of the tapes. Thus at the end of the first phase of the balanced merge sort, the four tapes are as follows: tape 1 is empty, tape 2 is empty, tape 3 has three substrings, tape 4 has three substrings. The tapes are now balanced, containing either ordered substrings or being empty.

In the next phase the first substrings from tape 3 and tape 4 are merged and written onto tape 1, leaving two substrings on both tape 3 and tape 4. Next the second substrings from tapes 3 and 4 are merged onto tape 2, leaving one substring on each. Finally, the remaining substrings are merged onto tape 1, leaving tapes 3 and 4 empty. At the end of this phase tape 1 has two (larger) substrings, tape 2 has one (larger) substring, and tapes 3 and 4 are empty. Merging continues until one tape contains the entire (ordered) string (see Figure 7.7).

Repeated passes and merges reduce the string to one sorted string in $\log_T s$ phases, where s is the number of initial strings and $T = t/2$. This method is similar to the internal merge sort, except that here half the tapes are merged at once.

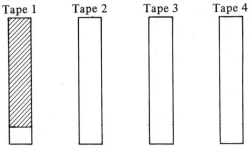

(a) Initial configuration of four tapes about to be used in
    a balanced merge sort. Tape 1 contains the unordered file.

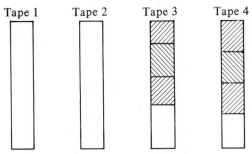

(b) First step of the balanced merge that produces six
    substrings. Tapes 3 and 4 each have three ordered substrings.

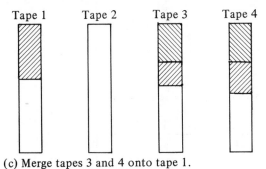

(c) Merge tapes 3 and 4 onto tape 1.

Figure 7.7 Configuration of a balanced merge sort

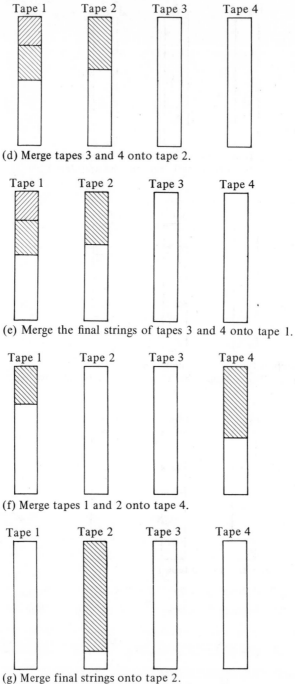

(d) Merge tapes 3 and 4 onto tape 2.

(e) Merge the final strings of tapes 3 and 4 onto tape 1.

(f) Merge tapes 1 and 2 onto tape 4.

(g) Merge final strings onto tape 2.

Figure 7.7 (continued)

CASCADE

The cascade merge sort operates on all tapes at once. First it distributes the initial sorted strings on all but one of the tapes and then merges them onto the remaining tape. The merge stops when one of the tapes runs out of data. Assuming there are t tapes, a subsequent pass begins by merging $t - 2$ of the unmerged tapes onto an empty tape. Repeatedly $t - 3, t - 4$, and so on tapes are merged until none remain. The final phase is to copy all the merged tapes onto one.

POLYPHASE

For installations with six or fewer tape drives the polyphase sort is best.[1] The initial strings are distributed on $t - 1$ tapes in amounts corresponding to a generalized Fibonacci sequence (see Figure 7.8). Like the cascade merge, all $t - 1$ tapes are merged onto the remaining tape until one is emptied. The empty tape is used as the output or merge tape on the next pass. Unlike the cascade merge, each pass uses $t - 1$ tapes.

k	Total number of strings at start of merge $a_k{}^{(0)}$	Tape 1 $a_k{}^{(1)}$	Tape 2 $a_k{}^{(2)}$	Tape 3 $a_k{}^{(3)}$
1	3	1	1	1
2	5	1	2	2
3	9	2	3	4
4	17	4	6	7
5	31	7	11	13
6	57	13	20	24
7	105	24	37	44

Figure 7.8 Polyphase table for $t = 4$. The general form of the Fibonacci sequence is

$$a_k^{(i)} = \sum_{\tau=1}^{t-1} a_{k-\tau}^{(i)}; \quad a_k^{(1)} = 1, \quad i = 2, 3, \ldots ,$$

$$k = t, t + 1, \ldots , \quad a_1^{(0)} = t - 1$$

[1]D. L. Shell, "Optimizing the Polyphase Sort," *Comm. ACM* 14, no. 11 (November 1971):713–719.

The number of strings to be merged is computed by a generalized Fibonacci sequence, where each number in the sequence is the sum of the $t - 1$ numbers preceding it. For example, if $t = 4$, the Fibonacci sequence for total number of initial strings is 1, 3, 5, 9, 17, 31, . . . It is not often that unordered strings come in Fibonacci sequence sizes, so D. L. Shell has offered a near optimum algorithm for the initial tape assignment. The optimum assignment algorithm is very complex and offers only a 3% improvement over the *horizontal distribution* method given by Shell.

An example of a polyphase merge of nine numbers with four tapes appears in Figure 7.9. Pass 0 shows the data in its original order on tape 1. Pass 1 writes the initial strings of length $a_3^{(1)} = 2$, $a_3^{(2)} = 3$, and $a_3^{(3)} = 4$ (these are from table in Figure 7.8). Pass 2 merges the data to tape 1 until tape 2 is empty. Pass 3 merges the data to tape 2 until tape 3 is depleted, and pass 4 shows the results of the final merge.

OSCILLATING SORT

The oscillating sort is applicable *only* to tapes which can be read in either the forward or reverse direction. Initially one string is written on all but one of the tape units and then merged to the empty tape. Then more of the string is written to the tapes and then merged. The term oscillating

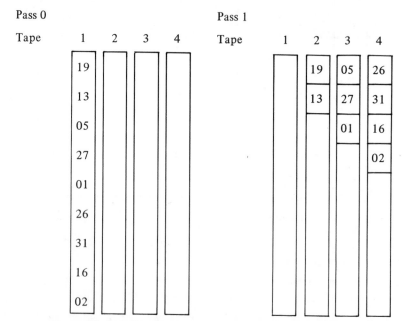

Figure 7.9 Polyphase merge of nine numbers with four tapes

Pass 2

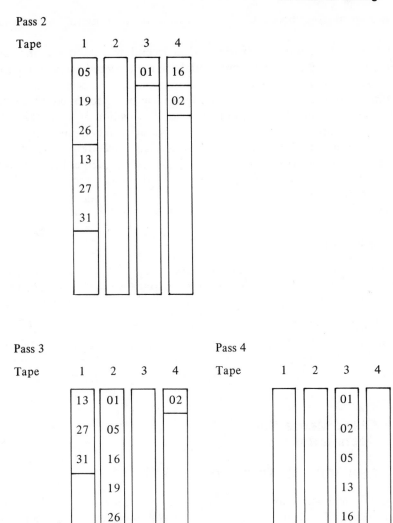

Figure 7.9 (continued)

sort is derived from the switching back and forth from internal to external sorts.

Figure 7.10 illustrates an example of an ascending order oscillating sort applied to 12 numbers and 5 tapes. Initially the unordered list is on tape 1. In the first pass numbers are written onto all but one of the remaining tapes. The tapes will be read in reverse order instead of being rewound, as shown by the dots in Figure 7.10. The dots indicate the position of the read/write head of each tape drive. During pass 2 the sorted numbers are merged to tape 2, but notice that the numbers are merged in descending order. Pass 3 distributes more values to tapes 2, 4, and 5, and pass 4 merges them to tape 3. The sorting and merging continues until all values are merged into ascending order in pass 9.

EXERCISES

1. Perform a balanced, cascade, and polyphase merge sort on two files: one initially of eight strings and one initially of nine strings. Assume $t = 4$ tapes. How do the methods compare?

2. Extend the table of Figure 7.8 for (a) $t = 4$ and $k = 8$, (b) $t = 5$ and $k = 4$.

3. Read the article by D. L. Shell, and then perform the horizontal distribution algorithm for polyphase merge sort, when there are $t = 4$ tapes and 13 initial strings.

7.4
Other Merge Sort
Techniques

REPLACEMENT-SELECTION

The replacement-selection algorithm produces an output tape containing one or more ordered strings from an unordered input tape. The technique depends on three lists:

1. The input string

2. An internal string of numbers

3. The last number written to the output tape

Before giving the algorithm we will perform a replacement-selection sort on the data in Figure 7.11 (page 131). Initially the unordered string is stored on tape 1 as shown. An internal list is obtained by reading the first few numbers into memory, as shown in the second snapshot of Figure 7.11.

Pass 0	Original data			
1	2	3	4	5
29				
23				
15				
27				
01				
26				
31				
16				
02				
46				
10				
22				

Pass 1	Sort			
1	2	3	4	5
27	(29)	(23)	(15)	
01				
26				
31				
16				
02				
46				
10				
22				

Pass 2	Merge			
1	2	3	4	5
27	29			
01	23			
26	15			
31				
16				
02				
46				
10				
22				

Pass 3	Sort			
1	2	3	4	5
31	29		(01)	(26)
16	23			
02	15			
46	(27)			
10				
22				

Pass 4	Merge			
1	2	3	4	5
31	29	27		
16	23	26		
02	15	01		
46				
10				
22				

Pass 5	Sort			
1	2	3	4	5
46	29	27		(02)
10	23	26		
22	15	01		
	(31)	(16)		

Pass 6	Merge			
1	2	3	4	5
46	29	27	31	
10	23	26	16	
22	15	01	02	

Pass 7	Sort			
1	2	3	4	5
	29	27	31	
	23	26	16	
	15	01	02	
	(46)	(10)	(22)	

Pass 8	Merge			
1	2	3	4	5
	29	27	31	46
	23	26	16	22
	15	01	02	10

Pass 9	Merge			
1	2	3	4	5
01				
02				
10				
15				
16				
22				
23				
27				
29				
31				
46				

Figure 7.10 Oscillating sort of twelve numbers using five tapes

The first output number is selected by taking the smallest number from the internal list and replacing it with the next number read from the input tape. Thus in Figure 7.11, 09 is output to tape 2 and is replaced by 02 from the input tape.

At each pass of the algorithm, we must select from the internal list the smallest number that is larger than the last number written to the output tape. The smallest number is written and replaced by the next number to be read from the input tape.

In Figure 7.11 we successively select 11, 16, 21, 26, and 31 as the smallest numbers that are larger than the number previously written out. After 31 has been written, we notice that the internal list is 01, 27, 02 all of which are smaller than the last output number 31. In this case we start a new string by beginning over again.

The first number placed in the new output string is the smallest number selected from the internal list. In Figure 7.11 we replace 01 with 05, and 02 with 13. The complete string is 01, 02, 05, 13, 19, 27.

The key to replacement-selection is finding the smallest number in the internal list that is larger than the last number written out. This fact is reflected in the following replacement-selection algorithm.

Replacement-Selection   T1 is the input tape and T2 is the output tape. Here, n is the size of the internal list (we used $n = 3$ in Figure 7.11).

1.   Initially read n numbers from T1 and store them in a memory list called LIST.

2.   Repeat the steps below until T1 becomes empty:
    (a)   Select the smallest number from LIST and call it MINIMAX.
    (b)   Output MINIMAX to T2 and replace it with a number from T1. Set SELECTION = 'SUCCESS'.
    (c) Repeat the step below until SELECTION = 'FAIL'.
        i.   If there is a smallest number in LIST that is larger than MINIMAX, replace MINIMAX with this number, output it to T2, and replace the smallest number with a number read from T1
            otherwise,
            set SELECTION = 'FAIL'.
    (d)   Output a file mark to T2.

3.   Order the $(n - 1)$ largest numbers in LIST and write the ordered list to T2. Output a file mark to T2.

Replacement-selection produces ordered strings of various lengths that can be optimally merged into one ordered string by forming a minimal merge tree. Such minimal trees are called *Huffman trees* in coding theory because they represent the fastest decoding trees for coded messages.

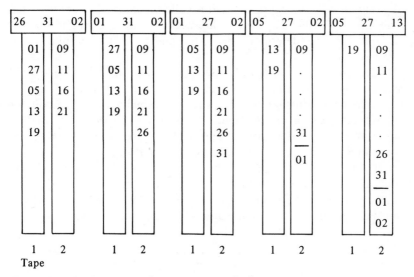

Figure 7.11 Replacement-selection sorting which generates two strings

OPTIMAL MERGE TREE

Suppose we use a replacement-selection algorithm to produce strings of lengths 28, 25, 13, 10, 8, 7, 6, and 3. Each string is stored on a different tape with an extra tape left blank after the replacement-selection. Of the eight full tapes we arbitrarily select three of them to be merged onto the blank tape. The question arises, Which three tapes do we merge first?

Suppose we start with the largest strings first and merge them onto the blank tape. This will create an ordered list of length $28 + 25 + 13 = 66$. The strings to be merged on a second pass are of lengths 66, 10, 8, 7, 6, and 3. If we continue to merge the three largest strings first, we produce 84, 7, 6, and 3; then 97 and 3; and finally 100.

We can draw a tree representing the steps in merge-sorting, using three tapes at a time. This tree contains terminal nodes that represent the initial strings. The value of a terminal node is the length of the string it represents. Internal nodes represent merged strings, and their value is the sum of the values of their successor nodes. See Figure 7.12 (a) for the merge tree created by merging, as we have suggested above. The root is at level zero to make our calculations easier.

Suppose we perform the merge as shown by the tree in Figure 7.12 (b). The first strings merged are the shortest strings of length 6 and 3. They form a string of length 9 that is merged with the next smallest strings of lengths 8 and 7. The resulting string of length 24 is merged with strings of length 13 and 10. Finally we obtain the ordered string of length 100 as we did before.

The merge tree of Figure 7.12 (b) is called a *minimal* or *optimal merge tree* because fewer move operations are needed when merging in the order shown. How can we determine this order, and how can we build optimal merge trees?

To determine the number of moves, we notice that every level in the merge tree represents a move (merge). To move the elements of an initial string to the final string, we must merge the terminal nodes repeatedly until we merge into the root node. Hence to move an element from an initial string, it must be elevated from its level in the merge tree to the root level.

A terminal node at level L must be moved L times to reach the root level. If a terminal node has a value of v_i, Lv_i is the number of moves needed to copy all v_i elements from the initial string to the final string.

Let L_i be the level number of terminal node i, and v_i be the value (length) of terminal node i. The value of a tree with r levels is:

$$\text{value} = \sum_{i=1}^{r} L_i v_i$$

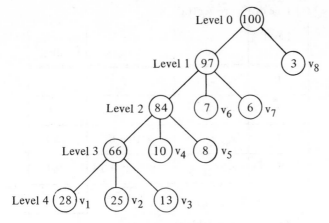

(a) A merge tree for a
three-way tape merge

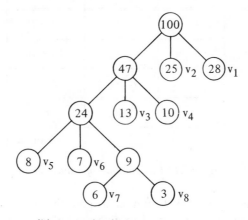

(b) An optimal merge
tree for a three-way
tape merge

Figure 7.12 Two merge trees for a three-way tape merge

A minimal or optimal merge tree is a tree constructed with terminal nodes (representing strings of length v_i) arranged so that the value of the merge tree is as small as possible.

The values of the trees of Figure 7.12 are shown by the computations in Figure 7.13. In each case the value of nodes at level n are summed and

(a) Tree of Figure 7.11(a)

Level number	Nodes	Values	Product
1	v_8	3	3
2	v_6, v_7	6 + 7	26
3	v_4, v_5	10 + 8	54
4	v_1, v_2, v_3	28 + 25 + 13	264
		Value =	347

(b) Tree of Figure 7.11(b)

Level number	Nodes	Values	Product
1	v_1, v_2	28 + 25	53
2	v_3, v_4	13 + 10	46
3	v_5, v_6	8 + 7	45
4	v_7, v_8	6 + 3	36
		Value =	180

Figure 7.13 Computation of values for two merge trees

multiplied by the level number to give the total value at that level. The level products are summed to give the value of the tree.

The formula for merge tree value gives us a means of checking the value of a tree to determine if it is minimal. The second problem is to determine how we construct minimal trees.

A two-way merge produces a binary tree, while a three-way merge produces a ternary tree. In general, a c-nary tree represents a c-way merge. A minimal merge c-nary tree is constructed by grouping together the c nodes of smallest value and calling these the *filial set*. The c smallest values are summed, and the sum becomes the value of the father node of the filial set. Again we select the c smallest nodes from all nodes remaining and call this the filial set. We form the father of this filial set and assign it the value equal to the sum of the filial set values. This procedure is repeated until only one node remains.

Often the number of terminal nodes does not equal a multiple of c. When this is true, we must select the size of the first filial set as follows: If $(r - 1)$ modulo $(c - 1) \equiv 0$, the first filial set contains c nodes, otherwise the size of the first filial set is $1 + [(r - 1)$ modulo $(c - 1)]$. An example of constructing the optimal tree of Figure 7.12 (b) is given in Figure 7.14. Since $r = 4$ and $c = 3$, the first filial set size is $1 + [(4 - 1)$ modulo $(3 - 1)]$ $= 2$.

DISK SORTING

An optimal merge strategy for disk files is easily found with the aid of a minimal merge tree if we ignore seek time. Unfortunately, seek time is of major significance in accessing disk files. How can we minimize seek time, rotational latency, and repetitive manipulation of records to be sorted?

First, we know that the tracks of a disk are organized as cylinders to avoid switching from track to track. If we control the placement of records on the disk, we can specify that each disk file be placed on a contiguous set of tracks contained within a single cylinder. In this way the cylinder may be treated exactly like a tape, and the methods useful for tapes are also useful for disk sorting.

If the initial strings are short enough to be fully contained within each cylinder, the sort-by-merge algorithms result in a minimal number of seeks. In addition, if extra output space is provided on each cylinder along with the input string's space, we realize an additional saving while performing the merge.

Often data-processing programmers attempt to decrease the size of a file by separating the key fields from the remainder of each record. The key field and a pointer to the corresponding master record are then sorted. The idea is to reduce the size of the file that is active in the sort. This is called *keysort* or *tagsort*.

The unfortunate part of keysorting is the rearrangement of the master file records necessary after the sort. Each record must subsequently be moved to its proper place in order.

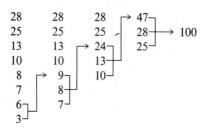

Figure 7.14 Derivation of minimal merge tree

It has been theoretically shown that the rearrangement overhead induces as much overhead as sorting without splitting off the keys first. For a file of N records, B records per file block, and a main memory buffer of M records we must perform about

$$\frac{(N \log_2 B)}{M}$$

block reading operations to rearrange the records after the keysort.

In most multiprogramming systems the user has little control over the order in which disk accesses are made or the placement of large files on disk. Hence we must design a sort strategy that is intrinsically optimal. To do this we note that the "cost" of merge sorting a disk file is a combination of the number of seeks and the number of strings merged. In the tree terminology we used before, the cost of sorting on disk is expressed as the number of node degrees D and the external path length E in all paths of the merge tree. We wish to minimize:

$$\alpha D + \beta E$$

α = constant of proportionality related to the overhead in a seek.

β = constant of proportionality related to the overhead in a merge.

D = sum over all terminal nodes of the internal node degrees along the path from terminal to root node.

E = sum over all terminal nodes of the path lengths from terminal to root node.

We cannot construct the minimal merge tree as we did before because of the added restraint placed on node degree. We can minimize the transmission time (time to access and copy from disk into a main memory buffer) by increasing c in the c-nary merge tree. However, we must remember that main memory is limited compared with the size of the file to be sorted.

Suppose we wish to sort ten strings all of the same length. We show the construction of three minimal merge trees in Figure 7.15. In each of these trees we have set $\alpha = \beta = 1$ to emphasize seek time over transmission time. The tree of Figure 7.15 (b) is best in this case because its E + D value is the lowest of the three trees. Therefore the best strategy is to perform two three-way merges, one four-way merge, and then one three-way merge.

The trees of Figure 7.15 are constructed by modifying the merge trees of the previous section for c = 2, 3, 4. At first sight it would appear that a Huffman tree of optimal degree satisfies the minimum E + D criteria, but this is not so.

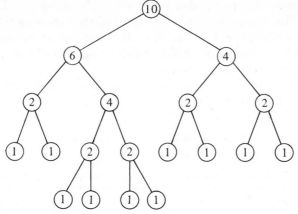

(a) A minimal binary tree with
E = 2(3) + 4(4) + 2(3) + 2(3) = 34
D = 2(6) + 4(8) + 4(6)   = 68
               E + D = 102

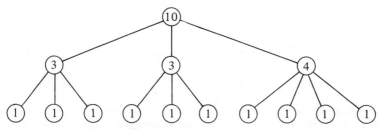

(b) A minimal 3-nary tree with
E = 10(2)   = 20
D = 6(6) + 4(7) = 64
       E + D = 84

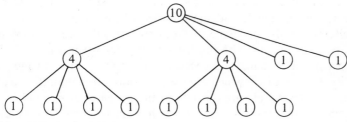

(c) A minimal 4-nary tree with
E = 8(2) + 2   = 18
D = 8(8) + 2(4) = 72
       E + D = 90

Figure 7.15 Modified minimal merge trees for ten terminal nodes and of order (a) two, (b) three, and (c) four

We construct the optimal disk sort tree by calculating $E + D$ for every tree with ten (in general n) terminal nodes, and then selecting the tree with the smallest value. Note, however, that all subtrees of an optimal tree are also optimal. Thus we can recursively construct optimal disk sort trees from a relatively brief table of optimal subtrees.

Table 7.1 contains a list of optimal subtrees for disk sorts on initial strings all of the same length.

Table 7.1   Optimal disk sort subtrees

n	Degree of root node of subtree	Son #1	Son #2	Son #3	Son #4	Son #5
				Filial set size		
2	2	1	1			
3	3	1	1	1		
4	4	1	1	1	1	
5	5	1	1	1	1	1
6	2	3	3			
7	3	1	3	3		
8	3	2	3	3		
9	3	3	3	3		
10	3	3	3	4		
11	3	3	4	4		
12	3	4	4	4		
13	4	3	3	3	4	
14	4	3	3	4	4	

Source: D. E. Knuth, *The Art of Computer Programming,* vol. 3, *Sorting and Searching* (Addison-Wesley Publishing Co., 1973), p. 369.

If we consult Table 7.1 for $n = 10$, we find that the optimal tree is one with three branches leaving the root node. The subtrees formed by son number 1, son number 2, and son number 3 have degree 3, 3, and 4, respectively. To obtain the shape of the three son subtrees, we look up the cases $n = 3$ and $n = 4$. The result is the tree shown in Figure 7.15 (b).

In specific cases it may be necessary to apply a different measure of optimality. In such cases (which are the rule more often than the exception) we would construct trees appropriate to the measure of optimality.

In general, total transmission time is minimized if we let c be as large as possible in the c-nary merge tree. Increasing c also increases the amount of main memory required, and so we have competing effects to consider.

A complete c-nary merge tree is optimal if the initial strings are all the same length, but if replacement-selection is used to create the initial strings this will not generally be the case. Merge patterns for unequal-sized initial strings can be obtained from the Huffman tree (no seek time considered) or from the minimum E + D trees that are experimentally derived (no method other than enumeration exists for finding minimum E + D trees when the initial strings are of different length).

Finally, methods other than merge-sorting may be useful in disk file sorting for particular instances. The radix sort, for example, is sometimes used when the range of key values is so small that all records with a given key value exceed main memory by roughly a factor of two.

We will again state the rule that there is no single sort algorithm that is best in all cases; this is equally true for disk sorting. Know the various methods and select the one that best fits your needs.

EXERCISES

1. Perform a replacement-selection sort on the records given by the keys: 10, 20, 15, 25, 30, 12, 2. What is the number of comparisons needed to sort these keys? Assume $n = 3$.

2. Use the list of Exercise 1 to construct a binary Huffman minimal merge tree. Compute the tree's value and then the number of comparisons needed to sort the keys.

3. Suppose your computer installation had $t = 5$ tape units. A certain payroll application requires merge-sorting 25 strings initially of length $L_0 = 1024$. Draw a minimal merge tree for this application. What are c and r? (*Caution:* Remember that one tape must always be free to store the merged output.)

8
SEARCHING

8.1
Search
Effort

Searching is the process of scanning a data structure or file to find a particular atom. The efficiency of a search algorithm depends on the data structure and, in turn, the data structure depends on how the data is manipulated (searched or updated). Therefore it is not clear which comes first—selection of the search algorithm or design of the data structure.

Chapter 8 will concentrate on the search algorithm alone. We will give examples that use a dense list data structure. However, the use of this structure is not always necessary. The measure of performance used is independent of the data structure. Instead, we will consider space requirements, algorithm complexity, and number of operations (MOVE, COMPARE).

One measure of search algorithm performance is the *average search length:* the expected number of comparisons needed to locate an item in the data structure. This is a statistical measure, so some searches will take longer than others because of the data involved. The average search length is only one way to compare different algorithms.

Suppose a dense list of social security numbers is stored and accessed frequently as shown in Figure 8.1. Perhaps these are part of an employee table maintained by a company or records kept by the Internal Revenue Service. The access frequency shows the number of times each record is accessed. With these numbers it is possible to compute an average search length for various algorithms.

From the table in Figure 8.1 we can estimate the probability of accessing an element (p_i) by dividing its access frequency (f_i) by the total number of accesses. Thus for any element:

Index	Social security numbers	Access frequency (f_i)
1	542-92-2241	100
2	381-82-1105	55
3	662-21-5503	10
4	212-55-3891	250
5	442-52-4122	125
6	588-29-9953	300

Figure 8.1 Sample list with access frequency counts

$$p_i = \frac{f_i}{\sum\limits_{i=1}^{n} f_i} \qquad \text{for } i = 1, 2, \ldots, n$$

We assume there are n items in the table.

For the table in Figure 8.1 we can compute the following probabilities. The first step is to calculate

$$\sum_{i=1}^{n} f_i = 100 + 55 + 10 + 250 + 125 + 300 = 840$$

and then

$$p_1 = \frac{f_1}{840} = \frac{100}{840} = .119$$

$$p_2 = \frac{f_2}{840} = \frac{55}{840} = .065$$

$$p_3 = \frac{f_3}{840} = \frac{10}{840} = .012$$

$$p_4 = \frac{f_4}{840} = \frac{250}{840} = .298$$

$$p_5 = \frac{f_5}{840} = \frac{125}{840} = .148$$

$$p_6 = \frac{f_6}{840} = \frac{300}{840} = .357$$

We can define the average search length L as follows:

$$L = \sum_{i=1}^{n} c_i p_i \qquad (8.1)$$

where n is number of table entries; c_i is number of comparisons needed to reach the ith entry; and p_i is probability of accessing the ith entry. Computing c_i depends upon the search algorithm. In the following sections we compute L for different search methods.

EXERCISES

1. Give three measures of search effort that might be used to compare search algorithms.

2. Write a computer program to compute the average search length for any search method. Let c_i and p_i for $i = 1, 2, \ldots, n$ be inputs to your program. Given n, compute L.

3. Let $c_i = i$ and compute L for the six social security numbers shown in the text.

8.2
Comparison of
Search Algorithms

SEQUENTIAL SEARCH

The simplest search algorithm is the *sequential* or *linear search*. The entries in the table in Figure 8.1 are compared with the desired key until a match is found. The table is scanned sequentially beginning with the first element. When the matching key is found, the search returns the address of the item, or if no match occurs an appropriate signal is returned. A sequential search of a file returns the address of the record. Thus whether working with files, tables, or lists, we use a similar procedure.

The search effort for this algorithm is computed by substituting into Formula (8.1) in Section 8.1. The number of comparisons needed to reach the first entry is one, the second entry two, and so on. In general, to reach the ith entry i comparisons are necessary. For the sequential search the average search length is:

$$L = \sum_{i=1}^{n} c_i p_i = \sum_{i=1}^{n} i p_i$$
$$= 1 \cdot p_1 + 2 \cdot p_2 + 3 \cdot p_3 + \cdots + n \cdot p_n$$

For the example in Figure 8.1:

$$L = 1(.119) + 2(.065) + 3(.012) + 4(.298)$$
$$+ 5(.148) + 6(.357)$$
$$= 4.36$$

In other words, 4.36 comparisons are required on the *average* to locate each desired record. For this example $n = 6$ and the search method requires searching over half the table *most of the time.*

Consider the frequency counts in the table in Figure 8.1. The most frequently accessed entry is the last in the table. Suppose the table is ordered by frequency: The most frequently accessed items are placed at the beginning. Then the value for L shows an improvement:

$$L_{ordered} = 1(.357) + 2(.298) + 3(.148) + 4(.119)$$
$$+ 5(.065) + 6(.012)$$
$$= 2.27$$

This nearly doubles the speed of the sequential search algorithm, but we no longer have freedom to choose how the items are placed in the table. Such ordering by frequency restricts the update characteristics of the list in exchange for improved search speed. What is the limit of improvement? Can we exchange other "freedoms" of list construction for speed? Assume that we know nothing about the frequency (and hence probability) of access. The worst possible case is that all items are accessed equally often. This means that

$$p_i = \frac{1}{n} \quad \text{for } i = 1, 2, \ldots, n$$

The average search length for the sequential search algorithm now becomes:

$$L_{random} = \sum_{i=1}^{n} c_i p_i = \sum_{i=1}^{n} i\left(\frac{1}{n}\right) = \frac{1}{n} \sum_{i=1}^{n} i$$
$$= \left(\frac{1}{n}\right)\frac{n(n + 1)}{2} = \frac{n + 1}{2}$$

Hence total ignorance (and complete freedom of placement of items) leads to an anticipated search length equal to approximately one half the length of the table.

Example What is the expected time to find an item in a table of length 1000, assuming uniform access probability and 10^{-3} second per comparison?

$$\text{time} = 10^{-3} L_{random}$$
$$= 10^{-3} \frac{1000 + 1}{2}$$
$$\approx 10^{-3} \frac{10^3}{2}$$
$$\approx \frac{1}{2} \text{ second}$$

BINARY SEARCH

We are concerned with improving access time by some method of ordering the data. Suppose that the data is ordered lexicographically, either alphabetically by letters or numerically by numerals. Given a key and the request to find its record in a file of n records, suppose we look at the middle record in the file, that is, the item nearest location $n/2$. The key of item $n/2$ is either larger or smaller than the given key. In either event we can eliminate either the first half or the second half of the total number of records from further consideration. By successively halving the lists we can close in on the desired item.

Suppose we are given the following list and are asked to search for the key $= 47$:

$$3 \quad 18 \quad 47 \quad \underline{54} \quad 65 \quad 83 \quad 94 \quad 97$$
$$\uparrow \qquad\qquad\qquad\qquad\qquad\quad \uparrow$$

The middle record is found by noting that 54 is nearest location $n/2$. Since 54 is greater than 47, we eliminate the right half and consider:

$$3 \quad \underline{18} \quad 47$$

Since 18 is at the center of the list and 18 is less than 47, we discard the left portion and are left with 47. Thus we have made a match in only 3 comparisons!

If we begin with a list of n elements and discard half the elements with each comparison, how long will it take us to discard all the elements? If we find the element we are searching for, we stop the search and do not go through the entire list. But if the item is not there, how many comparisons must we make before determining that fact? This is equivalent to asking how many times we can successively divide n (and its quotients) by 2, and the answer is:

$$c = \log_2 n$$

Another way of expressing this is $2^c = n$.

This searching technique is known as a *binary search*. It succeeds by successively halving the lists until a sublist of length one occurs. That sublist either contains the desired item, or the desired item is not in the list.

The maximum search length we can have is $\log_2 n$. If the key corresponds to the middle element, the search length is one. Suppose the list is very long. How many entries can be located by a binary search algorithm in exactly one comparison? in exactly two comparisons? This information is summarized in the following table.

Comparison	Number of Items Which Can Be Found
1	$1 = 2^0$
2	$2 = 2^1$
3	$4 = 2^2$
.	.
.	.
.	.
k	2^{k-1}

But what is the *average* search length? Let us assume that $n = 2^k - 1$, and that the probability of searching for each key is equally likely. Then statistically speaking, we would expect to have searched for each item exactly once after processing n requests. The average search length is the total number of comparisons divided by n:

$$L = \frac{\text{total comparisons}}{n}$$

To calculate the total number of comparisons required to access all items in the list, notice that the middle element contributes one comparison to the total. Each of two elements contributes two comparisons; each of four elements contributes three comparisons; each of eight elements contributes four comparisons, and so on. Thus:

$$L = \frac{\sum_{i=1}^{k} i\, 2^{i-1}}{n}$$

Without going through the derivation, we evaluate L as:

$$L = \frac{n+1}{n} \log_2 (n+1) - 1$$

Since not every list has length $2^k - 1$, and our other assumptions introduce errors into the above analysis, it is common to accept the following approximation, provided that n is large ($n > 50$):

$$L = \log_2 (n+1) - 1$$

The exact formula for a list of arbitrary length n is given by the formula[1]

$$L = \log_2{(n + 1)} - \frac{1}{n}\left(2^{[\log_2{(n+1)}]} - [\log_2{(n + 1)}] - 1\right)$$

where the brackets [ ] mean take the integer part of the contents of the brackets.

In summary, the binary search algorithm owes its search performance to the loss in flexibility incurred by ordering the list. The price for rapid access is the difficulty in keeping the list ordered after repeated updates.

BLOCK SEARCH

For rapidly changing files which are not accessed too often, there is a compromise between the sequential search and the binary search. The search method is the block search. The data is divided into blocks; within each block we do not have to order the data, but we must keep the blocks in order. This means that all items in the first block are less than all items in the second block, and so on, assuming the list is in ascending order. If the list is in descending order, all items in the first block would be greater than all items in the second block, and so on.

To facilitate the search we must know the largest value in each block (if the list is in ascending order). Searching the list means comparing the key against the largest value in each block until the key is less than some largest value. Having located the block which should contain the key, we use a sequential search within the block. If the key is found, we return its location. If the key not found, we return an appropriate value to signal that the key is not in the list.

For example, suppose we have the list pictured in Figure 8.2. The column labeled POINTER contains pointers to the largest value in each block. Each block contains five values. To search for the value 60, we first compare it to 22 (largest value in block one), then to 44 (largest value in block two), and finally to 74 (largest value in block three). This means that 60 is in the third block, if it is in the list at all. Next we search the third block sequentially and find 60 in location 12.

The average search length for a block search reveals that it is an improvement over the sequential search, but not nearly as efficient as the binary search. The block search involves two searches: one to find the correct block and one to find an item within the block. Thus the average search length

$$L_{\text{block}} = L_b + L_w$$

[1]For a fuller treatment of this formula see C. V. Ramamoorthy and Y. H. Chin in References.

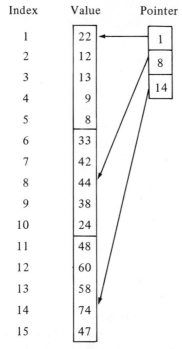

Index	Value	Pointer
1	22	1
2	12	8
3	13	14
4	9	
5	8	
6	33	
7	42	
8	44	
9	38	
10	24	
11	48	
12	60	
13	58	
14	74	
15	47	

Figure 8.2 List prepared for block search

where L_b is the average search length for blocks, and L_w is the average search length within blocks. Let us say that the list contains n elements, s elements per block, and b blocks, where $b = n/s$. If the probability of searching for an element is the same as that of searching for any other element, then the probability of accessing any block is $1/b$ (or s/n) and

$$L_b = \sum_{i=1}^{b} (i)\left(\frac{1}{b}\right)$$

The probability of accessing any item within the block is $1/s$. Only $(s - 1)$ items need be compared because one in each block is used to search from block to block. Thus:

$$L_w = \sum_{i=1}^{s-1} (i)\left(\frac{1}{s}\right)$$

Then the average search length for any item is:

$$L_{\text{block}} = \sum_{i=1}^{b} (i)\, \frac{1}{b} + \sum_{i=1}^{s-1} (i)\, \frac{1}{s}$$

$$= \frac{1}{b} \sum_{i=1}^{b} i + \frac{1}{s} \sum_{i=1}^{s-1} i$$

$$= \frac{1}{b}\, \frac{b(b+1)}{2} + \frac{1}{s}\, \frac{(s-1)s}{2}$$

$$= \frac{b+1}{2} + \frac{s-1}{2}$$

$$= \frac{b+s}{2}$$

$$= \frac{1}{2}\, \frac{n}{s} + s$$

$$= \frac{n + s^2}{2s}$$

Thus the average search length depends not only on n but also on s, the number of elements in each block. For a given list n is constant, but s may vary. To minimize L_{block} we use some results from calculus. First we set the derivative of L_{block} with respect to s equal to zero and solve for s:

$$\frac{\mathbf{d} L_{\text{block}}}{\mathbf{d} s} = \frac{1}{2}\left(1 - \frac{n}{s^2}\right) = 0$$

Then $s = \sqrt{n}$ provides a minimum average search length. Substituting $s = \sqrt{n}$ in the formula for L_{block}, we find that the average search length L^*_{block} is:

$$L^*_{\text{block}} = \frac{n + (\sqrt{n})^2}{2\sqrt{n}}$$

$$= \frac{2n}{2\sqrt{n}}$$

$$= \sqrt{n}$$

For example, a block search on a list of 10,000 entries requires on the average 100 comparisons to retrieve an item. This assumes that there are 100 entries/block and a total of 100 blocks.

BINARY SEARCH TREE

Another alternative that allows both rapid search and ease of update is the binary search tree. In Chapter 5 it was referred to as the binary sort tree because we wanted to convert a list into a tree structure in such a way that the nodes would be ordered, if scanned in an LNR-recursive scan. Updating and searching the tree are simplified because of the way it is defined. Recall that in a binary tree each node is either terminal or has at most two immediate successors; the successors are labeled left and right successors. A binary search tree is constructed so that a node's immediate left successor is less than the node, and its immediate right successor is greater than the node. Thus all the elements on a node's left subtree are always less than all the elements on the node's right subtree. Searching the tree for a particular item is a binary-type search. We begin at the root and, depending on the result of the comparison, eliminate either the left or right subtree. We continue the search until either the item is found or a terminal node is reached.

For example, Figure 8.3 illustrates the binary search tree constructed from the list of numbers {4, 2, 3, 6, −1, 12, 8}. Recall that a different ordering of the same numbers would produce a different tree structure because nodes are added in the order that they are found in the list.

In Chapter 5 we discussed the addition of nodes to the tree. We now turn our attention to the problem of deleting nodes because this structure gives us both update flexibility and search speed. After a deletion, the tree must remain a binary search tree so that other insertions or searches may occur with ease. Figure 8.4 shows before and after pictures of various binary search trees. See if you can determine how the shape of the tree changes.

Visually, the basic rule of deletions involves replacing the deleted node with a terminal node. The terminal node chosen is the rightmost terminal node in the deleted node's left subtree. In this way the tree remains a binary search tree. If the deleted node is already terminal, no replacement occurs.

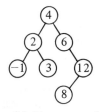

Figure 8.3 Binary search tree

(a) Before deletion of 2   (a) After deletion of 2

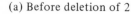

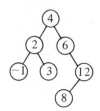
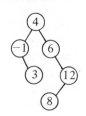

(b) Before deletion of 5   (b) After deletion of 5

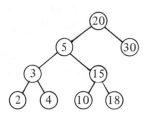
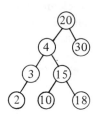

(c) Before deletion of 30   (c) After deletion of 30

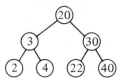

Figure 8.4 Deletion of nodes from binary search trees

Since this may seem confusing, refer to the examples in Figure 8.4. In Figure 8.4 (a) the rightmost node of the deletion node's ② left subtree is nil so that the right pointer of node ② is copied into the right pointer field of node ⊝1. Similarly in Figure 8.4 (b) the right and left pointer of node ⑤ is copied into the right and left pointer field of node ④ because ④ is the rightmost node of the left subtree beginning at ⑤. Every rightmost node will have a nil pointer.

Each time a deletion takes place, we must search the left subtree emanating from the deletion node to find the rightmost node. We summarize these steps below by noting that D = deleted node. (D − 1) = predecessor of D, (D + 1) = left successor of D, and R = rightmost node in subtree (D + 1).

1. Search the subtree of (D + 1) for R.

2. Copy the right pointer of D into the right pointer field of R.

3. Copy the left pointer of D into the left pointer of R.

4. Change the pointer in (D − 1) that points to D, and make it point to R, now.

One possible application of a binary search tree is the storage of an airline's rapidly changing reservations file. Assume that each flight has its own binary search tree containing the names and telephone numbers of passengers. Making a reservation creates an additional node on the tree. Canceling a reservation deletes a node from the tree. Last names determine the ordering. A name appears on a node's left subtree if it precedes the node alphabetically; a name appears on the right subtree if it follows the node alphabetically.

Whether adding or removing a name or just checking a particular person's confirmation for a flight, we must search the tree. Can we estimate the average search length for a typical binary search tree? Here we assume that reservations and cancellations occur randomly. It can be shown (although we will not do it here) that for a binary search tree, the average search length is bounded by:

$$L_{\text{tree}} \leq 1.4 \log_2 (i - d)$$

where we begin with an empty tree and make i random insertions and d random deletions.

For the airline's binary search tree, if we assume 250 passengers and 10% cancellations, then the average search length is:

$$L_{\text{tree}} \leq 1.4 \log_2(250 - 25)$$
$$= 1.4 \log_2(225)$$
$$= 10.94$$

This means that the search length for the airline's binary search tree is approximately 11. We can only estimate L_{tree} because the tree is constantly changing in size. The more insertions there are, the larger the average search length.

The binary search tree organization does compare favorably in average search length with the binary search. However, the memory requirements are nearly twice that of a dense list organization because we must provide room for the pointers.

Another problem of the binary search tree is that the tree grows in the order in which insertions occur. Compare the two binary search trees in Figure 8.5. The tree in Figure 8.5 (a) results from the list {10, 60, 30, 70, 20, 50, 40}; the tree in Figure 8.5 (b) results from {40, 20, 60, 30, 70, 50, 10}. The binary tree (a) is not balanced because it is not symmetric, while the binary tree (b) is symmetric and therefore balanced. An unbalanced binary search tree results in longer search lengths and slower updates. Is there some way to balance a binary search tree?

Algorithms for balancing binary search trees are given by W. A. Martin and D. N. Ness (see References) and will not be discussed here. Also note that binary search trees are a special kind of AVL (Adel'son, Vel'sky, and Landis) tree. These trees have been studied extensively for their searching and sorting properties.

SUMMARY

To summarize the searching algorithms, consider the following: Programming a dense list sequential search is simple and is perhaps the "best" method to use on short lists. The average search length is proportional to the length of the list.

The binary search is rapid because it requires very few comparisons. However, it will work only on an ordered list. Therefore it is best suited to a dense list structure which does not change or changes slowly. Updates to an ordered list are slow because they must preserve order.

A block search can be optimized to provide moderately fast searches and moderately flexible update capability. The storage requirements and programming simplicity of a block search make it an alternative to a binary search tree.

A binary search tree allows rapid lookup and ease of insertion and deletion. It requires a tree structure, which needs extra memory for pointers. Thus memory requirements increase in exchange for speed and flexibility.

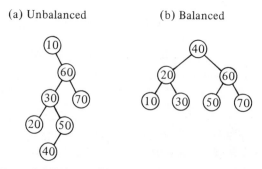

(a) Unbalanced   (b) Balanced

Figure 8.5 Balanced versus unbalanced binary search tree

Features / Algorithm	Search length	Memory space	Programming complexity	Main advantages
Sequential	$\dfrac{n+1}{2}$	n	simple	programming
Block	$\sqrt{n}$	$\sqrt{n} + b$	moderate	programming and updating
Binary	$\log_2(n+1) - 1$	$n + 2$	moderate	search length (speed)
Search Tree	$1.4 \log_2(i - d)$	$\approx 2n$	difficult	search length (speed) and updating

EXERCISES

1. Write an algorithm for one of the search algorithms.

2. Write a program for one of the search algorithms and try it on different data sets. Compute the theoretical average search length and compare it to the empirical average produced by the program runs.

3. What assumptions were made about the access frequency for each average search length calculation?

4. What is the expected number of moves needed to insert a new item in the list searched with a binary search? What are your assumptions?

5. Suppose a table is ordered by access frequency and a copy is ordered lexicographically. Which table can be searched faster? Qualify your answer by saying something about the access frequencies and the maximum search lengths.

6. How many different binary search trees can be constructed from the numbers 10, 20, 30, 40, 50? Compute the expected search length for each tree and show which one is smallest.

7. What are the optimal block sizes for a block search on a list of 144 items? Suppose that the same list has blocks of eight items each. What is the average search length now? What is the percentage loss in average search efficiency?

8. Suppose that the block search uses a binary search to determine the correct block and then a sequential search within the block. What is the average search length?

9. Write programs for each search algorithm and compare their performance, space requirements, and programming complexity.

8.3
Hashing

We have seen how the average search length can be affected by keeping the data in order. It is conceivable that other methods might yield even better search characteristics. The key-to-address transformation or hashing[2] (see also Chapter 6) is one in which the data need not be ordered but which provides high-speed searching capability.

Suppose that a file is to be designed for which rapid insertion, deletion, and lookup are of paramount importance. If we are willing to sacrifice memory, hashing has a remarkable potential. We will go into some of the more common techniques first, then analyze the search characteristics of hashing.

DIGIT ANALYSIS

Assume we have a list of social security numbers as shown in Figure 8.6. It would be most convenient to use the numbers themselves as addresses. Therefore 542-42-2241 is stored in memory location 542422241, 542-81-3678 in 542813678, and so on. This means that the few numbers in our example would need close to a billion locations. Unquestionably this approach is fast: The maximum search length is one. But let us see how we can eliminate some of the wasted space from the example.

Suppose we have only 1000 memory locations available and want to define an address for each of the numbers in Figure 8.6. The first three digits are all the same, so we eliminate them immediately. The next six digits would be all right, but we really need only three (000-999). How can we intelligently fit these six social security numbers into 1000 locations? A closer look at the numbers reveals a preponderance of number 7 in the second column from the right. Since the digits in that column do not help spread the numbers out, we will eliminate that column also. We continue to examine the key set for other columns with nonrandom patterns. If none are obvious, we arbitrarily eliminate some others, e.g., 4, 5, and 8. The key-to-address transformation (pick columns 6, 7, and 9) for the example (Figure 8.6) appears in Figure 8.7.

We are illustrating the principle that only those digits which have the most uniform distribution are selected. The digits with the most nonuniform (skewed) distribution are deleted from the key until the desired number of digits is obtained. A program can be written to perform digit analysis, but this requires advanced knowledge of the keys. A change in the key set

---

[2]We will use the terms hashing and key-to-address transformation interchangeably.

542-42-2241
542-81-3678
542-22-8171
542-38-9671
542-54-1577
542-88-5376
542-19-3552

Figure 8.6 Social security numbers for hashing

requires a new digit analysis, so this method really does not meet our requirement of rapid insertion and deletion capability.

FOLDING

It often happens that the key is longer than the number of digits in the address range. If the distribution of digits in the key is roughly uniform, the choice of which digits to ignore is rather arbitrary. One alternative (upon which there are countless variations) is to arbitrarily select some columns and use the remaining ones by adding them to the chosen ones. Figure 8.8 demonstrates two methods of folding social security numbers into an address space of 4 digits (0000–9999). The intention is to use all the digits to help scramble the addresses uniformly across the address space. If the sum produces overflow digits, they are usually discarded.

DIVISION

One of the earliest and easiest key-to-address transformations is division by the number of possible addresses. For example, division of any number by n always leaves a remainder in the range of zero to $n - 1$. The transformation of a number to its remainder after division by a fixed number is the central idea in modular arithmetic, popular in the "new mathematics."

Key	Address
542-42-2241	221
542-81-3678	368
542-22-8171	811
542-38-9671	961
542-54-1577	157
542-88-5376	536
542-19-3552	352

Figure 8.7 Key-to-address transformation on social security numbers

(a) Before folding, creases are selected

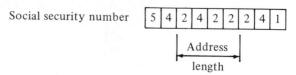

(b) Fold-boundary with sum

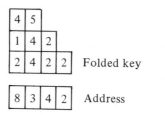

(c) Fold-shifting with sum

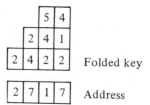

Figure 8.8 Fold-boundary and fold-shifting transformation

For example, we say that:

$$18 = 0 \ (\text{mod } 6)$$

$$19 = 1 \ (\text{mod } 6)$$

$$20 = 2 \ (\text{mod } 6)$$

because division by six leaves remainders of 0, 1, and 2, respectively. Most hashing experts suggest division by a prime number, slightly larger than the table size. We will see later that there are definite advantages in selecting a prime number for table length; thus a list of primes appears in Figure 8.9.

PSEUDORANDOM

The division algorithm is reminiscent of the way multiplicative pseudo-random number generators work. Typically such a generator has the form:

$$y = (ax + c) \bmod p$$

Replacing x by the key produces y for its address. Typically p is a power of two of the form 2^n and $c = -1$. If we select $a \equiv 1 \pmod 4$, it is possible to generate every number from zero to $p - 1$ exactly once by starting with any number in the same range. To use this formula as a hashing function, we let:

$$\text{address} = (a \cdot \text{key} + c) \bmod p$$

$$a \equiv 1 \pmod 4$$

$$c = \pm 1$$

$$p = 2^n = \text{table size}$$

This method is often used as a standard against which the randomizing effect of other hash algorithms is measured.

Other methods of hashing which may offer advantages in some extreme cases have been proposed. You may invent a personalized hashing function of your own. However, the division technique is fairly simple and is quite effective for most applications.

n	2^n	$(4k + 3)$ prime $< 2^n$
3	8	7
4	16	11
5	32	31
6	64	59
7	128	127
8	256	251
9	512	503
10	1024	1019
11	2048	2039
12	4096	4091
13	8192	8191
14	16384	16363
15	32768	32719
16	65536	65519
17	131072	131071
18	262144	262139
19	524288	524287
20	1048576	1048571
21	2097152	2097143
22	4194304	4194287
23	8388608	8388587
24	16777216	16777207

Figure 8.9 List of primes near a power of 2 and of form $4k + 3$

Since the purpose of hashing is to squeeze a potentially large key space into a small address space, it is inevitable that *collisions* will occur. That is, two or more keys are transformed into the same address. Before a complete file structure based on hashing can be implemented, we must decide what to do when collisions occur. Once we make that decision, insert, delete, and search algorithms are all basically the same.

Suppose we are in the process of building a file using some hashing function. We are given a record and use the hash function on the key to generate an address. What can we do if something is already stored at that address? Or suppose we are searching for a particular record; we hash its key to give an address, but the record stored at that location is not the one we wanted. Where do we look next?

There are many methods for solving these problems. For example, if the computed address is full, check the next address, then the next, and so on, until a vacant spot is found for the new record. Searching is done the same way. If the computed address does not contain the desired record, check the next record, then the next, and so on. This is a simple scheme but it has some drawbacks. If several keys hash to the same address, the sequential searching which follows can become too costly. This effect is called *primary clustering,* and it occurs when the hashing function does not spread the addresses uniformly throughout the address range.

Another alternative is an extension of the pseudorandom hashing technique. If the computed address collides with a table occupant, a subsequent location is interrogated by computing a number called an *offset,* which is added to the original location. The various methods of handling collisions differ only in the manner of calculating offsets.

In pseudorandom probing, the offset x_i is computed from the following formula in which n is the table length:

$$x_i = (ax_{i-1} + c) \bmod n$$

The first time a collision occurs, we compute an offset of x_1 from the above formula, assuming $x_0 = $ key. The next address interrogated is the hash address plus x_1. If that produces a collision, we compute another offset x_2 and add it to the hash address. If needed, several offsets might be computed before we meet with success (or failure). Simpler random-number generators are possible, but they do not guarantee that every location of the table will be scanned before the original location is scanned again. The table length n must be a power of two, and a and c must be selected properly to assure a full table scan.

The pseudorandom probe requires lengthy calculations and serves only to spread primary clusters over the entire table. If several keys hash to the same address, and if the method of computing the offset traces out the same search sequence for these synonyms, the result is called *secondary clustering*.

Several investigators have noticed the buildup of secondary clustering and have proposed methods for eliminating it; these methods use additional information about the key. J. R. Bell proposes a variable offset that changes from one synonym to another. His *quadratic quotient search* employs a prime division hashing function and sets the offset equal to the quotient obtained after division. Thus the original probe is:

$$\text{key} \ (\text{mod} \ n)$$

and the *i*th offset is given by

$$qi^2$$

where $q = \text{key}/n$ and n is a prime of the form $4k + 3$. This technique guarantees a scan of only half the table, but eliminates primary and secondary clustering. It is possible to adapt this technique to get a full table scan.

The quadratic quotient hash eliminates primary and secondary clustering because it produces a different offset for synonyms. The fact that a quadratic offset is computed is of secondary importance. A linear offset that uses $q = $ (quotient of prime division) also eliminates clustering and is fast. The linear quotient hash algorithm is given below:

1. Let $R \leftarrow \text{Key} \ (\text{mod} \ p)$, $Q \leftarrow \text{Key}/p$. If $Q = 0$, set Q to some constant > 0.

2. Set the probe counter, $i \leftarrow 1$.

3. While $i < p$ do the following:
   (a) Investigate TABLE(R); if found, done.
   (b) Increment $i \leftarrow i + 1$.
   (c) Increment $R \leftarrow R + Q \ (\text{mod} \ p)$.

Step 3(a) of the algorithm carries out either an insertion/deletion or a simple look-up, depending upon the desired operation. You are cautioned to note that a deletion must be marked with a flag to prevent an error during look-up. This flag prevents the termination of a search when a chain of probes is established during an insert and then one of the chain "links" is deleted before a subsequent look-up is done.

AVERAGE SEARCH LENGTH

You were promised that hashing is fast. To prove this we analyze the average search length needed to access a record. The secret to scatter storage is never allow memory to become full. In fact, as memory fills up, the average search length will increase.

Let us assume that there are n locations in memory, but only k of them are filled. Then the loading factor l is given by the relation:

$$l = \frac{k}{n}$$

where we assume that $k < n$. In addition, the probability of a collision is l. (We equate the probability of an additional scan with the probability of a collision.)

When no probes have been made, the probability of making an additional probe is 1. The probability of a collision on the ith probe is l^i, and the probability of locating a record in exactly i probes is $l^{i-1}(1 - l)$. The average search length is:

$$L = \sum_{i=0}^{n} il^{i-1}(1 - l)$$

$$\leq \sum_{i=0}^{\infty} il^{i-1}(1 - l)$$

$$= \frac{(1 - l)}{(1 - l)^2}$$

$$= \frac{1}{1 - l}$$

Observe that this formula expresses the search length as a function of the loading factor l, and not as a function of the number of records. For a fixed number of records k, we can make the loading factor l close to zero by making n larger; $l = k/n$. The penalty of course is the $n - k$ memory locations which are not used.

Example   A file is to be designed using a hashing function. The loading factor is limited to 3/4. If there are 30,000 records in the file, how many record locations will be required?

$$l = \frac{k}{n}$$

$$\frac{3}{4} = \frac{30,000}{n}$$

$$n = (30,000) \left(\frac{4}{3} \right)$$

$$= 40,000$$

What is the expected search length for each record?

$$L \approx \frac{1}{1 - l}$$

$$= \frac{1}{1 - \frac{3}{4}}$$

$$= 4$$

If there are 90,000 records, how much space is required and what is the expected search length?

The formulas above express search effort for a static table. The greatest advantage of a scatter table lies in its updatability. Hash tables fluctuate over a range of $0 \le k < n$ as they are built. What happens to our estimate of average search length when l is allowed to vary? Assume that a scatter storage table grows from $l_{init} = 0$ to $l = l_{max}$. Then the estimated search effort needed to insert and delete items in this table is:

$$L = \frac{1}{l_{max} - l_{init}} \int_{l_{init}}^{l_{max}} \frac{dl}{1 - l}$$

$$= - \left(\frac{1}{l_{max}} \right) \ln(1 - l_{max})$$

This assumes no clustering at all.

Although we have separated the chapters on files and searching, it should be evident that the topics are interrelated. A sequential file needs a sequential search; an indexed file requires something similar to a block search, and so on. Although we have given figures for average search length, other aspects of file design, such as total memory cost, may take precedence in the choice of the overall design. At this stage file design is still an art rather than a science and often reflects the designer's personal preferences or the hardware's limitations rather than a rational choice of alternatives.

EXERCISES

1. Define the following terms and tell how they relate:
   - (a) Synonym
   - (d) Secondary clustering
   - (b) Collision
   - (e) Key-to-address transformation
   - (c) Primary clustering

2. Design a search technique that uses buckets (see Chapter 6). It should compare to hashing in the same way that the block search compares to a sequential search. Compute the average search length.

3. Write an algorithm to perform file maintenance for a scatter storage file. It should provide for insertion, deletion, and search capabilities.

4. Write a program to implement the algorithm in Exercise 3. Test it with different sets of data and compute the average search length. Compare this length against the theoretical value.

5. Suppose the Highway Patrol wants to design a scatter storage file so that any record can be retrieved in an average of two probes. If they expect a total of 100,000 records, how much space must be provided for the file?

9
MEMORY
MANAGEMENT

9.1
The Fragmentation
Problem

In the preceding chapters we have been concerned with choosing data structures to efficiently use memory space. We have not considered the question of where that memory space comes from. We assumed that the computer system could always supply the necessary memory on demand. Of course this cannot be the case in a system with many users requesting space in a finite memory. The following discussion is an introduction to the problems which confront systems designers when they must implement procedures for allocation and release of space in memory.

Let us consider one portion of a simplified operating system in a multiprogramming environment. Since we anticipate that several jobs may be executing and others may be waiting in various stages of completion, we assume that the system reserves a small segment of memory in which it keeps tabs on all its jobs. The type of information kept in this segment might include the type of job (compile, execute, or edit), anticipated storage requirements, and other facilities required (tapes, disk, and so on). This information is to be stored as a dense list with a tag at the head to distinguish between jobs. The list for some jobs may be quite short, while for other jobs it might be quite lengthy. Usually no two jobs require the same amount of resources. The question is this: How does the system manage these lists within this fixed segment of memory?

In Figure 9.1 we imagine a snapshot of this area shortly after the system begins running. As new jobs enter and old jobs finish, we expect to see changes in the allocated space. In Figure 9.1(b) the available space is schematically represented as six units, which is a lot compared to the three to four units required for most jobs in the example. However, it is evident that there is not enough space for a job that requires only three units.

The exact procedure for allocation and release of area in the segment is unspecified, but it is easy to imagine that the procedure involves two linked lists, one for the allocated space and one for the available space. There would be an algorithm ALLOCATE to remove space from the available list and place it in the allocated list for new jobs. A RELEASE algorithm would remove space from the allocated list and place it on the available list when a job finishes.

Figure 9.1 shows something which can and does occur in such systems. A checkerboard pattern of allocated spaces interspersed with available spaces causes loss of usable memory. Even though the total space available might be considerable, often it is too fragmented to use. This type of memory waste is called *external fragmentation.*

If the problem of external fragmentation is really serious (see Exercise 3), we might consider an alternate scheme which helps alleviate the prob-

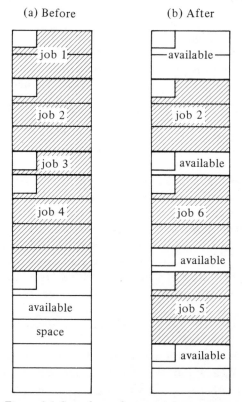

Figure 9.1 Snapshots of system job status area

lem. Instead of allowing variable size blocks for each job and keeping linked lists of available and free space, we could require every job to use one or more blocks of fixed size, as shown in Figure 9.2 (a). After a period of time, the configuration changes to that shown in Figure 9.2 (b). There is still some wasted space in blocks 4 and 6. Job 7 fills block 3, but only part of block 4. Job 5 needs only part of block 6 but gets the whole block. This type of memory waste is called *internal fragmentation.* In our efforts to eliminate external fragmentation we have succeeded in introducing a different kind of memory waste.

Assuming we are systems designers with these two methods available to manage the job status memory area, which one do we choose? How serious is external fragmentation? Does the second method of allocating fixed-size blocks eliminate external fragmentation? Is internal fragmentation less serious? What techniques can be used to help decide these questions?

EXERCISES

1. Explain the differences between external and internal fragmentation and the circumstances under which they appear.

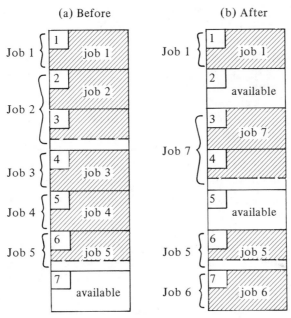

Figure 9.2 Snapshots of system job status area with fixed size blocks

2. Develop algorithms to maintain available and allocated lists for the two systems discussed above.

3. Use a random-number generator to produce requests for memory space and the length of time that the space will be occupied. Simulate the systems described in this section, allocating and releasing space as requested. If the memory area fills up, keep a queue of requests which cannot be filled until space becomes available. Use the same set of request sizes and hold times for each system and see which one can honor all the requests first. Compute such things as the amount of unallocated memory area, average queue length, and other values which would be useful in comparing the systems.

9.2
Garbage
Collection

If a system begins with a large block of memory and allocates areas toward one end of memory, the available space will be located at the opposite end of memory. As jobs complete, making their areas available and other jobs enter the system, memory becomes fragmented as shown in Figure 9.1 (b). The available space is unusable because it is separated into small disjoint pieces. A solution to this problem is to move all the allocated space up into a contiguous area, and collect the available space at the bottom, or vice versa. This process is called *compaction,* which is a form of garbage collection. *Garbage collection* refers to any technique which makes unused memory areas available for use.

For example, suppose we are given the linked list string storage area pictured in Figure 9.3. At the beginning of each atom are three numbers. The first is a link to the next string (which is a book title) in the list; the second tells the length of the string in number of characters; and the third is a valid flag (1 means the area is allocated, zero means it is free). The largest available space is 40 characters. To store a string longer than 40 characters, we would have to split the string and link it together with pointers. Because the pointers take up space and require special handling, we want to avoid this procedure if possible.

To keep the structure uniform, we collect the strings toward one end of the area and leave the rest as one large, free area. Before moving anything, we must decide whether to keep the strings in their same relative position or to rearrange them in the order specified by the pointers. For example, if they are rearranged, the strings would be in the order, ELEMENTS OF SCIENTIFIC DATA ANALYSIS, MURDER IN MIAMI, and SCORPION. Certainly it is not difficult to rearrange the titles since the pointers provide the correct ordering. As the strings are moved, we can change the links to represent the correct values. However, if we transfer the first string into the beginning of the storage area, we run the risk of wiping out all or part of the string already stored there. If we decide to perform compaction, we are faced with the problem of readjusting the links. These problems are simplified if there is another memory area into which the strings can be rearranged and compacted. Then the entire block of locations pictured in Figure 9.3 can be released.

Decisions concerning when and how to perform garbage collection are equally important. Some systems wait until there is little contiguous storage available before they stop processing and begin garbage collection. To make more efficient use of the control processor, it might be feasible to

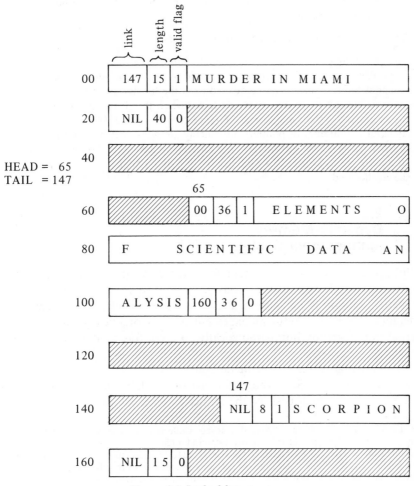

Figure 9.3 Linked list structure

collect memory whenever the CPU is idle, e.g., waiting for input. In any event, the strategy should be designed to produce efficient use of the computer while meeting the needs of the user.

EXERCISES

1. Write an algorithm to move linked lists (such as the one pictured in Figure 9.3) around in memory so that the first atom in the list is placed in the beginning location of the area. Be sure to reset the links where necessary. All available space should be connected into a single block of memory.

2. Write an algorithm to perform garbage collection on a linked list, such as the one pictured in Figure 9.3. Keep all atoms in their same relative positions, but reset links as necessary.

3. Investigate several garbage collections schemes.[1]

4. In a multilinked list each atom contains pointers to one or more atoms. If it is possible for a single atom to be pointed to by several atoms, then an atom which is not referenced can be deleted from the list. Its space can then be freed and reallocated when necessary. To know when to release the space allocated to an atom, a system may use a reference counter. The *reference counter* keeps track of the number of pointers referencing an atom. If it is zero, the atom can be deleted. Discuss advantages and disadvantages of the reference counter. If a node points to itself (like the header of a nil circular list), can its space ever be deallocated?

9.3
Dynamic Memory
Management Systems

Garbage collection is a treatment for external fragmentation. Because it is expensive and has bad side effects, it should be used only as a last resort. A better solution is prevention. Prevention means better management of memory. Through careful management we can practically eliminate external fragmentation but, paradoxically, internal fragmentation becomes a problem.

Early memory management designers tried to solve the problem by using this strategy: Scan the entire list of available memory areas and choose the one which best fits the requested size. Allocate the amount re-

---

[1]R. Fenichel and J. Yochelson, "A LISP Garbage Collection for Virtual-Memory Computer Systems," *CACM* 12, no. 11 (November 1969):611–612.

Kenneth Knowlton, "A Fast Storage Allocator," *CACM* 8, no. 10 (October 1965):623–625.

H. Schorr and W. Waite, "An Efficient Machine Independent Procedure for Garbage Collection in Various List Structures," *CACM* 10, no. 8 (August 1967):501–506.

quested and return any leftover space to the available list. If the leftover space is "too small" to be of any use, allocate the entire block. This approach is known as Best Fit strategy.

Scanning the entire list to find the best fit could use an excessive amount of time, so it might be simpler to take the first available block that is large enough to hold the request. The unused portion can be returned to the list of available memory blocks. This approach is called First Fit method. Surprisingly, First Fit method is often better than Best Fit strategy. For example, suppose we have available the following list of blocks:

$$1200$$
$$1000$$
$$3000$$

and our list of requests is:

$$700$$
$$500$$
$$900$$
$$2200$$

Best Fit strategy allocates storage in the following way:

1. Allocate 700 words from the 1000 word block.
    Result: 1200
            300
            3000

2. Allocate 500 words from the 1200 word block.
    Result: 700
            300
            3000

3. Allocate 900 words from the 3000 word block.
    Result: 700
            300
            2100

4. Cannot allocate storage to the 2200 word block.

However, First Fit method would first allocate 700 words from the 1200 word block, then 500 words of the remainder. Nine hundred words would be removed from the 1000 word block, and 2200 words from the 3000 word block. This is one instance when First Fit method works better than Best Fit strategy. There are examples where the reverse is true (see Exercise

1). Simulations with a variety of requests have shown that First Fit method is better in terms of number of requests filled per unit time.[2]

With the splitting of available blocks and return of the unused portion to the list, we might expect memory to be subject to severe external fragmentation. What we need is something short of garbage collection to perform this function: If two adjacent blocks (perhaps too small to be useful) become available, combine them into a single block because the larger block is more useful than the two small blocks. Of course it may be difficult to locate adjacent blocks. In fact, the search mechanism may be very time-consuming. What we need is a systematic method of splitting and coalescing small available blocks into larger ones. Ideally the system would allocate small amounts of memory for small requests, yet could still allocate large blocks of memory as necessary. This system is called a *dynamic memory management system.*

The feature that makes a memory management system dynamic is the capability of closely matching allocated space to requested space. This feature contrasts with the arbitrary allocation of one or more blocks of the same size to every request. In practice, a dynamic memory system may include characteristics of both systems. That is, it may prefer to allocate blocks of certain sizes, but there are enough different sizes to match closely most requests.

The number of distinct block sizes is sometimes called the number of levels of the system. All blocks of the same size are considered to be at the same level.

Example   A Five-level Dynamic Memory Management System. Suppose a memory of 1000 words has blocks of sizes 200, 400, 600, 800, and 1000. Blocks at level 1 can be coalesced into blocks at level 2; blocks at levels 1 and 2 can combine into a block at level 3, and so on.

Level	Size	Number of Possible Blocks
5	1000	1
4	800	1
3	600	1
2	400	2
1	200	5

[2]Donald E. Knuth, *The Art of Computer Programming*, vol. 1, 2d ed. (Reading, Mass.: Addison-Wesley Publishing Co., 1973), pp. 445–451.

One memory management system which incorporates these considerations is the Buddy system.[3] In the Buddy system, memory is always allocated in sizes which are a power of two. If a block is much larger than a memory request, it can be split into two blocks, each block size being a power of two. These blocks are called *buddies*. If both buddies become available, they can be recombined into one larger block. Because blocks are always a power of two (2, 4, 8, 16, 32, . . .), it is easy to compute the location of a block's buddy and then determine whether or not a larger block can be formed.

Initially we assume that the entire memory is available and has size $m = 2^n$. This forms an n level system which offers the following assortment of possible block sizes: 2^n, 2^{n-1}, 2^{n-2}, . . . , 8, 4, 2. However, at any given moment this does not mean that a block of each type is available or is even in the system. To know which blocks and sizes are available, we use n linked lists whose headers are AVAIL[1], AVAIL[2], . . . , AVAIL[n]. In general, AVAIL[i] points to the location of an available block of size 2^i. If the AVAIL[i] pointer is nil, then no block of size 2^i is free (but could possibly be obtained by splitting a larger block). Thus initially AVAIL[1], AVAIL[2], . . . , AVAIL[$n - 1$] have nil pointers and AVAIL[n] = zero. (We assume that the memory has addresses 0 through 2^{n-1}, as is normally done on computers.) Within each block is a field to specify whether or not the block is free. In this we use:

$FREE_k = 1$ if the block beginning at location k is available.

$FREE_k = 0$ if the block beginning at location k is not available.

Since it is possible that several blocks of the same size may be available, we include a link within each block to point to the next available block of that size. Because there is only one block of size 2^n, that block's link field is always nil. For convenience, the FREE and LINK fields would be part of each block. Since they cannot contain data, we consider them as overhead for the memory management system. The AVAIL list is also overhead.

As an example, assume we begin with a memory 32 units long ($32 = 2^5$). Its addresses are 0 through 31, or 00000 through 11111 in binary notation. If the first request is for a block of size 8, the block of size 32 is split into two blocks of size 16. One of these is placed at the head of the AVAIL[4] list, and the other is split into two blocks of size 8. One of these can be allocated, and one can be placed at the head of the AVAIL[3] list. If the next request is for a block of size 4, we find the smallest block which will fill that request. In this case it is a block of size 8. It must be split, one part

[3]Kenneth Knowlton, "A Fast Storage Allocator," *CACM* 8, no. 10 (October 1965):623–625.

allocated, and one part placed on the AVAIL[2] list. After these operations our AVAIL list is now:

$$AVAIL[1] = nil$$
$$AVAIL[2] = 12$$
$$AVAIL[3] = nil$$
$$AVAIL[4] = 16$$
$$AVAIL[5] = nil$$

and memory appears as below:

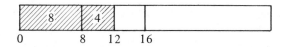

As a block is split, its right half (the part with the large address) remains free and the left half allocated. Now suppose a request for a block of size 8 is made. To fulfill this request, the block beginning at location 16 is split and memory is now allocated in the following way:

If the block at location 8 becomes free, it can be recombined with its buddy to form another block of size 8. It cannot be combined with the block beginning at location 24, since these blocks are not buddies. However, they can be linked together on the available list. AVAIL[3] will be 8; the block at location 8 will point to the block at location 24, whose link is nil. Memory can be visualized as shown below. The ground symbol ($\rightleftharpoons$) represents the nil link.

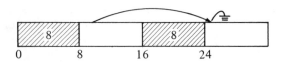

To understand the location of a block's buddy, consider Figure 9.4 which shows a possible configuration of memory after many allocations and releases have occurred. The boxes below the addresses in Figure 9.4 (a) give the address in binary. The tree structure in Figure 9.4 (b) helps us visualize the blocks which are buddies. The FREE field shows which blocks are available (FREE = 1) and which are allocated (FREE = 0). We see that there are two available blocks of size 8 and one of size 4. In the tree, nodes which are preceded by the same parent node are buddies. For example,

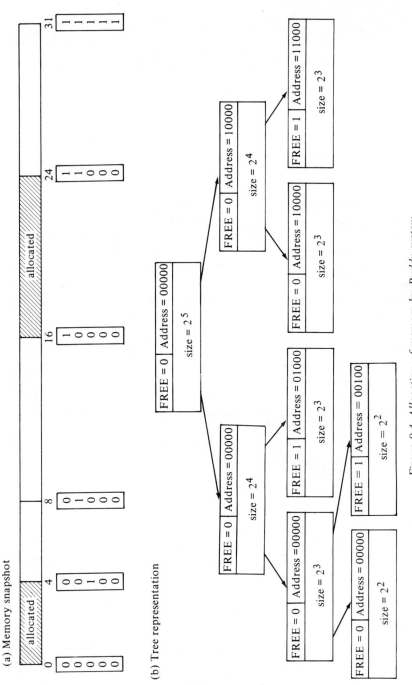

(a) Memory snapshot

(b) Tree representation

Figure 9.4 Allocation of memory by Buddy system

nodes at addresses 0 and 4 (00000 and 00100) and nodes at addresses 16 and 24 (10000 and 11000) are buddies. Each pair of addresses differs by only a single bit in the ith position, where i is the level number of the block and 2^i is the size of the block. (Here the low-order (rightmost) bit is numbered 0.) A block of size 2^i beginning in location k has a buddy at either location

$$k + 2^i \text{ if the } i\text{th bit of its address is 0.}$$

or $\qquad\qquad\qquad k - 2^i \text{ if the } i\text{th bit of its address is 1.}$

If the buddy is free, the two buddies can be recombined into a block of size 2^{i+1}. As long as $i + 1 < m$, the new block is not the entire memory area, and more recombinations may be possible.

The Buddy system shows an adaptive feature in its ability to split large blocks and coalesce buddies. However, it may suffer some external fragmentation if free blocks of the same size cannot be recombined because they are not buddies. If requests are not a power of two, the result is internal fragmentation. Even though we cannot eliminate fragmentation, the Buddy system minimizes memory waste by adapting to request sizes as nearly as possible.

The topics and questions presented here are intended to emphasize the use and misuse of data structures. Very often designers or programmers select a particular data structure because they are familiar with it, or perhaps "feel" it is better. What we need is evidence to back up these feelings. One way we can get such evidence is by designing simulation experiments to measure the advantages or disadvantages in question. (See, for example, Exercise 3 at the end of Section 9.1. For another approach to selection of an efficient memory algorithm see Section 9.5.)

EXERCISES

1. Find an example of available blocks and request sizes which show that sometimes the Best Fit method yields a better allocation than First Fit strategy.

2. Write an algorithm to grant a memory request based on the Best Fit method.

3. Write an algorithm to allocate memory based on the First Fit strategy.

4. Is it possible to have external fragmentation with the Buddy system? Discuss ways to measure external and internal fragmentation.

5. Design algorithms to allocate and release space in the Buddy system.

6. In view of examples, such as occur in Exercise 1, of what real value is simulation? How should the results of a simulation be interpreted?

7. Perform the following simulation by hand. Assume a memory of 20 words. Each time unit, the system receives a new request for memory. When a request is allocated, it holds its location for five time units. Unfulfilled requests go in a queue, followed by any new requests.

Use both the First Fit and Best Fit strategies. Take the request sizes from the first 20 digits of π; for example, the first 3 request sizes are 3, 1, and 4. Adjacent available blocks should be recombined (why?).

9.4
Fibonacci Memory Management Systems

We now generalize the Buddy system memory management algorithm. We present the generalized Fibonacci system and demonstrate the use of data structures in memory allocation during program execution. The algorithms given below were obtained from Hinds[4], Hirschberg, and Knowlton.

The Fibonacci system creates blocks of size F_n, where

$$F_n = F_{n-1} + F_{n-k-1}$$
$$F_0 = 0, F_1 = F_2 \ldots F_{k+1} = 1$$

for some arbitrary k. In the case $k = 0$ the Buddy system is realized with blocks of size $F_n = 2^n$. Although the algorithms described below are general for any value of k, we will use the case $k = 1$ as a demonstration. Thus the set of blocks, 1, 1, 2, 3, 5, 8, 13, 21 . . . would replace 1, 2, 4, 8, 16, 32 . . . in the Buddy system discussed earlier. Indeed, we can view the tree of adjacent Fibonacci blocks in a manner similar to the Buddy system tree (see Figure 9.5).

The central problem encountered with generalized Fibonacci systems is not in allocating but in locating adjacent "buddies" for coalescing into

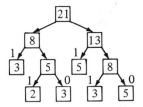

Figure 9.5 A Fibonacci tree for $k = 1$ in the Fibonacci allocation system

[4]James A. Hinds, "A Design for the Buddy System with Arbitrary Sequences of Block Sizes," Technical Report No. 74, State University of New York at Buffalo, Computer Science Department.

free blocks. Therefore in Figure 9.5 the subtrees of each node are the adjacent blocks in the Fibonacci system. For example, at the lowest level, 2 and 3 coalesce to yield 5, 5 and 3 yield 8, and 5 and 8 yield 13.

A method which assures that left and right buddies are matched uses a "left buddy counter" that is zero for all terminal nodes with a left buddy, and nonzero for all terminal nodes with a right buddy. In Figure 9.5 we see that only two nodes have a left buddy. We can extend this notion so that it will be useful during "split" and "free" operations. We maintain the counter as follows:

1. The root node (the largest block) is assigned a LEFT-BUDDY-COUNT of zero.

2. At each split, assign the LEFT-BUDDY-COUNT of the LEFT and RIGHT BLOCKS recursively:

$$\text{LEFT-BUDDY-COUNT (RIGHT-BLOCK)} = 0$$

$$\text{LEFT-BUDDY-COUNT (LEFT-BLOCK)} =$$

$$\text{LEFT-BUDDY-COUNT (PARENT)} + 1$$

Therefore we can now draw the tree of Figure 9.5, applying the rule above in order to obtain the LEFT-BUDDY-COUNTS prescribed (see Figure 9.6).

The two buddies that have a LEFT-BUDDY-COUNT of zero and nonzero are candidates for coalescing. If they both become free, they are coalesced, and the LEFT-BUDDY-COUNT of the coalesced pair is one greater than the count of the left subtree.

EXERCISES

1. Design a linked list AVAIL structure for the Fibonacci allocation system and give an ALLOCATE and FREE algorithm.

2. Generate the first ten block sizes from the $k = 2$ Fibonacci system. Assume $F_0 = 0, F_1 = 1, F_2 = 1, F_3 = 1$.

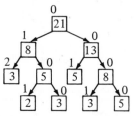

Figure 9.6 The left-buddy-count of the tree of Figure 9.5

3. Show that the formula $F_n = C\alpha^n$ satisfies the Fibonacci recurrence formula for any value of k (specified beforehand). The integers in the sequence are given by this formula by rounding to the nearest integer. (*Hint:* α is the root of $X^{k+1} - X^k - 1 = 0$, and C is obtained by noting $F_0 = 0, F_1 = \ldots F_{k+1} = 1$.

9.5
Optimal Memory
Management Systems

This section should be read only by those who have the mathematical background. While it contains an analytical method of block size selection, it is not essential for understanding memory management. However, it is a fascinating application which will interest the Fibonacci number enthusiast.

We can design a memory management scheme based on the kth Fibonacci sequence and modeled after the Buddy system. Initially, memory is the size of an appropriate Fibonacci number, and requests for smaller pieces of memory are serviced by using the formula for F_n to split and reassemble blocks. Does this improve utilization of memory? Table 9.1 shows there is a greater variety of block sizes as k increases, but that system overhead increases.

For the moment we will disregard the overhead and examine the cost due to internal fragmentation. Let $\{F_i\}$ for i from 0 to n be the collection of block sizes, with $F_0 = 0$ and $F_n = m$, the memory size. If the system services a request for a certain number x of memory locations, it will allocate a block of size F_i, where $F_{i-1} < x \leq F_i$. The waste involved is $(F_i - x)$.

The requests for memory space are always for an integral number of locations, but for convenience let us assume that the request sizes are given by a continuous probability function $pdf(x)$. Then the expected average waste per request $\overline{w}$ is given by Hirschberg (see References):

$$\overline{w} = \sum_{i=1}^{n} \int_{F_{i-1}}^{F_i} (F_i - x)pdf(x)\, dx$$

Rewriting this, we obtain:

$$\overline{w} = m - \overline{x} - \sum_{i=1}^{n} (d_i)cdf(F_{i-1})$$

where

$$m = \text{maximum memory size}$$

$$\overline{x} = \int_0^m x\, pdf(x)\, dx = \text{average request size}$$

**Table 9.1   Generalized Fibonacci Sequences Giving Block Sizes
1 Through 250 (approx.)**

i	F_i				
Level	$k = 0$	$k = 1$	$k = 2$	$k = 3$	$k = 4$
1	1	1	1	1	1
2	2	1	1	1	1
3	4	2	1	1	1
4	8	3	2	1	1
5	16	5	3	2	1
6	32	8	4	3	2
7	64	13	6	4	3
8	128	21	9	5	4
9	256	34	13	7	5
10		55	19	10	6
11		89	28	14	8
12		144	41	19	11
13		233	60	26	15
14			88	36	20
15			129	50	26
16			189	69	34
17			277	95	45
18				131	60
19				181	80
20				250	106
21					140
22					185
23					245

n = number of distinct block sizes

$d_i = F_i - F_{i-1}$

$$cdf(z) = \int_0^z pdf(x)\, dx = \text{cumulative distribution function}$$

The objective of memory management is to minimize $\overline{w}$ for a given $pdf(x)$. If we restrict our attention to Fibonacci-type systems, we can gain some additional insight into minimizing $\overline{w}$.

To solve for F_n in closed form, we must investigate the characteristic polynomial, $x^{k+1} - x^k - 1 = 0$, of the kth Fibonacci sequence. The polynomial (for fixed k) is known to have $(k + 1)$ distinct roots, which yield a closed form expression for the nth Fibonacci number. Note that $f(x) = x^{k+1} - x^k - 1$ has a real root between 1 and 2, since $f(1)$ is negative and

$f(2)$ is positive. By Decartes' rule of signs, this is the only positive root, which will be denoted by α_1. Thus $1 < \alpha_1 \leq 2$ ($\alpha_1 = 2$ if $k = 0$). Let the other roots of $f(x)$ be $\alpha_2, \alpha_3, \ldots, \alpha_{k+1}$. It is easy to establish that α_1 is the root of largest modulus and, in fact, $|\alpha_i| < 1$ for $i = 2, 3, \ldots, k + 1$.

Evidently, any sequence of numbers $\{u_i\}$ satisfying $u_i = c_1\alpha_1^i + c_2\alpha_2^i + \ldots + c_{k+1}\alpha_{k+1}^i$ will be a kth Fibonacci sequence for F_n. Specifying the initial $(k + 1)$ terms of the sequence determines the constants $c_1, \ldots, c_{k+1}$, or specifying the constants determines the sequence. For the particular sequence $\{F_i\}$ in Table 9.1, we can write $F_i = c_1\alpha_1^i + \ldots + c_{k+1}\alpha_{k+1}^i$. Since $|\alpha_i| < 1$ for $i = 2, 3, \ldots, k + 1$, it follows that for sufficiently large i:

$$F_i \cong c_1\alpha_1^i$$

Some approximate values of c_1 and α_1 are given in Table 9.2. The initial segments in Table 9.1 can be obtained from the formula $F_i = c_1\alpha_1^i$ (rounded to the nearest integer).

Table 9.2   Generators for Fibonacci Sequences

	$k = 0$	$k = 1$	$k = 2$	$k = 3$	$k = 4$
$c(k)$	1	.44721	.41724	.39663	.38119
$\alpha(k)$	2	1.61803	1.46557	1.38028	1.32472

Consider now the value of α_1 for different values of k. Let this root be denoted by $\alpha(k)$. We have observed that $1 < \alpha(k) \leq 2$. We see that $\alpha(k) = 1 + \left(\dfrac{1}{\alpha(k)}\right)^k$, and it follows that $\alpha(k + 1) < \alpha(k)$ for every k. In fact, $\lim\limits_{k \to \infty} \alpha(k) = 1$.

Let us apply the preceding observations to a particular example, in which the distribution of request sizes is given by the uniform distribution $pdf(x) = 1/m$. Then $cdf(x) = x/m$, and $\bar{x} = m/2$. Let k be arbitrary but fixed. We write $\alpha(k) = \alpha$ and $c(k) = c$, so that $F_i \cong c\alpha^i$, and $F_n = c\alpha^n = m$. Then:

$$\bar{w} = m - \bar{x} - \sum_{i=1}^{n} (d_i)cdf(F_{i-1})$$

$$= m - \frac{m}{2} - c\left(1 - \frac{1}{\alpha}\right)\sum_{i=1}^{n} \alpha^i \, cdf(c\alpha^{i-1})$$

$$= \frac{m}{2} - c\left(1 - \frac{1}{\alpha}\right)\sum_{i=1}^{n} \alpha^i \frac{c\alpha^i}{\alpha^m}$$

If we assume that $m \gg 1$, then $\alpha^2 m^2 - 1 \cong \alpha^2 m^2$, and $\overline{w} \cong \dfrac{m}{2} - \dfrac{m}{\alpha + 1}$.
Thus $\overline{w}$ can be made as small as desired by increasing k, since α approaches 1 as k increases.

Intuitively, this is to be expected, since for any finite memory size m, if $k > m$, the kth Fibonacci sequence contains all the integers from 1 through m, and $\overline{w}$ should be zero. However, this leads to extreme overhead in memory management and places unreasonable demands on the search mechanism for allocation and release of area in memory.

The waste function $\overline{w}$ measures only the cost of internal fragmentation. Let us assume that the overhead associated with a memory system is given by a function of n, the number of distinct block sizes. Then a more complete cost function is:

$$w = m - \overline{x} - \sum_{i=1}^{n}(d_i)cdf(F_{i-1}) + f(n)$$

This raises the possibility of optimizing the collection $\{F_i\}_{i=0}^{n}$ by considering the equations:

$$\frac{\partial w}{\partial F_j} = 0 \qquad \text{for } j = 1, 2, \ldots, n - 1$$

and the boundary conditions $F_0 = 0$, $F_n = m$. The solution is given by the "state equation":

$$F_{j+1} = F_j + \frac{cdf(F_j) - cdf(F_{j-1})}{pdf(F_j)}$$

Continuing with the simple example of the uniform request distribution, let us assume conveniently that $f(n) = \beta \cdot n$, where $\beta > 0$ is a constant. We obtain:

$$F_{j+1} = F_j + \frac{\dfrac{F_j}{m} - \dfrac{F_{j-1}}{m}}{\dfrac{1}{m}} = 2F_j - F_{j-1}$$

The difference equation is not of the Fibonacci type, but does have a closed form solution:

$$F_j = \frac{m}{n}j \qquad \text{for } j = 0, 1, \ldots, n$$

So it is possible to optimize the collection $\{F_j\}$, which minimizes w, provided we know the nature of $f(n)$.

Unfortunately, other request distributions and other functions $f(n)$ do not lead to such nice solutions. Indeed, the difference equations resulting from the state equation are, in general, extremely difficult to solve analytically. For certain $pdf(x)$, however, solutions are of considerable importance to computer systems designers, and where closed-form solutions of the difference equations are not feasible, it is still important to apply numerical techniques to these problems.

EXERCISES

1. Write a computer program to compute F_n for any n and any k.

2. Write a computer program to compute $\bar{w}$ for any value of n, any $pdf(x)$, and any F_i.

3. Devise an algorithm to ALLOCATE and FREE the blocks that are optimal for $pdf(x) = 1/m$.

4. Assume $pdf(x) = \dfrac{1}{\sigma m}e^{-x/m}$ for $0 \leq x \leq m$, and

$$\sigma = \int_0^m \frac{1}{m}e^{-x/m}\,dx.$$

Calculate the optimal block sizes for this system when $n = 10$.

10
ADVANCED APPLICATIONS

The following sections cut across three phases of computer programming: preparation, translation, and execution. We wish to demonstrate how data structures permeate these three phases, and to integrate your ideas about the material covered in previous chapters.

We follow an evolutionary development of the growth of data structures and table operations required in computer programming. In this way, a student of data structures can see the relationships among the many parts already described. In particular, these parts are bound together by our need to add, delete, and change information within computer memory.

PROGRAM PREPARATION

The design of a computer program begins with problem definition and organization of the tasks to be performed. We use a flowchart to describe the tasks identified by our analysis. The flowchart shows how data is to be manipulated. The operations used in manipulation determine what structure is most efficient for data storage. Therefore an awareness of data structure techniques is necessary at the earliest stage of computer programming: program preparation.

We demonstrate three data structures imposed by program preparation for three diverse applications. In the analysis, we assume no programming language considerations (this may be unrealistic). The applications are numerical calculations on sparse arrays, updating operations on a structure for display graphics, and text editing of source statements. The applications may be studied in any order since they are independent examples.

10.1 Sparse Arrays

We will study a common problem in numerical calculations: efficient storage of sparse arrays. Suppose a two-dimensional array of 100 by 100 elements is needed to do a certain calculation. The array space for a dense list implementation would require 10,000 memory locations. Suppose further that all but three diagonals of the array contain zero. An array containing many zero elements and few nonzero elements is termed a *sparse array*. We define a tridiagonal array with elements $a_{i,j}$; $i = 1, 2, \ldots n$ and $j = 1, 2, \ldots n$ as the form shown below.

$$
A = \begin{bmatrix}
a_{11} & a_{12} & 0 & \cdots & & 0 \\
a_{21} & a_{22} & a_{23} & \cdots & & 0 \\
0 & a_{32} & a_{33} & & \ddots & \\
0 & & & \ddots & \ddots & \\
\vdots & & & & & \\
\vdots & & & & a_{n-1,n-1} & a_{n-1,n} \\
0 & & & & a_{n,n-1} & a_{n,n}
\end{bmatrix}
$$

In the array under discussion, $(98 \times 3) + 4 = 298$ entries are nonzero, while $10{,}000 - 298 = 9{,}702$ entries are zero in the 100×100 array. Much space is being wasted in storing zeros. Is there a data structure that will save memory in this case? Let us use a 3×3 array example to show how we could save space in the 100×100 array problem.

Figures 10.1 and 10.2 demonstrate a multilinked list structure for storage of a 3×3 array. In Figure 10.2 only two atoms are nonzero, hence only two atoms are included in the list.

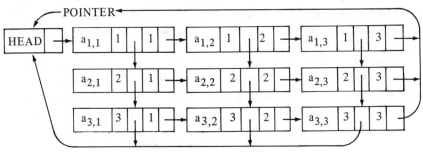

Figure 10.1 Data structure for a 3 × 3 matrix

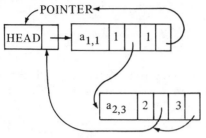

Seven words of memory are saved by using linked lists instead of array structure for a sparse matrix.

Figure 10.2 Data structure for a 3 × 3 matrix with (1, 1) and (2, 3) elements nonzero

The row pointers of Figure 10.1 establish a ring structure for rows, while column pointers encircle vertical columns. Notice that additional overhead is needed to label each atom with appropriate subscripts. These are needed to identify which element of the matrix is nonzero. The $a_{i,j}$ entries would contain the actual value stored in the i,j position of the matrix.

If we assume that each atom of data in Figure 10.1 requires two words of space (one for $a_{i,j}$ and one for (i,j) plus pointers), then the density of an $n \times n$ array is as follows:

$$d = \frac{n^2 \text{ words of data}}{2n^2 \text{ words of data structure}}$$

$$= \frac{1}{2}$$

On the other hand, the density of a dense list is 1.0. The break-even point for "sparseness" is 50%. In the case of a 100×100 array, if more than 5000 entries are nonzero, a dense list implementation saves as much space. In general, if the density of the sparse array multilinked list is d, then $d \cdot n^2$ nonzero entries is the break-even point.

In our example, 298 nonzero elements are to be stored and manipulated as a tridiagonal matrix. Storage as a doubly linked list requires $2 \times (298)$ = 596 words, as opposed to 10,000 words! What price do we pay for this saving?

Suppose we wish to add together two tridiagonal (or any sparse matrix) matrices stored as shown in Figure 10.1. Mathematically we want to add together corresponding elements and store the sum back in one of the arrays:

$$a_{i,j} \leftarrow a_{i,j} + b_{i,j} \qquad \text{for all } i,j$$

Let us assume matrices A and B contain only the nonzero elements $a_{i,j}$ and $b_{i,j}$, respectively. Thus the following algorithm must be performed to accomplish the addition indicated above.

1. Set $i \leftarrow 1, j \leftarrow 1$. (The subscripts must range over all possible pairs for $i,j = 1, 2, \ldots n$.)

2. While $j \le n$ perform steps 2 through 4. Search A for $a_{i,j}$, B for $b_{i,j}$. (This is done by tracing the pointers first along the "i-direction" and then down the "j-direction" until a match occurs between the i,j key and the values of i,j stored in an atom, or until it is discovered that no match exists.)

3. Do one of the cases below:
   (a) If $a_{i,j}$ and $b_{i,j}$ are located in A and B, respectively, perform the addition and store the result in $a_{i,j}$.
   (b) If both $a_{i,j}$ and $b_{i,j}$ do not exist, do nothing.
   (c) If only $b_{i,j}$ exists, create a new atom for $a_{i,j}$ and insert it into structure A. Copy the value of $b_{i,j}$ into $a_{i,j}$.
   (d) If only $a_{i,j}$ exists, do nothing.

4. Increment i. If $i = n + 1$, set $i \leftarrow 1$ and increment j.

Operations on sparse matrices stored as linked lists are more complex and time-consuming. Therefore we should use dense structures, unless storage is limited or the application warrants storage-minimizing usage.

In preparing a computer program for processing a sparse array, we must choose the data structure and then implement a search algorithm analogous to the one given above (unless the programming language incorporates the search mechanism). The selection of structure is made during analysis and design of the computer program, that is, during program preparation.

EXERCISES

1. Devise an algorithm for locating the (i,j)th element of a sparse matrix stored in a multilinked list.

2. Use the results of Exercise 1 to write an algorithm to multiply two sparse matrices.

3. Design a data structure for a sparse vector, and then for a three-dimensional array. What can you say about the density of each and their storage efficiency break-even point? Devise a hashing algorithm that transforms the subscript values of (i,j) into a table address corresponding to the $a_{i,j}$th element of a sparse array, A. Discuss this approach as compared with the linked list approach.

10.2
A Display
Graphics Structure

The application of linked lists to display graphics data demonstrate again the usefulness of linked lists and the need to analyze a problem fully before programming. Two-dimensional input/output, employing a televisionlike device for output and a light pen device for input, is a good means for displaying large volumes of data to people. Such large volumes of data require sophisticated structuring to make the data presentable or viewable.

Either a refresh-type display (the picture must be "repainted" 30 or 40 times a second to keep it from fading) or a storage-type display (the picture is painted once and remains until "erased") is used to display data stored in structures appropriate to the device.

We will discuss data structures that are especially suitable for refresh-type cathode-ray tube (CRT) terminals. Storage-type CRT terminals are also used in a slightly different manner, but the data structuring is quite similar.

Before a single point or line can be drawn on the face of a CRT, a convention for coding output data must be known. These conventions are called plotting modes.

Modes are established by the CRT hardware. The modes of Figure 10.3 show some of the possibilities for plotting points, vectors, and lines. In all cases, a grid of Cartesian coordinate points is assumed to be transparently superimposed on the face of the CRT. Each point on the grid represents a point that may be referenced by a plotting mode word.

The basic modes that use this invisible grid are:

POINT: Plot a point at location (X, Y).

VECTOR: Draw a line from the current point (X, Y) (last point drawn) to the point $(X + \Delta X, Y + \Delta Y)$.

LINE: Draw a line from (X_1, Y_1) to (X_2, Y_2).

INCREMENT: Draw short line segments in steps of size R, where R = resolution (size of a grid "square").

The escape bit is used to switch from one mode to another. Normally the CRT plotting hardware assumes a mode setting given at the beginning of a sequence of plots.

The relative merits of different modes depend upon the application and attempts to conserve bits. The best mode may be a combination of all of the modes given. For example, 150 lines may be drawn in INCREMENT mode and then, using the escape bit to signal a change, 28 lines are drawn in the LINE mode.

POINT-PLOTTING

0	1	10	11	20	21
I	X		Y		E

I   Intensity (on or off)

X   10-bit X-coordinate ⎱ Any point on a

Y   10-bit Y-coordinate ⎰ 1024 × 1024 grid

E   Escape bit

VECTOR MODE

0	1	2	8	9	10	16	17
I	S	ΔX		S	ΔY		E

I   Intensity

S   Sign bits

ΔX   Change in horizontal position ⎱ Updated from

ΔY   Change in vertical position ⎰ previous point

LINE MODE

0	1	10	11	20	21	30	31	40	41
I	X_1		Y_1		X_2		Y_2		E

I, E   As before

X_1, Y_1 Starting point ⎱ Line drawn

X_2, Y_2 Stopping point ⎰ between

INCREMENT MODE

0	1	2	3	5	6	7	8	10	11
I	N_1		D_1		N_2		D_2		E

I, E   As before

N_1, N_2 Number of steps in direction D_1, D_2

D_1, D_2 Direction of steps (in 45° increments)

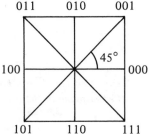

Figure 10.3 Data structure of CRT plotting modes

The data structure is actually built as a bit string, usually in multiples of bytes or fractions of words to conserve space. The CRT hardware prepares a point for plotting by storing a plotter word in separate *display registers,* called the *x* and *y* axis registers. The *x*-display and *y*-display registers are separately converted from digital into analog signals, which position and fire an electron beam. Often the electron beam is passed through *character templates* to become shaped into a character.

An example, demonstrating a data structure for line mode, is given for the "graph" of Figure 10.4. This picture, in graph form, is composed of components defined in the data structure using BACKWARD pointers (see Figure 10.5). The significant point here is that the BACKWARD pointers are used to group together components of the picture.

Component 1 consists of lines 1 through 6. These lines are represented in the data structure of Figure 10.5 by atoms 1 through 6. The BACK-WARD pointer of atom 6 points back to the HEADER, thus signifying a component. Component 2 consists of lines 7 through 9 and is represented by atoms 7 through 9 in Figure 10.5. The BACKWARD pointer of atom

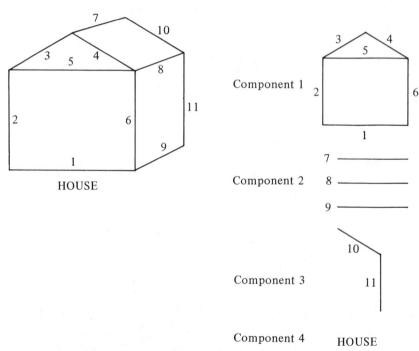

Figure 10.4 Graph of a house to be displayed. Each component is on a different plane in the orthographic projection

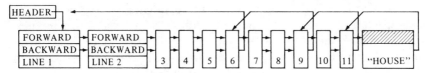

Figure 10.5 Simplified representation of data structure for the graphic display of Figure 10.4

9 groups together all atoms in component 2. In this way we can either manipulate an atom or a component of data.

The CRT display algorithm paints a picture from the data structure of Figure 10.5 by scanning the FORWARD pointers. Each atom is accessed in turn and a value copied into the x, y display registers.

The data provided in Figure 10.5 is not detailed enough to specify how lines are to be actually drawn (painted), but serves only to demonstrate the overall structure of data atoms. As a demonstration, let us propose a format for the atoms of Figure 10.5. In Figure 10.6 we see that each atom in the data structure is composed of fields.

Header

1	2
3	
4	

Data Atom

5	6
7	8
9	
10	
11	
12	
13	

Legend
1. User code (console number)
2. FORWARD pointer (next HEADER for another picture)
3. BACKWARD pointer (previous HEADER for previous picture)
4. Atom size (number of words in atom)
5. Display code $=\begin{cases} 0 \text{ do not paint} \\ 1 \text{ paint} \end{cases}$
6. FORWARD pointer (next atom)
7. Plane number (which component)
8. BACKWARD (for grouping components)
9–12. X_1, Y_1, X_2, Y_2 for LINE mode (other modes could be used)
13. Mode switch (set Escape or not)

Figure 10.6 Data organization for the structure of Figure 10.5

The algorithm for drawing the picture of Figure 10.4 operates on the data structure of Figure 10.5 containing atoms structured as shown in Figure 10.6. By tracing the FORWARD pointers, the algorithm locates x, y values for the x, y display registers. If the display code (item 5) is set to one, the electron beam is directed to paint the given line.

The last component spells "HOUSE" by furnishing the CRT hardware with codes for "H", "O", "U", "S", and "E." If special hardware exists for character generation, these characters are painted in a manner similar to the other components in the picture.

Notice that the data structure helps us select lines, components, and pictures as a simple unit of information. This demonstrates how careful design of a data structure can help ease the programmer's burden.

EXERCISES

1. Give a vector mode sequence of plotting words for the "house" of Figure 10.3. Make up your own scale factor and resolution.

2. How might we expand the INTENSITY field of the plotting mode words to include three colors?

3. Suggest several plotting modes for a polar coordinate graphics CRT.

4. How might a polar coordinate CRT be used to display complex plane data (imaginary as well as real valued)?

10.3
Text
Editing

Once the proper data structure has been selected for a given problem, a program must be written and debugged. An aid to program construction using on-line systems is the text editor. A text editor is a program that helps us type programming language statements into a file that will be processed by a language translator. (We use the term "translator" to include compilers, interpreters, and symbolic assemblers.)

The variety of text editors that currently exist are usually capable of manipulating text in many ways. We wish to discuss the data structuring necessary to do three basic text-editing operations: insertion, deletion, and replacement. These three operations are basic to all text editors, and they also motivate designers of editors to construct elaborate data structures. Suppose we wish to type in the following segment of source statement program for processing by a PL/I compiler.

.
.
.

$DECLARE$ A(10) $FIXED$;
$GET LIST$ (A);
A(1) = (A(1) − A(2)/A(1)*5) + 3;

.
.
.

This segment shows that A is an array of ten integer (FIXED) numbers. The values of A are input by the GET LIST command, and then A(1) is computed as:

$$A(1) - \frac{A(2)5}{A(1)} + 3$$

The text above is input by the editor as follows. Each statement is numbered in ascending order and input, e.g., through a keyboard terminal. Errors are corrected by either deleting a line or replacing parts of a line. The final version might appear as below.

10    $DECLARE$ A(10) $FIXED$;
20    $GET LIST$ (A);
30   A(1) = (A(1) − A(2)/A(1)*5) + 3;

This appears innocent at first glance, but we see upon closer examination that the dynamic nature of this process causes problems for memory organization. Suppose, for example, we delete statement 20. The adjacent statements, 10 and 30, must be moved to contiguous locations. Suppose further we wish to increase the length of statement 20 by inserting a comment. How is space expanded? A data structure that allows interaction with the characters of each line is needed. We propose here only one of many possible ways to organize text. (Other methods are discussed in Section 2.3.)

Figure 10.7 (a) shows how memory is utilized in text editing. The HEADER is a dense list (often called a dope vector) containing a FLAG, STATEMENT NUMBER, and ADDRESS field. The FLAG field indicates whether the statement has been inserted or deleted.

$$FLAG = \begin{cases} 0 \text{ inserted statement} \\ 1 \text{ deleted or empty} \end{cases}$$

The STATEMENT NUMBER corresponds to the number used in entering the statement. This number is used to identify the entire statement.

(a) Layout of test editor memory

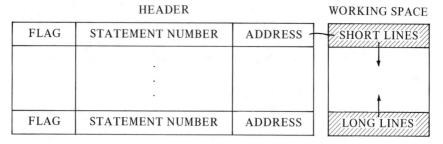

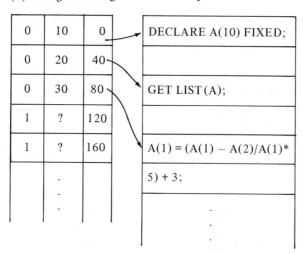

(b) Storage of text given as an example

Figure 10.7 A possible data structure for text editing

Therefore, string operations (see Chapter 2) are performed by referring to this number. The ADDRESS is an index into the WORKING SPACE.

WORKING SPACE is divided into two levels: SHORT LINES are text of 40 or less characters, LONG LINES are text of 41 to 80 characters. This method causes memory loss due to internal fragmentation of the WORKING SPACE, but has the advantage of allowing large numbers of updates (increase or decrease the statement length) without the need to move large numbers of characters.

More economical usage of memory is possible using a multilevel system (see Chapter 9 on memory management). Note that the SHORT LINE space grows from the "top" of our SPACE, while the LONG LINE space grows from the "bottom." When these two areas meet, the WORKING SPACE is said to have overflowed.

When overflow occurs, we must compact the two areas into less space. The FLAG field is used for this purpose. FLAG $= 1$ indicates that the area pointed to by the ADDRESS field is available for use. If, however, all FLAGS equal zero, the system is saturated and garbage collection is of no use.

Suppose we wish to insert a statement numbered 15 into the structure of Figure 10.7 (b). We have two choices: We can move everything below 10 "down" to make room for insertion of statement 15, or we can place statement 15 in the first available location in the dense HEADER list. If we do the first (move), we incur overhead in moving. If we do the second, we incur overhead in searching for statement 15 later.

This data structure must be flexible enough to allow renumbering of statements, creation of ordered lists, and substring searching. We have outlined merely one approach to this problem, called the *dope vector* method. Other approaches may use hashing, multiple linked lists, or techniques to compress the text. In each case, the structure is selected because it is necessary for the operations to be performed.

EXERCISES

1. Compute the expected internal fragmentation (use layout of Figure 10.7) if the probability distribution for statement length is $e^{-x/5}/5$; $x > 0$.

2. Give INSERT, DELETE, and REPLACE algorithms for the data structure suggested in Figure 10.7. The REPLACE operator must find a substring s_0 and replace it with string s_1. Keep in mind that the replacement string may be null.

3. Discuss limitations or drawbacks to the method of Figure 10.7.

4. Design a text editor system based on hashing instead of the dope vector method presented here.

5. Write a computer program to perform INSERT and DELETE operations on a data structure. What problems did you encounter?

10.4 Symbol Tables

Let us use the program segment of Section 10.3 as an illustration of the ideas here. We assume that these statements are part of a program entered into a text editor file. This file is processed by a translator that reads source statements and generates object statements for a particular computer. The recognition of source language statements of a high-level programming language is our main concern.

> *DECLARE* A(10) *FIXED*;
> *GET LIST* (A);
> A(1) = (A(1) − A(2)/A(1)*5) + 3;
> .
> .
> .

The source statements above will be used to demonstrate symbol tables for use in translation, templates or dope vectoring arrays, and parsing of arithmetic expressions by a push-down stack automaton.

Each variable name in a program must be associated with an attribute list. The attributes include the location address, type of variable, and sometimes an initial value (and other attributes not discussed here). To rapidly access the attribute list during translation, a means of building a table containing names is imperative.

In Figure 10.8 we see such a symbol table. Since access is made during construction, we need a method that works well when the table entries are constantly changing. The following hashing technique is suggested.

1. Fold-shift NAME so that it fits into one computer word.

2. Set R ← remainder of the division NAME/N. Q = quotient from division. If Q = 0, set Q ← 1.

3. Set INDEX ← R.

INDEX	NAME	TYPE	ADDRESS
0			
1			
2			
		.	
		.	
		.	
(N − 1)			

Figure 10.8 Symbol table format

4. Examine TABLE (INDEX). All calculations are done modulo N, so if the desired TABLE (INDEX) is *not* found, then add Q to INDEX and repeat this step again. Otherwise continue on to step 5.

5. If N probes have been unsuccessful, the name does not exist in the table. Stop.

Let us perform the hashing algorithm above for the array 'A' and the literals '5' and '3' as given in the sample program segment. The EBCDIC coding for these is (in hexadecimal);

Character	EBCDIC
'A'	$C1_{16}$
'3'	$F3_{16}$
'5'	$F5_{16}$

We will assume a word with four bits of precision and therefore must shift and fold the two hex digits as follows.

Character	Fold-shift
'A'	$C + 1 = D_{16}$
'3'	$F + 3 = 2_{16}$
'5'	$F + 5 = 4_{16}$

Since 'A' is encountered first, then '5', and finally '3', we will perform the hash on these names in the order: 'A', '5', '3'. The algorithm produces the following results, assuming $N = 11$ (B in hexadecimal).

Variable	Calculation	
R	$D_{16}/B_{16} = 2_{16}$	
Q	$D_{16}/B_{16} = 1$	For 'A'
INDEX	$= 2_{16}$	

Variable	Calculation
R	$2/B_{16} = 2$
Q	$2/B_{16} = 0$; set to 1
INDEX	$2 + Q = 3$

For '3'

Note that the hash value of INDEX in the case for '3' collides with the INDEX for 'A'. The collision is resolved by addition of Q, as indicated in step 4 of the algorithm.

Variable	Calculation
R	$4/B_{16} = 4$
Q	$4/B_{16} = 0$; set to 1
INDEX	$= 4$

For '5'

The final result of storing these names in the symbol table appears in Figure 10.9. Note that we have also filled in the other information to demonstrate a possible outcome for a compiler. We have used the character form of information to assist in reading. The address field represents locations where additional information about the array A and the constants 3 and 5 are stored.

It would appear that the information in Figure 10.9 has solved' our problem of translating symbolic names in a high-level language into attributes, such as type and address. Notice, however, that 'A' is an array. We have not supplied information about the length of A or how many subscripts A has declared. For this reason, an additional descriptor called the *dope vector* is used.

EXERCISES

1. Write a computer program to perform the symbol table hashing algorithm given in the text.

2. Use the program of Exercise 1 to study the performance of hashing as the loading factor is changed from $\alpha = 0.5$ to $\alpha = 0.9$. Compute the average number of comparisons expected when inserting a symbol.

INDEX	NAME	TYPE	ADDRESS
0			
1			
2	'A'	'ARRAY'	0A54
3	'3'	'CONSTANT'	0BC0
4	'5'	'CONSTANT'	0BC4
. . .		. . .	
10			

Figure 10.9 Result of hashing into symbol table

3. Construct a symbol table based on a binary search tree rather than a hash code table. Show how the tree would appear for the data in Figure 10.9.

4. Create a symbol table for names 'B', 'J', and '9', using the same parameters given in Figure 10.9.

5. Why is Q set to 1 when the quotient is zero in the hashing algorithm?

10.5
Dope
Vectors

In Figure 10.9 the address field of name 'A' points to a dense list containing additional information about array A. In particular, the dense list (called a dope vector, template, or various other names) contains subscript and location information. A possible dope vector for our example is shown in Figure 10.10.

The general dope vector of Figure 10.11 (a) and the example of Figure 10.11 (b) show how a d-dimensional array is dope-vectored. The dope vector may be partially filled in during translation, and during execution the remainder of the parameters may be computed and stored in the dope vector.

A column-major order mapping for the dope vector of Figure 10.11 is given in terms of the parameters M_i:

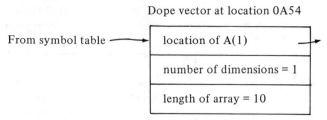

Dope vector at location 0A54

From symbol table ⟶

| location of A(1) |
| number of dimensions = 1 |
| length of array = 10 |

Figure 10.10 A dope vector for the array of Figure 10.9

$$a = \sum_{i=1}^{d} M_i(j_i - LB_i)$$

j_i = subscript of array reference

M_i = block size of multiple columns

LB_i = lower bound

UB_i = upper bound

This formula is analogous to the row-major order formula given in Chapter 3.

EXERCISES

1. Compute the dope vector parameters for an array B declared as B(10, 20, 10).

2. Compute the density of the structure in Exercise 1.

10.6
Parsing

Now that the names are resolved into attributes, it is the task of the language translator to separate the parts of each statement into basic units that can then be converted into machine language instructions. The process of separating statements into syntactic units is called *parsing*. The syntactic units that we use here as a demonstration will be restricted to simple variables and operators.

Suppose we simplify the assignment statement given in the sample program segment so that it appears as below.

$$A = (A - B/A*5) + 3;$$

In order for the translator to generate the necessary '=', '−', '*', and '+' operations, it must separate the names from the operators and establish

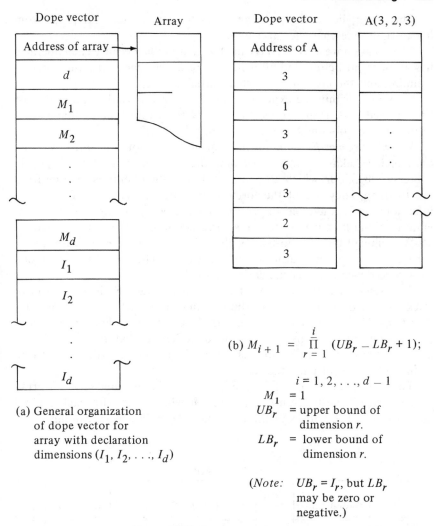

(b) $M_{i+1} = \prod_{r=1}^{i} (UB_r - LB_r + 1);$

$i = 1, 2, \ldots, d - 1$

$M_1 = 1$

UB_r = upper bound of dimension r.

LB_r = lower bound of dimension r.

(a) General organization of dope vector for array with declaration dimensions $(I_1, I_2, \ldots, I_d)$

(*Note:* $UB_r = I_r$, but LB_r may be zero or negative.)

Figure 10.11 Dope vector for arrays

an order for the operations. We can see that the order needed here is as follows:

First operation:	B/A	divide
Second operation:	(B/A)*5	multiply
Third operation:	A − (B/A)*5	subtract
Last operation:	(A − (B/A)*5) + 3	add

This order, however, is not apparent to a computer that reads from left to right, one character at a time.

The notation we have used is called *infix notation,* because each operator has an operand before and after it. This results in backward and forward scanning and the creation of nested partial results, as shown above; e.g., B/A is nested within the expression, and yet it is a partial result that must be obtained first. How are we to simplify the expression so that partial results may be obtained as we move from left to right?

We will use *postfix notation* (a form of Polish notation introduced by the logician Łukasiewicz) to overcome the problem of nesting. A postfix expression is one in which all operators follow the operands reading from left to right. They are of the form (OP) (OP) . . . (OPERATOR). The infix notation is converted to postfix, and the postfix is then used to generate machine language statements corresponding to the steps needed.

We will call the infix-to-postfix algorithm a *transducer,* because it converts an input into an output of different form. The transducer is guided by a precedence table as shown in Figure 10.12.

Two stacks are operated by the transducer; stack S_1 is a push-down stack which stores the output of the machine, and stack S_2 is a temporary "scratchpad" memory used by the transducer during operation. For simplicity, only operands in the form of identifiers, operators $(+, -, *, /)$, and parentheses will be allowed as input. The output set will consist of all of the above except parentheses.

The precedence table of Figure 10.12 may be encoded into an array which "drives" the transducer by telling it what to do with each symbol as it is input. The entries in the table have the following meaning:

INPUT SYMBOL

		\<Identifier\>	=	+, −	*, /	(	)	End of statement	
	"null"	S_1	S_2	ERR	ERR	ERR	ERR	ERR	
TOP of S_2	=	S_1	ERR	S_2	S_2	S_2	ERR	U_2	
	+, −	S_1	ERR	U_1	S_2	S_2	U_c	U_2	
	*, /	S_1	ERR	U_1	U_1	S_2	U_c	U_2	
	(	S_1	ERR	S_2	S_2	S_2	U_c	U_2	

Figure 10.12 Next state function for pushdown stack transducer

S_1 = stack input onto S_1

S_2 = stack input onto S_2

ERR = error occurred, input not valid

U_1 = unstack $S_2 \rightarrow S_1$, do another comparison

U_c = unstack, $S_2 \rightarrow S_1$ repeatedly until (is encountered; discard (

U_2 = unstack $S_2 \rightarrow S_1$ until S_2 empty

Let us demonstrate the operation of the transducer in Figure 10.12. The steps in Figure 10.13 show how S_1 and S_2 grow and shrink as the expression is scanned from left to right. The infix expression is shown along the bottom of each table of Figure 10.13, and two stacks, S_1 and S_2, rise above each character in the infix expression. The operation performed after reading each syntactic unit (identifier or operator) is indicated below the character read from infix form. The final result (output in postfix) is found in stack S_1 when S_2 is empty and no other inputs are made.

Let us follow through the example of Figure 10.13. The first syntactic unit is the identifier 'A'. Since the top of stack S_2 is null, the table in Figure 10.12 tells us that the operation is "stack A onto S_1." The next value is '='. Referring to the table again, we see that '=' should go onto stack S_2. Now the top of S_2 is the '=' unit, and the input is the unit '('. This results in an operation of S_2.

We continue in this fashion until S_1 contains all the input and S_2 is empty. Note that identifiers are stored on S_1 as they are read left to right. Operators, on the other hand, are always diverted to S_2 before going onto S_1. The diversion to S_2 is how parenthesis nesting is avoided. The rules for unstacking S_2 are determined by precedence of the operators. Bracketing is done by parentheses and causes every operator between parentheses to be pushed onto S_2, temporarily.

The result in S_1 contains no parentheses and no nesting that cannot be resolved by left-to-right scanning. Let us see how the postfix string of S_1 is interpreted so that appropriate operations can be generated in machine language:

$$S_1: A\ A\ B\ A\ /\ 5\ *\ -\ 3\ +\ =$$

The storage element S_1 is now treated as a queue by reading from bottom to top, or as shown above, from left to right. The interpreter algorithm below uses S_2 again as a push-down stack element for temporary storage. The interpreter must scan from left to right by storing operands in S_2 until an operator is found, apply the operator to the top atoms of the temporary storage stack S_2, and push the resulting value onto S_2. This is repeated

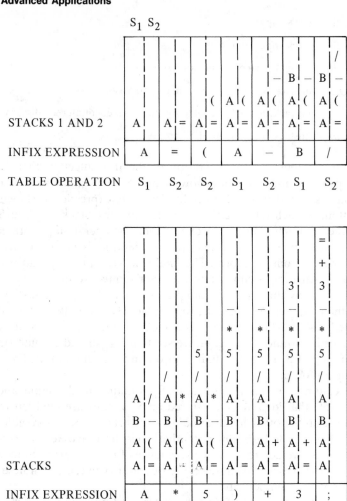

Figure 10.13 Demonstration of infix-to-postfix notation

iteratively until S_1 has been scanned and S_2 is empty. The interpreter algorithm is given below:

1. While S_2 is not empty, do steps 2 and 3.
2. Take a unit from S_1 by removing it from the "left." Call this X.
3. If X is an identifier, then push X onto S_2. If X is an operator, perform the

operation on the top two elements on S_2 and replace them with the result of this operation.

An example of scanning the sample string is given in Figure 10.14. Note that S_2 grows until an operator unit is encountered. The operator unit takes the top two elements off S_2 and performs an operation. The result is placed back onto S_2 and the entire procedure repeated.

In practice, the precedence table and the syntactic units are coded to conserve storage. The codes used for identifier name and operators are called *token-codes*. The tokens must be recognized as either name or operator. Recognition of tokens is sometimes done with the aid of a symbol table as discussed previously.

We have now shown the steps in program preparation and translation. The next step is to show how data structures play a role in program execution. During execution, when a structure is part of a machine's hardware program it is called a computer structure; when part of a software program, a data structure.

EXERCISES

1. Write a program to recognize assignment statements as given by the parsing transducer. Assume names are single character alphabetic, and binary operators are $+$, $-$, $*$, $/$. Allow any level of parentheses nesting.

2. Write a program to interpret the output string S_1 from Exercise 1. How have you coded the tokens?

3. Devise a precedence table for the *IF* source statement of the form: *IF* e_1 *THEN* e_2 *ELSE* e_3;. Assume e_1, e_2, e_3 are simple expressions, such as A < B or X = Y, so that only two names and one infix operator are allowed.

				A		5					
			B	B	B/A	B/A	$B/A*5$		3		
		A	A	A	A	A	A	$A-T_1$	$A-T_1$	T_2	
S_2	A	A	A	A	A	A	A	A	A	A	$A=T_2$
S_1	A	A	B	A	/	5	*	$-$	3	+	=
Operation	Stack	Stack	Stack	Stack	Divide	Stack	Mult	Sub	Stack	Add	Assign

Figure 10.14 Interpretation of S_1 where $T_1 = B/A*5$ and $T_2 = (A - T_1) + 3$

10.7
I/O Processing

Most computers must manage the flow of data to and from peripheral devices, as well as compute arithmetic results. Unfortunately, the speed of peripheral devices differs vastly from the internal working speed of a computer. For this reason, it is necessary to provide structures called buffers for input/output (I/O). A *buffer* is a storage element used to temporarily save data that is being written or read. Once the transfer from a peripheral has taken place, the buffer is referenced by the user's program to obtain data. Our second topic in program execution is the structure necessary for buffering.

Modern computers have the capability to simultaneously transfer data to and from main memory while processing other data. For example, a lengthy numerical calculation requires very little input/output, but very much arithmetic capability. Hence an I/O operation may take place simultaneously with calculations to increase the computer system throughput. On the other hand, I/O is typically slower than the arithmetic component of a computer, and so it is desirable to transfer large blocks of data at one time.

A method of input called *buffered I/O* will be used to demonstrate a useful data structure for increasing the processing speed of a computer system. Assume that two buffers (blocks of temporary storage) are used in the following manner:

> Buffer A is being used for input while
> Buffer B is being read by the program

and then when A is full and B has been processed their roles are reversed:

> Buffer B is being used for input while
> Buffer A is being read by the program.

The ping-pong effect of these two buffers increases throughput because it allows simultaneous operation of the program and I/O (see Figure 10.15).

In Figure 10.15 we see that two areas of memory are set aside for input buffers. In addition, three pointers are needed to indicate the INPUT buffer: ACTIVE, which points to the input space and the displacements within A and B of the data being accessed. The two buffers are being accessed simultaneously: A by the input processor which is transferring data from an outside source to location NEXT A, and B by the output processor which is moving the word in NEXT B to an executing program.

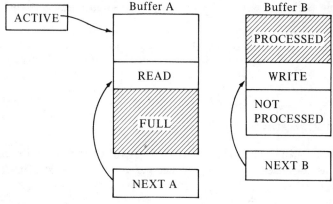

Figure 10.15 Double buffering in operation

In Figure 10.16 the buffers have just completed a cycle. Buffer A is full and buffer B is "empty" (processed). The input is now made to B, and the processing is done on the contents of A. The ACTIVE pointer tells us which buffer is to receive the input data. Once all input has been made and all of A has been processed, the cycle is completed and ACTIVE switches back to buffer A.

EXERCISES

1. What should be the size of buffers A and B of Figure 10.15 when I/O is performed at 20,000 bytes/second and processing is done at 40,000 bytes/second? Assume that it takes 1/40 second to switch from buffer A to buffer B. (*Hint:* Let I/O time = switch time + process time for each buffer.)

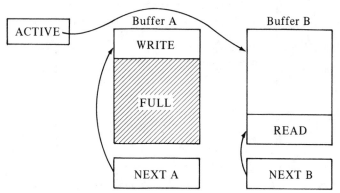

Figure 10.16 State of double buffers at beginning of next cycle

2. Explain what happens if data rates exceed the processing rates in a double-buffer system.

3. Show how 3, 4, . . . and more buffers can be used in a multiple-buffer system that provides for data overrun (*data overrun* is the process of exceeding the capacity of the processor to process data as fast as it is transferred into a buffer).

10.8
Recursion

As a second example of data structures useful for program execution we illustrate stacks used for recursion. *Recursion* is the process of nesting subprogram calls within one another. A *recursive subprogram* is a subprogram that calls itself.

The topics of recursion and I/O buffering are two features of a system that executes programs. Such features are part of the run-time environment of a computer system. The support of run-time environments is an important topic of computer science and involves extensive use of data structures. As these structures become known and understood, they are incorporated into hardware and become computer structures. Indeed, many of the operations mentioned below will be operations performed by hardware instead of software.

Consider this recursive problem: The number 518 is stored in computer memory as a binary number (1000000110). Our problem is to separate the decimal equivalents into 5, 1, and 8, and print them out as characters. In other words, we want to convert from binary to decimal and code the decimal digits for output. A table for the ASCII-7 character set is shown in Figure 10.17.

Character (decimal)	ASCII-7 (octal)
0	60
1	61
2	62
3	63
4	64
5	65
6	66
7	67
8	70
9	71

Figure 10.17 ASCII-7 codebook for numerals zero through nine

To solve the problem by recursion, assume that division produces a remainder and a quotient. Repeated division of 518 by 10 produces first 8, then 1, then 5 as remainders.

1. Set the quotient Q to the number, initially. Q ← number.

2. While Q ≠ 0 do step 2 (a):
   (a) Divide Q by 10 and obtain R, the remainder, and a new Q, the quotient. Save R and Q on a stack.

3. Since we have saved Q and R after each division by 10, we can now encode the remainders and print them out as follows. Unless the stack is empty do step 3 (a):
   (a) Pop an R value from the stack, add 60_8, and print the character.

The recursive nature of the algorithm above is not apparent. Let us see how the run-time environment of this "program" might operate. Assume that a push-down stack is used to store results and operands, and to save the return address of subprograms. A "call" will be a jump to a subprogram that preserves the return address on the stack. A "return" pops the stack to obtain the return address. We will allow parameters to be passed forward by referencing the stack from the top element. Therefore to obtain a single parameter from the top-of-stack (indexed by TOS) we can index, (TOS − 1) to obtain the second element on the stack. The steps in our binary-to-decimal conversion algorithm may now be rewritten in terms of the stack environment.

MAIN 1. Push 518 onto stack.
          2. Call conversion routine, CNVT.
          3.   .
                    .
                    .

CNVT 1. IF top of stack (TOS − 1) is zero, return.
         2. Divide the (TOS − 1) element by 10. Place the remainder R and the quotient Q on the stack.
         3. Call CNVT (recursively).
         4. Delete TOS element. (This is the quotient left by recursion.)
         5. Add 60_8 to TOS and output code to printer. (Delete from TOS).
         6. Return.

Carefully study the recursion above. The routine is "nested" by successive calls at step 3 and "unwinds" in step 1. Steps 4 to 6 are performed when step 1 invokes a return followed by successive returns in step 6. Observe the snapshots of the stack in Figure 10.18. The RTN (return) addresses of Figure 10.18 must be carefully observed. The final RTN branches back to the MAIN program, step 3.

The stack output is 65_8, 61_8, and 70_8 just as expected. The elegant point, however, is that the algorithm produces remainders in the exact opposite order desired, but with the stack the order is again reversed as needed.

The algorithm increases the stack in steps 1 to 3 and decreases the stack in steps 4 to 6. Contrast this with the interpretation of postfix notation as discussed in Section 10.6. The use of a stack has greatly simplified processing.

EXERCISES

1. Write a recursive subroutine to perform the binary to decimal conversion of CNVT.

2. How long will the stack get for an n-digit number?

Stack	Program step		Unstack step
518	MAIN: 1		MAIN: 3
RTN MAIN: 3	MAIN: 2		CNVT: 6
8	CNVT: 2		CNVT: 5
51			CNVT: 4
RTN CNVT: 4	CNVT: 3		CNVT: 6
1	CNVT: 2		CNVT: 5
5			CNVT: 4
RTN CNVT: 4	CNVT: 3		CNVT: 6
5	CNVT: 2		CNVT: 5
0			CNVT: 4
RTN CNVT: 4	CNVT: 3		CNVT: 1

Growth (downward, left side)   Decrease (middle)

(a)   (b)

Figure 10.18 (a) Final state of the run-time stack at the time CNVT determines that (TOS − 1) is zero and a RTN is needed, (b) decrease in stack as recursion "unwinds"

3. Give an algorithm and a simple example ($n = 3$), for $n! = n \cdot (n - 1)!$, where 0! is defined to be 1. (*Note:* $n!$ is read n factorial.)

10.9
Minimal Path
Algorithms

Computing the shortest path from one node to another in a graph has become a very important problem since the advent of computers. Shortest path algorithms are not necessarily difficult, but the number of computations required is often unwieldly. Applying these methods to problems such as transportation or communication networks would be too tedious without the aid of a computer.

In this section we will discuss two shortest path algorithms. The first one was published by Edgser Dijkstra in 1959 and is generally considered to be the most efficient method for finding the shortest distance between a pair of nodes. The second was published by Robert Floyd in 1962 and shows how to compute the shortest path between every pair of nodes in a graph.

COMPUTING THE SHORTEST PATH
BETWEEN A PAIR OF NODES

Let us assume that the nodes in the graph are numbered 1, 2, . . . , n and that we wish to find the shortest path from node 1 to node n. The lengths of the edges in the graph are given by an incidence matrix D, in which the entries d_{ij} give the distance from node i to node j. If there is no path from i to j, let d_{ij} be "∞," meaning infinite or any large value.

The algorithm involves dividing the nodes into two classes. Class 1 nodes are those whose minimum distance from node 1 has already been determined. Class 2 nodes remain to be examined. In addition to class, each node has a value. For class 1 nodes the value is equal to the node's distance from node 1 along a shortest path. For class 2 nodes the value represents the shortest distance found thus far. As the algorithm progresses, the value of class 2 nodes will decrease if a shorter path is found. After the value of each class 2 node has been adjusted, the one with smallest value is reclassified as class 1. This most recently reclassified node we will call the *pivotal node,* and its value is used to adjust the value of the remaining class 2 nodes. The algorithm terminates when node n is placed in class 1.

Algorithm A   Shortest Path from Node 1 to Node n

1. Place node 1 in class 1 and all others in class 2.

2. Set the value of node 1 to zero and all others to "∞."

3. Do the following until node n is placed in class 1.
   (a) Define the pivotal node as the one most recently placed in class 1.
   (b) Adjust all class 2 nodes in the following way.
      1. If a node is not connected to the pivotal node, its value remains the same.
      2. If a node is connected by an edge to the pivotal node, replace its value by the minimum of:
         i. its current value.
         ii. the current value of the pivotal node plus the distance from the pivotal node to the node in class 2.
   (c) Choose a class 2 node with minimal value and place it in class 1.

If the algorithm stops only after all nodes are in class 1, the value of each node is the length of the shortest path from node 1 to the given node. The algorithm gives only the length of the shortest path, it does not tell what the path is. However, if we record a node's immediate predecessor whenever its value changes in step 3 (b.2), the shortest path can be traced back to node 1 (see Exercise 5). The algorithm requires at most $n(n - 1)/2$ additions and $n(n - 1)/2$ comparisons.

SHORTEST PATH BETWEEN PAIRS OF NODES

The following algorithm works with the adjacency matrix D which contains elements d_{ij}, the distance from node i to node j. If there is no edge connecting i and j, then d_{ij} is defined as "∞." The algorithm proceeds by inserting nodes one at a time into a path only if the new path yields a shorter distance. For example, the graph in Figure 10.19 has $d_{13} = 12$, but the distance is shorter if the path taken from 1 to 3 includes node 2.

The algorithm produces a sequence of matrices, which we will label $D^{(0)}, D^{(1)}, \ldots, D^{(n)}$. A typical element in $D^{(k)}$ is $d_{ij}^{(k)}$, where k is some value between 0 and n. $D^{(0)} \leftarrow D$ the adjacency matrix. At any step, $D^{(k)}$ represents the distance between all pairs of nodes resulting from the possible inclusion of nodes $1, 2, \ldots, k$ in the path to make it shorter.

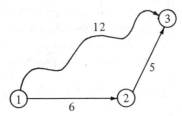

Figure 10.19 Directed graph with lengths of edges given

Algorithm B *Shortest Path Between All Pairs of Nodes*

1. Define $D^{(0)} \leftarrow D$ the adjacency matrix.
    ($d_{ij}^{(0)} \leftarrow d_{ij}$ for all i, j between 1 and n)

2. Do the following as k ranges from 0 to $n - 1$.
    (a) Define $D^{(k+1)}$, where

    $$d_{ij}^{(k+1)} \leftarrow \text{minimum of:} \quad \text{i.} \quad d_{ij}^{(k)}$$
    $$\text{ii.} \quad d_{i,k+1}^{(k)} + d_{k+1,j}^{(k)}$$

    for all i, j between 1 and n.

The algorithm does not specify which paths produce the shortest distances, but merely determines the distances. To find out how the paths can be found see Exercise 6. This algorithm requires $n(n - 1)(n - 2)$ comparisons and additions.

EXERCISES

1. Use the following nondirected graph to find the shortest distance between node 1 and node 6.

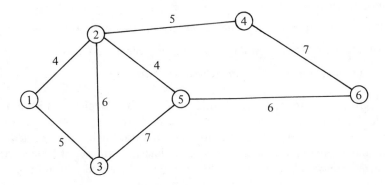

2. Use the nondirected graph in Exercise 1 and compute the shortest distance between every pair of nodes.

3. What would happen if in step 3 (c) of Algorithm A there were several nodes with the smallest value?

4. Write a program to implement either Algorithm A or Algorithm B.

5. How can Algorithm A be modified so that the minimum path can be determined?

6. How can Algorithm B be modified so that the minimum paths can be recorded?

10.10
B-Trees

The searching methods discussed in Chapter 8 deal primarily with data stored in internal memory. A good internal searching technique may be extremely slow when applied to data residing on a direct access storage device. For example, a binary search requires on the average $\log_2 n$ comparisons before locating the specified element. In a disk file containing 100,000 records this means approximately 17 disk accesses for each search, and each access involves seek time and rotational delay. A possible solution to external searching is to keep a partial index of selected records in memory. Assuming the records are ordered, the index determines (before making any access to the disk) the approximate location of the record. The indexed sequential file organization uses this strategy with two levels of indexes. The higher-level index locates the cylinder and the lower-level index, the track. Then the track is read to find the record. For an example of this strategy see Section 6.3.

Another organization that makes searching and updating of files relatively easy is the B-tree. A *B-tree of order n* has the following properties:

1. Every node has no more than *n* immediate successors.

2. Every node, except for the root and the terminal nodes, has at least *n*/2 immediate successors.

3. The root has at least two immediate successors (but can have none).

4. All terminal nodes are on the same level and contain no keys.

5. A nonterminal node with *k* immediate successors has $k - 1$ keys.

Figure 10.20 pictures a B-tree of order 6. The values depicted in each node are the keys and each key is unique. In a node the keys are in order and there is one more branch than the number of keys. Each node can have no more than 6 immediate successors, so each has a maximum of 5 keys. Since the terminal nodes hold no data, they can be represented with nil pointers.

The general form of each node is the following:

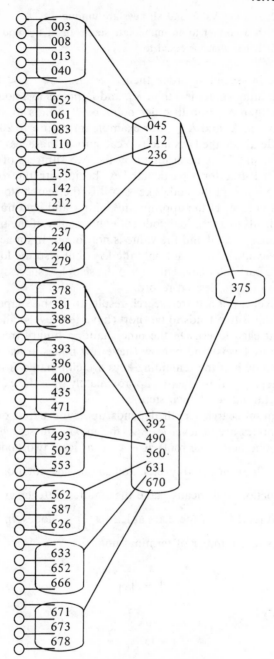

Figure 10.20 A B-tree of order 6

where K_i is a key value and all keys are unique.

P_i is a pointer to an immediate successor of the node.

j is less than or equal to $n - 1$.

If the keys are in ascending order, then $K_1 < K_2 < \ldots < K_j$. P_0 points to a node containing values less than K_1, and P_j points to a node containing values greater than K_j. For all other pointers, P_i points to a node whose values are between K_i and K_{i+1}. For example, in Figure 10.20 the pointers of the root node divide the keys into two categories: those less than 375 and those greater than 375 as determined by the two subtrees of the root.

To search a B-tree for a particular key, begin with the root node and see if the value is one of the node's keys. If it is, the search stops and is successful. If it is not, select the appropriate pointer and continue the search. If the pointer leads to a terminal node (or equivalently, if the pointer is nil), the search is unsuccessful and the value is not found. In an actual application the nodes could contain not only the keys but also the location of the record with the particular key. Thus when the search is successful, we would be able to retrieve the desired record.

The effectiveness of a B-tree search results from the shape of a B-tree. By definition the B-tree tends to be short (have few levels) and wide (have many nodes at each level). On the other hand, a binary tree tends to be long (have many levels) and narrow (have few nodes at each level). In a binary search only half the remaining keys are eliminated from consideration at each step. In a B-tree search approximately $(n - 1)/n$ of the remaining keys are eliminated at each step.

The maximum search length depends upon the depth of the tree. If the terminal nodes are at level $k + 1$, the maximum search length is k. There is only one node (the root) at level 1, at least two nodes at level 2, $2\left\lceil \dfrac{n}{2} \right\rceil$ at level 3, $2\left\lceil \dfrac{n}{2} \right\rceil^2$ nodes at level 4, and so on. The notation $\left\lceil \dfrac{n}{2} \right\rceil$ is called the ceiling function and means "take the smallest integer greater than or equal to $\dfrac{n}{2}$." At level $k + 1$ there are at least $2\left\lceil \dfrac{n}{2} \right\rceil^{k-1}$ nodes. In a B-tree containing N keys, the number of terminal nodes is $N + 1$, so

$$N + 1 \leq 2\left\lceil \dfrac{n}{2} \right\rceil^{k-1}$$

or equivalently

$$k \leq 1 + \log_{\lceil \frac{n}{2} \rceil} \dfrac{N + 1}{2}$$

This means that for a B-tree of order 256 a file containing 100,000 records the maximum search length is no greater than 3.

Inserting a key into a B-tree is quite simple and causes the tree to grow upward toward the root. In Figure 10.20 there is one more terminal node than the number of keys in the entire tree. The terminal nodes are place holders where insertions may appear. For example, insertion of the key 137 causes the node to change from

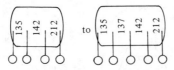

If, however, we had wanted to insert the value 460, we must use a different procedure because the node where the insertion should take place is already full. In this case we split the node into two halves and put the middle key into that node's predecessor node. In doing so it may be necessary to split the predecessor node and pass its key on up the tree. This process may continue until the root node has to split and a new root is defined for the tree. For example, when 460 is inserted, the node changes from

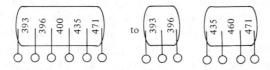

and 400 (the middle value) goes into the node's predecessor. Since the predecessor is full, it too must be split and a value carried up to the root. After this insertion, the changed portions of the tree appear in the following way:

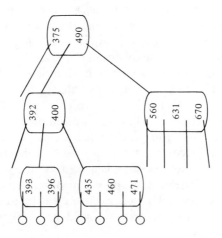

If a B-tree of order n has $i + 1$ levels (where the terminal nodes are on level $i + 1$), a key to be inserted goes into a node at level i. If that node contains n keys, split it into the following two parts

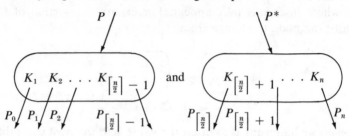

and insert key $K_{\lceil \frac{n}{2} \rceil}$ into the node's immediate predecessor. The pointer associated with the key $K_{\lceil \frac{n}{2} \rceil}$ is P^*, the pointer to the newly created node. If the insertion of $K_{\lceil \frac{n}{2} \rceil}$ causes the predecessor node to be full, split it in a similar manner and continue the process until no more divisions are necessary. This may mean that the root node splits causing a new root to be added to the tree.

Deletion is handled in a similar manner. If a key is not at the lowest level (immediately above a terminal node), replace it with the key's successor and delete the successor. If a key is at the lowest level, its removal from a node may cause the node to contain less than $n/2 - 1$ keys. In this case we use the node's left or right brother and move the keys so that each of the two nodes are approximately the same size. In doing so it may be necessary to remove a key from the node's predecessor, which in turn may cause another removal, and so on.

The step between a B-tree and the implementation of a directory structure with the search characteristics of a B-tree is complicated by the fact that directories usually contain considerably more information than the keys and pointers. In some files, for example, a record is protected by lists of users authorized to read from or write into the record. Such extra information can be quite voluminous, and if stored in the nodes near the root, can seriously affect the time to search through a node.

The nodes farther from the root also have problems. If we imagine that the records in the file are stored on a disk file, at some level a node in the index corresponds to a block of records which are transferred to and from disk as a unit. The fact that the keys are kept in order in the nodes reflects the fact that the records within each transfer block are also kept in order. Problems arise when records must be added or deleted. To facilitate the insertion of records, some free space can be allocated within each transfer block. When a record is deleted, its space is incorporated into this free space. To illustrate some of the differences between a B-tree structure as defined and its application to a file structure, consider the following example.

One of the basic features of this file structure is the allocation of extra space within the nodes to keep storage management to a minimum. Inserted records may use up the empty areas but deleted records create empty areas. If necessary, additional space can be added, but the tendency is to have the B-tree grow in width, not length. Assume each record has a unique key which determines the ordering of the records. Retrieval of the records can be in a sequential manner or in a random manner, as determined by key value. The lowest level of the tree contains the actual records in key sequence. The higher levels of the tree contain pointers and key values to facilitate file storage, retrieval, and update. Figure 10.21 pictures a three-level structure. The second-level index contains the highest key value in each of its successor record blocks; it also contains a pointer to the location of each record block. Some of the record blocks may be entirely empty, and some may have space included at one end. Similarly, some of the second-level index nodes may be empty, or only partially full. The horizontal pointers on the second-level index permit sequential access to the records without having to refer to the first-level index.

Characteristics of the secondary storage device help determine the size of the nodes. At the lowest level the size of a node is the amount which is transferred to and from main memory and depends on the length of the records and the amount of storage allocated for I/O buffers, as well as the device where the file is stored. The lowest level nodes are grouped so that they occupy an integral number of tracks. Normally this is a cylinder to limit the amount of head movement. To save space, keys in the index level nodes are stripped of those beginning and ending characters which do not help distinguish them from adjacent keys. Thus more information can be packed into a single index node. Control information is kept as part of each record node so that the records can have either fixed or variable length.

Each second-level index node points to the same number of record nodes which may or may not be full. If an insertion causes the splitting of a record node, approximately half the data will be copied into an empty node and the insertion made. The empty node and the split node must have the same predecessor. If there is no empty node available, the predecessor node is split, and approximately half its record nodes assigned to a new index node. This splitting will create two index nodes, each of whose record nodes are half empty, thus avoiding further splitting for new insertions.

When records are deleted, the space is reclaimed and added to accumulate free space at the lowest level nodes. Within a node the data is shifted so that the free space is always at the end.

The above discussion pertains to the organization of a single file. In the overall system the directory of allocated files could be kept with the same sort of B-tree structure.

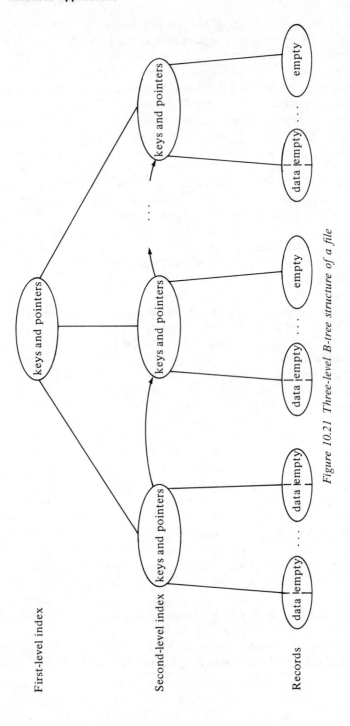

First-level index

Second-level index

Records

Figure 10.21 Three-level B-tree structure of a file

11
FORMAL DATA STRUCTURES

11.1
An Implementation Model

Graph theory provides a basis for a formal theory of data structures. You may skip the presentation of formal theory if your interests are applications of data structures. We use set theory for a more rigorous explanation of structure. We present two models and refine our earlier definitions.

A directed graph (digraph) is a triplet, $G = \{A, P, \Phi\}$, where $A = \{a_1, a_2, \ldots, a_k\}$ is a set of atoms, $P = \{p_1, p_2, \ldots, p_j\}$ is a set of pointers (called arcs), and

$$\Phi = \{p_{m_1} \sim a_{r_1} \& a_{s_1}, p_{m_2} \sim a_{r_2} \& a_{s_2}, \ldots, p_{m_t} \sim a_{r_t} \& a_{s_t}\}$$

is a mapping of arcs between atoms. We use $\sim$ to indicate an arc connection from node x to node y which is represented by x & y.

The mapping function Φ is simply a "connectivity table," which describes how atoms are connected via pointers. For example, consider the digraph of Figure 11.1. Atoms become labeled points and pointers become labeled arcs of the digraph. The mapping Φ is simply a correspondence (in order) between atoms. The example of Figure 11.1 may be interpreted as a ring (circular list) by tracing the circuit beginning at a_1 and scanning a_2 and a_3 before returning to a_1. Notice that $a_1 \& a_2$ is *not* the same as $a_2 \& a_1$, since in a digraph arcs are directed.

The digraph model of data structures is fine for describing relationships between atoms and pointers. This model does not, however, help in understanding what the structure means. A semantic component is needed to label atoms and pointers such that the labels give meaning to the graph arcs and nodes.

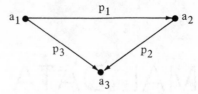

Figure 11.1 A digraph with $A = \{a_1, a_2, a_3\}$, $P = \{p_1, p_2, p_3\}$, and mapping function $\Phi = \{p_1 \sim a_1 \,\&\, a_2, p_2 \sim a_2 \,\&\, a_3, p_3 \sim a_1 \,\&\, a_3\}$

To demonstrate the idea of a semantic component, let us consider a simple array (dense list). According to the digraph model ARRAY(3) is a collection of three atoms as follows:

$$A = \{a_1, a_2, a_3\}$$

$$P = \{i | i = 1, 2, 3\}$$

$$\Phi = \{p_j = \text{'null'} | j = 1, 2, 3\}$$

Somehow we wish to show that A and P are related in the manner shown, and at the same time *label* the items in Figure 11.2. In other words, we want to attach meaning to each atom and pointer.

To attach meaning to each atom and pointer introduce a semantic map as follows: A semantic mapping is a correspondence T between a set S_σ and S_m, where S_σ are objects and S_m are meaning labels. The semantic map for Figure 11.2 is:

$$S_\sigma = \{a_1, a_2, a_3\}$$

$$S_m = \{A(1), A(2), A(3)\}$$

$$T = \{a_1 \sim A(1), a_2 \sim A(2), a_3 \sim A(3)\}$$

This map is a correspondence table showing which label A(i) to attach to each atom a_i. We have used the $\sim$ symbol to show correspondence.

Atom	Graph	Label
a_1	•	A(1)
a_2	•	A(2)
a_3	•	A(3)

Figure 11.2 A dense list, array, of three atoms. The null pointers are demonstrated by their absence

Actually, programmers are more accustomed to thinking in terms of pictures. The information in Figure 11.2 may just as well be described by the picture in Figure 11.3. This shows how data values might appear during a run of the program which manipulates the data structure.

We will use an attribute-value pair to assist in formalizing a picture model as demonstrated in Figure 11.3. An *attribute* is a semantic label. A *value* is a literal (self-defined) constant, that is, a number or alphanumeric. *Attribute-value pairing* is used to attach values to fields specified by semantic labels.

Once the data structure is defined, it must be possible to store data within it, and often to alter the structure itself. The attribute-value pairing operation is a means of binding data together with the field defined by an attribute (label). Let us demonstrate this by an example taken from our study of linked lists (see Figure 11.4).

Let us define a formal data structure as a digraph with a semantic transformation:

$$D = \{A, P, \Phi, T, V, \sigma\}$$

A = atom set T = labels (attributes)

P = pointer set V = values

Φ = pointer map σ = semantic map

The example of Figure 11.4 may be described formally as follows:

$A = \{a_1, a_2, a_3\}$

$P = \{p_1, p_2, p_3\}$

$\Phi = \{p_1 \sim a_1 \,\&\, a_2, p_2 \sim a_2 \,\&\, a_3, p_3 \sim \text{'null'}\}$

$T = \{\text{HEAD, NAME, LINK}\}$

$V = \{\text{NAMES, 101, MARTIN, 111, HUTTON, 000}\}$

$\sigma = \{a_1 \sim \text{HEAD}, (a_2, a_3) \sim \text{NAME}, (p_1, p_2, p_3) \sim \text{LINK}\}$

a_1	25.5	A(1)
a_2	10.3	A(2)
a_3	8.1	A(3)

Figure 11.3 A picture equivalent of Figure 11.2. Values of A (i) are included to show storage of data

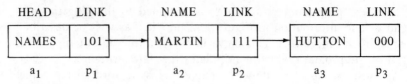

Figure 11.4 A linked list of names. This structure may be formalized
by a digraph with semantic labeling

The correspondence between attribute and value, e.g.,

$$A\text{-}V = \{HEAD = NAMES, NAME = (MARTIN,HUTTON),$$

$$LINK = (101,111,000)\}$$

is performed by an algorithm. To make a complete system out of our formalism, we need only define a set A-V as a computer program that performs the mapping, and we have completed our formal description. We will leave that task to you, and concentrate on the data structures aspects.

The model described here is static. We have given no mechanism for altering the structure itself once it is defined. It is a simple matter, however, to include an update transformation for data structure operations. We do this by "before" and "after" pictures.

Suppose we wish to formally define a stack. The structure in Figure 11.5 is a linked list that is treated as a stack by altering the atom pointed to by the HEAD atom. These operations can be described by "before" and "after" data structures, $D = \{A, P, \Phi, T, V, \sigma\}$ and $D' = \{A', P', \Phi', T', V', \sigma'\}$.

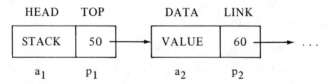

(a) Before push operation

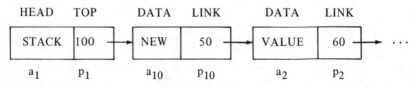

(b) After push of DATA = NEW atom

Figure 11.5 A "before" and "after" stack transformation

EXERCISES

1. Give the sets for D in the example in Figure 11.5.

2. Give the "before" and "after" maps corresponding to Figure 11.4 for a pop operation.

3. Give the after data structure, D', for Exercise 1.

4. Give an attribute-value pair set, A-V, for the digraphs in Figure 11.5.

5. How might this formalism be used to define a formal algorithmic language for describing data structures to a computer?

11.2
An Access
Model

The model previously described might properly be called an implementation model because it represents a picture of how the data is implemented in computer memory. Each atom corresponds to one or more cells in memory, and pointers are addresses.

An alternative model based on access of information has been proposed by Jay Earley.[1] This model employs the same notions of graphs and semantics, although the terminology is different. Let us construct an access model corresponding to the implementation model previously given. We need additional definitions.

A *V-graph* is a directed graph with names on the arcs. It has three kinds of objects: nodes, links, and atoms. The key feature of V-graphs is that they represent a set of data (information) atoms and they are not necessarily accessed in the way they are implemented. Thus we must relax our notions of storage efficiency and access algorithms based upon addresses.

We will study V-graphs primarily as they apply to arrays and linked lists. (We will ignore trees and multilinked lists; if you are interested, consult the References.) A special notation is used to indicate an atom, node, or link attribute (see Figure 11.6).

The representation of an array of three atoms (see Figure 11.3) would be done by the symbolic form shown in Figure 11.7 (a). The V-graph for a linked list is shown in Figure 11.7 (b).

Emphasis on accessibility is central to V-graph models. The actual implementation, e.g., dense list or linked list, does not concern a V-graph representation. For example, it is easy to describe a symbol table for a

[1]Jay Earley, "Toward an Understanding of Data Structures," *Comm ACM* 14, no. 10 (October 1971):617–627.

☐   Head node

○   Access node

5   Example of an atom (with value = 5)

CONT Contents

NIL   Null value

Figure 11.6 V-graph notation and its meaning

language translator independent of its implementation (which is left to the programmer).

Suppose a compiler has recognized J, SUM, and X1, as an integer variable, procedure name, and real variable, respectively. The compiler must store each of these names in a symbol table along with location and data-type information. Suppose further the locations are known to be 1002, 2000, and 1000, respectively. The V-graph representation of this portion of the symbol table is shown in Figure 11.8.

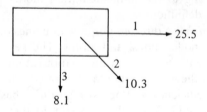

(a) Representation of the array of Figure 11.3

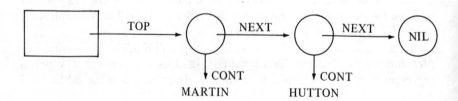

(b) Representation of the list of Figure 11.4

Figure 11.7 V-graphs for the implementation model of Section 11.1

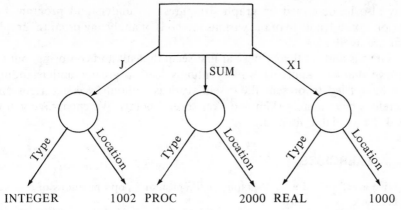

Figure 11.8 V-graph of a symbol table containing names, J, SUM, X1, and their attributes and storage locations

Set theory formalization of V-graphs is stated simply as a collection of sets: A V-graph is a 7-tuple:

V = {N, NT, nt, A, L, F, C}.

N = set of nodes.

NT = set of node-types.

nt = mapping of node-types to nodes: N → NT.

A = set of atoms.

L = set of pointers (links).

F = mapping of pointers and objects (the connectivity of the V-graph).

C = remainder of connectivity map (define what each pointer points to).

We can define the V-graph model of a data structure, D, as a pair consisting of a set of initial V-graphs and a set of transformations. The transformations in this definition are exactly the "before" and "after" pictures discussed earlier. When used to manipulate data, these transformations are captured in the form of a computer program.

The interested reader might like to refer to J. B. Dennis[2] for a treatment of programs that parallels this treatment of data structures. Since programs are stored in computer memory in the same way that data is stored, they

[2]J. B. Dennis, "Programming Generality, Parallelism and Computer Architecture," *Information Processing 68* (Amsterdam: North Holland Publishing Co., 1969) pp. 484–492.

may also be described by graph structures. To understand program behavior, take advantage of the various methods of analyzing program graphs that are available.

Graphs and set theory may at first seem difficult and confusing, but we believe that this approach will eventually lead to greater understanding. We have tried to present the essential ideas without excessive rigor and therefore have merely skimmed over several points. We encourage you to read the available literature.

EXERCISES

1. Give a before and after V-graph for the push and pop operations of a linked list stack.

2. Give a V-graph for the 3 × 2 array, ARRAY (3, 2), and show labeling.

3. Describe a tree-structured data structure using a V-graph and any special forms needed.

A
STRING PROCESSING WITH PROGRAMMING LANGUAGES

We will show how to program the string operations performed on the expression X = A1 + B of the example in Section 2.2. This can be done in a variety of ways and with a variety of programming languages. We will illustrate only a few string processing capabilities of SNOBOL and PL/I. For a complete explanation of SNOBOL or PL/I, consult a programming text.

As you may recall, the problem is to scan the expression string and separate the variables X, A1, and B from the operators, equals sign (=), plus (+), and "end of statement." The operators and variables will be placed in a separate storage area capable of storing strings. Thus we wish to find the substrings X, =, A, 1, +, B, and the terminating blanks, and then concatenate them into the substrings X, =, A1, +, and B.

PL/I

Let us see how we would do the separation and concatenation in PL/I. There are five basic constructions in PL/I that provide all the operations necessary for concatenation, insertion, deletion, replacement, indexing, and length determination. We give the form of each in Figure A.1.

In addition to the PL/I string functions, we will use PL/I statements for control, initialization, and assignment. You will have to get these statements from other sources. We only intend here to demonstrate string processing in a high-level language.

The program is developed by stepwise refinement beginning with a gross outline and then constructing modules. Each module will perform a

PL/I Function	Description	Example
A || B	Concatenate strings A and B	S = 'STR' || 'ING';
INDEX(S,SUB)	Integer index of first character of SUB embedded in S	N = INDEX ('ABC','BC'); result: N is 2
SUBSTR (STR,START,LENGTH)	(a) as a function SUBSTR returns the substring starting at START within STR and of length LENGTH	S = SUBSTR ('ABC',2,2); result: S is 'BC'
	(b) as a pseudo-variable SUBSTR replaces the substring within STR that starts at START and is of length LENGTH	SUBSTR ('ABC',2,2) = 'XY'; result: 'AXY'
DCL S CHAR(N) VAR;	This declares string S to be a CHARacter of maximum VARying length of N. N must be a constant.	DCL A CHAR(100) VAR; A can store up to 100 characters (or less)
LENGTH(S)	Integer valued length of S	N = LENGTH (STR);

Figure A.1 PL/I String Functions

specific function clearly defined by comments in the source code. In the final step we combine all modules into a working program. Let us start by defining the modules with the PL/I comment statement as shown in Figure A.2.

Starting with the comment modules of Figure A.2, we now begin to construct modules. The modules may contain additional submodules; we continue in this manner until we have finally constructed the refined PL/I code. The first module is shown refined in Figure A.3.

The data declaration module shows how we would define variables for string arrays of size 10, e.g., VARI(10) and OPER(10), to hold the separated

```
SCAN: PROCEDURE OPTIONS (MAIN);
            /*  DECLARE VARIABLES AND INITIALIZE  */
            /*  INPUT STRING AS: STRING = 'X = A1 + B'  */
            /*  DELETE BLANKS  */
            /*  SEPARATE CHARACTERS AND TEST  */
                 /*  EITHER ADD TO VARIABLE STRING OR
                     ADD TO OPERATOR STRING  */
            /*  OUTPUT STRINGS  */
      END;
```

Figure A.2 Body of PL/I Program to Scan a String

variables and operators. The CHAR attribute indicates that characters will be stored within the arrays or strings. VAR indicates that the string lengths are allowed to vary up to the maximum amount specified by the CHAR attribute. The initialized variables are set with an INITIAL parameter. For example, ten null strings are placed in VARI, and the characters 'A', 'B', and so on are placed in ALFA. The FLAG string is used to switch between operator separation and variable separation.

During the course of our stepwise refinement we may need to modify the data declaration module to reflect changes in the program design. It is assumed that a modular flowchart has been drawn beforehand, so we have a good idea what variables are needed.

The next module we need is the input/output code segment. Let us select the simplest PL/I I/O statements: GET DATA and PUT DATA. These constructions allow us to input the string by merely inputting STRING = 'X = A1 + B';. The output will be equally simple. Figure A.4 illustrates how this is done.

```
/*  DECLARE VARIABLES AND INITIALIZE  */
DCL VARI(10) CHAR(2) VAR INITIAL((10)(1)''),   /*  VARIABLE
    STRING  */
    OPER(10) CHAR(1) INITIAL((10)(1)''),   /*  THE OPERATOR
       STRING  */
    ALFA(6) CHAR(1) INITIAL('A','B','X','1','+','='),   /*
    ALPHABETICS  */
    STRING CHAR(80) VAR,   /*  INPUT TEXT  */
    WORK_STR CHAR(1).   /*  TEMPORARY CHARACTER  */
    FLAG CHAR(4) INITIAL('OPER');   /*  VARI OR OPER FLAG  */
/*  THIS MAY BE GENERALIZED BY CHANGING SIZES AND
       INITIAL VALUES  */
```

Figure A.3 The Data Declaration Module

(a) The Input Module

```
/*   INPUT STRING AND          */
/*   COPY STRING TO PRINTER    */
     GET DATA COPY;
```

(b) The Output Module

```
/*   OUTPUT STRINGS            */
     PUT DATA (VARI, OPER, STRING);
```

Figure A.4 Input/Output Modules

The input text may contain unwanted blanks. We will remove embedded blanks with a module that deletes blanks (Figure A.5). This module also demonstrates some very helpful string processing techniques in PL/I. Observe that string operators may be used both in a DO WHILE clause and as a string replacement operator.

The DO WHILE clause computes an index value for the first blank encountered when scanning STRING from left to right. As long as this value is not zero, the clause is executed. When all blanks have been deleted, the clause is skipped.

SUBSTR is used as a pseudovariable in the replacement step. First an index value for a blank (' ') is found, and then the blank is replaced by a null ('') character. In some implementations of PL/I this construction will not work, and we must use the statements below which replace the statement in the DO WHILE of Figure A.5.

```
LBLANK = INDEX(STRING,' ');
LONG = LENGTH(STRING) − LBLANK;
STRING = SUBSTR(STRING,1,LBLANK − 1)   ‖
         SUBSTR(STRING,LBLANK + 1,LONG);
```

Using either construction, the STRING is now packed (without blanks) and is possibly shorter. Notice that we declared STRING as VARying up to 80 characters.

The heart of our PL/I example is the module that separates the character string into individual characters and places them in the appropriate

```
/*   DELETE BLANKS   */
     DO WHILE (INDEX(STRING,' ') ¬ = 0);
        SUBSTR(STRING,INDEX(STRING,' '),1) = '';
     END;
     LONG = LENGTH(STRING);   /*   STRING MAY BE SHORTER   */
```

Figure A.5 Delete Blanks Module

```
/*  SEPARATE CHARACTERS AND TEST  */
    I_EQ = 0; I_OP = 0; FLAG = 'OPER';
    SCAN: DO J = 1 TO LONG;  /*  LONG DEFINED EARLIER  */;
             WORK_STR = SUBSTR(STRING, J, 1);
             IF WORK_STR = ALFA(5) | WORK_STR = ALFA(6)
                THEN  /*  MOVE TO OPER STRING  */;
                ELSE  /*  MOVE TO VARI STRING  */;
    END SCAN;
```

Figure A.6 The Separate Characters Module Including Submodules

VARI or OPER string arrays. In Figure A.6 we see that additional sub-modules are needed to complete the stepwise refinement.

The VARI string array is indexed with the integer variable I_EQ, and the OPER string array is indexed with I_OP. The FLAG indicator is used to direct the program to store WORK_STR as an operator 'OPER' or as a variable 'VARI'. J is an index into the STRING string. The value of J runs the full length of STRING which is given by LONG. In our simple example we have tested ALFA(5) and ALFA(6) for FLAG = 'OPER'. In a more difficult problem we would resort to a more sophisticated search mechanism.

For the final refinement we specify the /* MOVE TO OPER STRING */ and /* MOVE TO VARI STRING */ submodules. We note that an operator is only one character, while a variable may be one or more characters long. Each string of one or more characters is an element of an array. Therefore the submodules must be able to determine the array element index and the string index needed to concatenate characters into strings. We show how these two functions are performed in Figure A.7.

```
/*  MOVE TO OPER STRING  */
DO;
  FLAG = 'OPER';
  I_OP = I_OP + 1;
  OPER(I_OP) = WORK_STR;
END;

/*  MOVE TO VARI STRING  */
DO;
  IF FLAG = 'OPER' THEN
    DO;
        FLAG = 'VARI';
        I_EQ = I_EQ + 1;
    END;
    VARI(I_EQ) = VARI(I_EQ) || WORK_STR;
END;
```

Figure A.7 The Move Submodules

Now that the modules have been refined, let us see how they work. The essential steps of the algorithm are: Select a character from the STRING by scanning from left to right (J = 1 TO LONG). If the character is an alphabetic symbol, concatenate it to a VARIable string until an operator is scanned. If the character is an operator, store it in the OPER string array. Each time a unit (either operator or variable) is found, increment the appropriate string array index.

The remainder of the algorithm deals with packing (deleting the blanks) and input or output. The program must have data declaration information to tell PL/I that variables are used as string arrays and the length of the strings. You might like to compose the PL/I program and test it. The output of the variables and the operators should be the following:

$$VARI(1) = 'X' \qquad OPER(1) = '='$$

$$VARI(2) = 'A1' \qquad OPER(2) = '+'$$

$$VARI(3) = 'B'$$

SNOBOL

The SNOBOL language was developed to manipulate character strings. It contains operators to concatenate strings, perform pattern matching, and do replacement. Unlike PL/I, simple SNOBOL variables do not have to be declared. The SNOBOL language processor automatically allocates storage for strings and allows the strings to be of varying length during program execution. However, declarations are necessary if users want to set up arrays or define their own data structures (see Appendix C).

Figure A.8 lists some of the basic operations and functions in SNOBOL. Most of these will be used in the following example, in which we input a statement like

$$X = A1 + B$$

and separate out the variables X, A1, and B, and the operators = and +. It is not our intention to teach the SNOBOL language; we wish only to illustrate some of its string manipulation abilities. In Figure A.8 the word "pattern" denotes either a single string or several strings joined with the concatenation or alternation (|) operator.

SNOBOL Operation	*Description*	*Example*
string$_1$ string$_2$	concatenate string$_1$ and string$_2$; to denote concatenation there must be at least one blank between string$_1$ and string$_2$	'SUB' 'STRING' result: 'SUBSTRING'
subject pattern	pattern matching; result is either success (subject contains the pattern) or failure (subject does not contain the pattern)	TEXT 'BY' :S(A)F(B) result: if the string 'BY' is contained in the string named TEXT, then the next statement executed is A, otherwise the next executed is B.
SIZE(string)	gives the length of string	SIZE('BJS') result: 3
string$_1$ | string$_2$	generates a pattern which will match either string$_1$ or string$_2$	'ABC' | 'XYZ' will succeed if the string tested contains either the substring 'ABC' or 'XYZ'
var = INPUT	reads one card and stores it under the variable named "var"	TEXT = INPUT result: one card is read and can be referenced with the name TEXT
OUTPUT = string	prints one line containing the characters in string	OUTPUT = 'PAGE 1' result: writes PAGE 1
&TRIM = value	If &TRIM has a non-zero value and a card is read, trailing blanks will be deleted. Otherwise all 80 characters will be read.	&TRIM = 1 result: unless the value of &TRIM changes, all cards read will have trailing blanks deleted.

Figure A.8 Basic SNOBOL Operations

SNOBOL Operation	Description	Example
subpattern = obj	replacement statement; if the subject string (sub) contains the pattern string, the first occurrence of the pattern will be replaced with the object string (obj), otherwise the subject is not changed.	'ABCABC' 'AB' = 'XY' result: 'XYCABC'
subpattern · obj	conditional value assignment; if the pattern string matches a substring of the subject, the substring matched becomes the value of obj	'X = A + B' ('+'|'−') . OP result: OP = '+'
variable = value	assignment statement	NUMBERS = '0123456789'

Figure A.8 Basic SNOBOL operations (continued)

To locate the operators and variables in our example statement, we will assume the statement has the form:

$$\text{var op var op var} \ldots \text{op var}$$

where var is a variable and op is an operator. The statement

$$X = A1 + B$$

is the correct form.

The basic outline of our program is:

1. Input the statement.

2. Delete all blanks.

3. Remove the first variable from the statement and print it.

4. Repeat the following until the last operator is removed.
   (a) Remove an operator from the statement string and print it.
   (b) Remove a variable from the statement and print it.

To enable us to recognize variables and operators, we define these patterns: LETTERS contains all the letters of the alphabet, NUMBERS the digits 0 through 9, and OP the $+$, $-$, $*$ (multiplication), $/$ (division), and $=$ operators. NULL is the null character string, and BLANK is a single blank character.

> LETTERS = 'ABCDEFGHIJKLMNOPQRSTUVWXYZ'
>
> NUMBERS = '0123456789'
>
> OP = '+ − * / ='
>
> NULL =
>
> BLANK = ' '

To recognize a variable as either a single letter or a letter followed by a string of letters or numbers, we define the following:

> ALPHANUM = LETTERS NUMBERS
>
> VARIABLE = ANY(LETTERS)(SPAN(ALPHANUM)|NULL)
>
> OPERATOR = ANY(OP)

ALPHANUM is the string formed by concatenating LETTERS and NUMBERS and contains all the alphabetic characters and numeric digits. The statements above introduce the SNOBOL functions ANY and SPAN. The function ANY(string) forms a pattern that matches any single character appearing in its string argument. For example, ANY(OP) can be used to see if a string contains any of the characters $+$ $-$ $*$ $/$ or $=$. The function SPAN forms a pattern that will match a run of characters. For example, SPAN(ALPHANUM) will see if a string contains all letters and numbers. The statement

> VARIABLE = ANY(LETTERS) (SPAN(ALPHANUM)|NULL)

defines a pattern named VARIABLE which will succeed if the string tested contains a single alphabetic character followed by either a run of letters and/or numbers or nothing (the null string).

We begin by setting &TRIM to one so that all cards read will have trailing blanks deleted. Then we input the statement, store it in TEXT, and print it.

> &TRIM = 1
>
> TEXT = INPUT
>
> OUTPUT = TEXT

Next we remove all blanks from the line by executing the following statement: It checks TEXT to see if it contains a blank. If so, the blank is removed (replaced with the null character) and the statement is executed again. REMOVE is the label of the statement. If a blank is found in TEXT, the match is considered successful, and the machine returns to REMOVE to execute it again. Thus when all blanks are out of TEXT, the statement following REMOVE is executed.

> REMOVE TEXT BLANK = NULL   :S(REMOVE)

Now we begin to see if there is a variable in TEXT. If so, the string matching the VARIABLE pattern is placed in VAR. If there is no such variable found, the statement labeled ERROR is executed. ERROR is defined later.

> SEARCH TEXT VARIABLE . VAR   :F(ERROR)

Next we remove the variable from the text by replacing it with the null string and then output VAR.

> TEXT VAR = NULL
>
> OUTPUT = VAR

After finding and removing a variable from the statement, we proceed to look for an operator, remove it from the string, and print it. If there is no operator, we have found the variable at the end of the string, so we stop.

> TEXT OPERATOR . OPR   :F(END)
>
> TEXT OPR = NULL
>
> OUTPUT = OPR   :(SEARCH)

If an operator was found and printed, we proceed to the statement labeled SEARCH to look for the next variable. The following statement will print a message if an error occurred and the text did not end with a variable. The END statement halts execution.

> ERROR OUTPUT = 'ERROR IN STATEMENT'
>
> END

The complete program appears below.

```
        LETTERS = 'ABCDEFGHIJKLMNOPQRSTUVWXYZ'
        NUMBERS = '0123456789'
        OP = '+ -*/='
        NULL =
        BLANK = ' '
        ALPHANUM = LETTERS NUMBERS
        VARIABLE = ANY(LETTERS) (SPAN(ALPHANUM)|NULL)
        OPERATOR = ANY(OP)
        &TRIM = 1
        TEXT = INPUT
        OUTPUT = TEXT
REMOVE  TEXT BLANK = NULL          :S(REMOVE)
SEARCH  TEXT VARIABLE . VAR        :F(ERROR)
        TEXT VAR = NULL
        OUTPUT = VAR
        TEXT OPERATOR . OPR         :F(END)
        TEXT OPR = NULL
        OUTPUT = OPR                :(SEARCH)
ERROR   OUTPUT = 'ERROR IN STATEMENT'
END
```

B

PL/I LIST PROCESSING

B.1
PL/I
Constructs

You should accompany the reading of this book with programming examples and exercises that manipulate lists. However, we have chosen to write algorithms in programming language independent form for obvious reasons. As a supplement and an illustration of how to perform list processing, we present this appendix on PL/I.

We need to know three basic constructions of PL/I to understand the list processing capabilities of the language. These constructions are: how to define the fields of an atom, how to reference the fields of an atom, and how to allocate or release space for an atom. Once we know these three constructions, we can build any list, tree, or graph structure discussed in this book.

We will limit this discussion to three types of PL/I variables: pointer, numeric, and character. The pointer variables will be used exclusively for reference of an atom by address. The numeric and character variables will be used exclusively for reference of information contained in atoms. In addition, we will use other variables to control the execution of programs.

Let us see how to define the fields of an atom. The data aggregate declaration in PL/I provides a method of labeling fields while at the same time specifying their type: pointer, numeric, or character. An example in Figure B.1 shows how we use level numbers 1 and 2 to indicate an atom name or a field name.

It is important to understand that the declaration of Figure B.1 *does not* allocate memory space for the atom pictured in B.1(a). The declaration simply informs PL/I that *when* we allocate space for ATOM, we will refer to that space in the way shown.

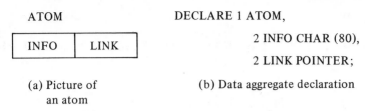

ATOM

DECLARE 1 ATOM,

2 INFO CHAR (80),

2 LINK POINTER;

(a) Picture of
an atom

(b) Data aggregate declaration

Figure B.1 How to define an atom in PL/I

Every linked list, tree, or graph that is allowed to change by updating the data structure must be anchored to a permanent HEADER atom. The PL/I compiler will provide this facility if we give it a BASED variable. This BASED variable is a pointer that emits from the HEADER (see Figure B.2).

Again we stress the fact that the DECLARE construct and BASED variable *do not* allocate the atom ATOM shown in Figure B.2. So far we have only told the compiler the format of ATOM if we decide to create it. Once it is created, we must learn to reference it. One way to reference ATOM is through the BASED pointer P.

The most common method of referencing an atom in PL/I is with the "→" operator. Each atom will have an address after it is created. The address is not known until the program is in execution. We therefore need pointer variables to store the addresses of atoms, and the "points to" (→) operator to reference an atom indirectly.

In Figure B.3 we assume that three identically formatted ATOMs have been created and are addressed by pointers P, Q, and R. The attribute PTR is an abbreviation for POINTER. The three INFO fields are referenced by different pointers. They read: P points to INFO, Q points to INFO, and R points to INFO. In each case a different string is assigned to a different atom in memory.

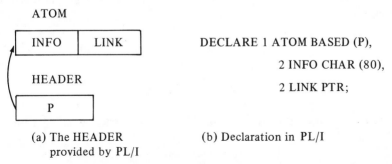

ATOM

DECLARE 1 ATOM BASED (P),

2 INFO CHAR (80),

2 LINK PTR;

(a) The HEADER
provided by PL/I

(b) Declaration in PL/I

Figure B.2 Anchoring a list to HEADER

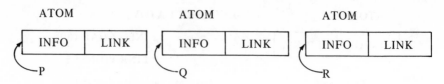

(a) Three identically formatted atoms
    with different addresses

DECLARE 1 ATOM BASED (P),

           2 INFO CHAR (80),

           2 LINK PTR,

      (Q, R) PTR;

ALLOCATE ATOM;

ALLOCATE ATOM SET (Q);

ALLOCATE ATOM SET (R);

      P → INFO = 'ELISE';

      Q = INFO = 'CLAIRE';

      R → INFO = 'MARTIN';

(b) Corresponding PL/I code referencing
    three different INFO fields through
    pointers P, Q, and R.

Figure B.3 Referencing atom in PL/I

We can link the atoms in Figure B.3 by assigning Q to the LINK field
of P → LINK, and R to the LINK field defined by Q → LINK. This is done
as follows:

          P → LINK = Q;

          Q → LINK = R;

          R → LINK = NULL;

The last assignment uses the built-in NULL pointer to set the last link to
null (or nil).

Now that we can define and reference atoms and their fields, let us
see how to create and discard them. The ALLOCATE name SET (pointer);

```
DECLARE 1 ATOM BASED(P),

          2 INFO CHAR(80) VAR,

          2 LINK PTR,

          (R,Q) PTR;

ALLOCATE ATOM SET(P);

ALLOCATE ATOM SET(Q);

ALLOCATE ATOM SET(R);

FREE Q → ATOM;
```

Figure B.4 A program segment that
creates the atoms of Figure B.3
and destroys the one addressed by Q.

construct is used to allocate a based data aggregate and set a pointer to it.
If the SET (pointer) phrase is left off, the construct assumes that the BASED
pointer is used in SETting the address. The FREE pointer → atom; construct reverses the process, thus freeing the atom addressed by a pointer.
If the "pointer →" phrase is left off the FREE statement, it assumes that
the BASED pointer P is used to address the atom (see Figure B.4).

B.2
A Linked
List Program

Consider now a PL/I program to create a linked list of N atoms, each atom
containing an integer corresponding to its order in the list. The program
is developed by stepwise refinement of modules as shown by the PL/I comments in Figure B.5.

The declaration module must define the format of ATOM and the
pointer variables needed to build the linked list. P and TAIL pointers are

```
BUILD: PROCEDURE OPTIONS(MAIN);
       /* DATA DECLARATIONS  */
       /* INPUT N  */
       /* CREATE N ATOMS  */
            /*  PLACE I=1 TO N IN ATOMS  */
       /* SCAN AND OUTPUT INFO  */
END;
```

Figure B.5 The modules needed to build a linked
list of length N.

```
/*    DATA DECLARATIONS    */
DCL 1 ATOM BASED(HEAD),
        2 INFO FIXED BINARY,
        2 NEXT PTR,
        (P,  TAIL) PTR;
/*    ATOM HAS TWO FIELDS:   INFO AND NEXT    */
```

Figure B.6 The Data Declaration Module

used to point to the atom most recently created (TAIL) and the atom immediately before it (P). The BASED pointer HEAD always points to the first ATOM created. This module is refined in Figure B.6.

We will use the simplest input and output commands in PL/I. These are performed by GET DATA(N); and PUT LIST(I); as shown by Figure B.7.

The central portion of the linked list program is the module that creates the ATOM space and references the INFO and NEXT fields of the space. The BASED variable HEAD must point to the first ATOM allocated, so we make this a special case. Subsequently every allocated ATOM is referenced through additional "sliding" pointers, P and TAIL. The pointer P is used to initialize the NEXT field in each atom as the atom is created.

The P pointer always keeps track of the predecessor of the last atom allocated. This is needed to access the NEXT field of the predecessor and set it to the TAIL (the last ATOM allocated).

The program builds N ATOMs that appear as shown in Figure B.8(b), where N = 3. The module of Figure B.8(a) provides the necessary PL/I coding.

Finally, let us refine the /* SCAN AND OUTPUT INFO */ module shown in Figure B.5. The scan starts with pointer HEAD and traces the chain of NEXT pointers until NEXT = NULL. The INFO field is output as we go along the chain; see Figure B.9.

The modules of Figures B.6 through B.9 are collected and placed in their proper order as shown in Figure B.5. The resulting program should be checked a final time before running it on a computer.

```
/*  INPUT N   */
GET DATA(N);

/*   OUTPUT INFO VALUE I   */
PUT LIST(I);
```

Figure B.7 The I/O modules

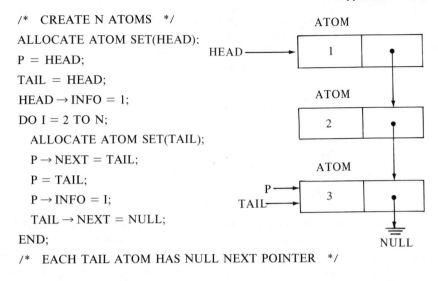

```
/*  CREATE N ATOMS  */
ALLOCATE ATOM SET(HEAD);
P = HEAD;
TAIL = HEAD;
HEAD → INFO = 1;
DO I = 2 TO N;
   ALLOCATE ATOM SET(TAIL);
   P → NEXT = TAIL;
   P = TAIL;
   P → INFO = I;
   TAIL → NEXT = NULL;
END;
/*  EACH TAIL ATOM HAS NULL NEXT POINTER  */
```

(a) The create module

(b) The linked list
for N = 3 atoms

Figure B.8 The create module and an example

B.3
A Binary
Search Tree Program

Taking an example from Section 5.2, we will use it to show how to construct
a binary tree in PL/I. Suppose we wish to insert a number into a binary
search tree so that the tree is in ascending order when scanned in LNR-
recursive order. You will recall (see Section 5.2) that this is done by comparing the DATA insert number with the NUMBRs stored at each node
of the tree. If DATA is smaller than NUMBR, take a LEFT branch; if

```
/*  SCAN AND OUTPUT INFO  */
P = HEAD;
DO WHILE (P¬ = NULL);
    I = P → INFO;
    PUT LIST(I);
    P = P → NEXT;
END;
/*  THE SCAN STOPS WHEN P = NULL  */
```

Figure B.9 The scan module for output

```
BINTREE: PROCEDURE(DATA);
/*  DECLARE NODES AND VARIABLES  */
IF  /*  EMPTY TREE  */  THEN
    /*  INSERT ROOT  */
ELSE
  DO;
    /*  SEARCH TREE                */
    /*  ALLOCATE A NODE FOR DATA  */
    /*  LINK NODE TO TREE         */
  END;
END BINTREE;
```

Figure B.10 Procedure For Binary Search Tree Insertion

larger, take a RIGHT branch. If the LEFT or RIGHT branch is NULL, insert the DATA value in a node created and addressed by the LEFT or RIGHT pointer.

Figure B.10 shows the least refined module for this problem. Observe that a special case is needed to take care of an empty tree. We must also maintain a FLAG to indicate a LEFT or RIGHT subtree.

We will again successively refine the modules of Figure B.10 until a final program is obtained. The declaration module is shown in Figure B.11. The NODE variable defines the fields of each atom in the tree. The PROBE and LAST pointers are used in the tree scan. PROBE eventually will point to the inserted node, and LAST will point to the father of the inserted node.

Initially the tree is empty and the BASED pointer P is NULL. We simply insert a root by allocating a NODE and placing DATA in the NODE at NUMBR. We make the LEFT and RIGHT pointers of the root NULL. The NULL value will be used to stop the tree search upon subsequent insertions (see Figure B.12).

The central part of the program is the tree search. Figure B.13 shows the tree search after it has been refined several times (we omit the intermediate refinements to save space). Initially PROBE points to the root, but is updated to either LEFT or RIGHT pointers. The value of FLAG indicates that a LEFT (FLAG = 0) or RIGHT (FLAG = 1) subtree is scanned.

```
/*  DECLARE NODES AND VARIABLES  */
DCL 1 NODE BASED(P),
        2 NUMBER,
        2 LEFT PTR,
        2 RIGHT PTR,
      (PROBE, LAST) PTR,
      DATA BINARY FIXED;
```

Figure B.11 The data declaration module

```
IF P = NULL THEN
  DO;
      ALLOCATE NODE SET(P);
      P → NUMBR = DATA;
      P → LEFT = NULL;
      P → RIGHT = NULL;
      ROOT = P;
  END;
```

Figure B.12 The If Empty Tree Module

```
DO;
   PROBE = ROOT;
   DO WHILE (PROBE¬= NULL);
      LAST = PROBE;
      IF PROBE → NUMBR >= DATA THEN
        DO;
            PROBE = PROBE → LEFT;
            FLAG = 0;
        END;
      ELSE
        DO;
            PROBE = PROBE → RIGHT;
            FLAG = 1;
        END;
   END;
END;
```

Figure B.13 The search tree module

The final modules are refined in two more steps; the result is given in Figure B.14. The allocated node is addressed by pointer PROBE. The value of PROBE must be stored in the LEFT or RIGHT link of the father node at address LAST. We test FLAG and insert PROBE in the proper link. The value of DATA is then stored in the allocated node and its pointers set to NULL.

```
ALLOCATE NODE SET(PROBE);
PROBE → NUMBR = DATA;
PROBE → LEFT = NULL;
PROBE → RIGHT = NULL;
IF FLAG = 0 THEN
   LAST → LEFT = PROBE;
ELSE
   LAST → RIGHT = PROBE;
```

Figure B.14 The Allocate a Node and Link Node Modules

```
            BINTREE: PROCEDURE(DATA);
            DCL 1 NODE BASED(P),
                    2 NUMBER,
                    2 LEFT PTR,
                    2 RIGHT PTR,
                (PROBE, LAST) PTR,
                DATA BINARY FIXED;
            IF P = NULL THEN
                DO;
                    ALLOCATE NODE SET(P);
                    P → NUMBR = DATA;
                    P → LEFT = NULL;
                    P → RIGHT = NULL;
                    ROOT = P;
                END;
            ELSE
                DO;
                    PROBE = ROOT;
                    DO WHILE (PROBE¬= NULL);
                        LAST = PROBE;
                        IF PROBE → NUMBR >= DATA THEN
                            DO;
                                PROBE = PROBE → LEFT;
                                FLAG = 0;
                            END;
                        ELSE
                            DO;
                                PROBE = PROBE → RIGHT;
                                FLAG = 1;
                            END;
                    END;
                    ALLOCATE NODE SET(PROBE);
                    PROBE → NUMBR = DATA;
                    PROBE → LEFT = NULL;
                    PROBE → RIGHT = NULL;
                    IF FLAG = 0 THEN
                        LAST → LEFT = PROBE;
                    ELSE
                        LAST → RIGHT = PROBE;
                END;
            END BINTREE;
```

Figure B.15 The completed tree search program

The complete binary tree insert procedure is given without comments in Figure B.15. The modules are indented to show how each unit developed by refinement fits into the finished program. Test the program by inserting the numbers given in the example of Section 5.2.

B.4
A Push-down
Stack Program

Section 4.2 shows how a linked list implementation of a stack operates (see Figure 4.5). The PL/I code for insertion and deletion is given in Figure B.16. Please note that this is an incomplete segment of code. The value of the pointer P must be defined before one uses this segment.

```
DCL 1 ATOM BASED(P),
       2 N,
       2 LINK PTR,
     NEW PTR;  /*  POINTER TO NEW ATOM  */
PUSH: INSERT: ALLOCATE ATOM SET(NEW);
             NEW → LINK = P;
             P = NEW;
POP: DELETE: NEW = P;
             P = P→LINK;
             FREE NEW → ATOM;
```

*Figure B.16 Segments for PUSH (INSERT) and POP
(DELETE) operations on a linked list stack*

C
SNOBOL
DATA STRUCTURES

In this section we discuss some of the structures (besides strings) which are available in SNOBOL. These structures are arrays, tables, and user-defined data structures. An array in SNOBOL resembles an array in any other programming language, but the value of an individual element may be either a number or a string. A single array may contain both numbers and strings. A table in SNOBOL resembles a list in which each element of the list is referenced by a unique key. The key can be either a number or a string. The ability of users to define their own data structures is a facility rarely found in programming languages. In SNOBOL the user can create a structure, define fields within the structure, and reference each part by name. Each field can contain a value or a pointer. If you are interested in data structures, you may wish to use SNOBOL for the assignments in this book.

It is not our intention to teach the SNOBOL language; we want only to illustrate through examples some of the available constructs. (For more information, consult References.)

C.1
Arrays

The SNOBOL function ARRAY permits the user to define arrays and give the elements of the array an initial value. Its general form is:

$$ARRAY(p,e)$$

where p is a prototype giving the bounds and dimensions of the array.

e is an expression giving the initial value of the array; each element is set to the same initial value.

For example, to define a vector V containing 100 elements, write

$$V = ARRAY(100)$$

Since the expression was omitted from the ARRAY definition, each element's initial value is the null string. The elements are named V<1>, V<2>, through V<100>.

To define a vector X indexed with the numbers −1 through 10, write

$$X = ARRAY('-1:10')$$

Note the use of the single quote marks around the prototype.

To define a 3 × 4 matrix M whose initial values are zero, write

$$M = ARRAY('3,4',0)$$

To reference any element of M, use two subscripts separated by a comma; for example, M<1,1> or M<I,J>.

An array element's value may be a number, a string, or a pattern. It is not necessary that the entire array contain the same type of value. For example, one element may be a string, and the second a number.

When defining an array, it is not necessary to use specific integers in the prototype. A variable is sufficient, as long as the variable has a value. For example, the following reads K and then defines an array B with K elements:

$$K = INPUT$$

$$B = ARRAY(K)$$

This means that during program execution, the SNOBOL interpreter allocates space for the array B. The amount of space allocated depends upon the value of K.

If an element outside an array is referenced, the reference fails. For example, the following program will print a message if J is greater than 50 or negative.

```
&TRIM = 1
X = ARRAY('0:50')
 .

 .

 .

J = INPUT
Z = X<J>                                      :F(ERR1)
 .

 .

 .

ERR1  OUTPUT = 'SUBSCRIPT OUT OF BOUNDS'
      OUTPUT = 'J = ' J
```

To reference one array with two different names, use the assignment statement with the array name. For example, the first statement below defines a vector X. The second statement says that Y refers to the same array as X. Thus X<1> and Y<1> are the same location in memory.

$$X = ARRAY(20)$$

$$Y = X$$

To make a copy of array X in array Y, use the COPY function

$$Y = COPY(X)$$

This creates a duplicate set of the values of X which can be referenced with the name Y. In this example, X<1> and Y<1> do *not* occupy the same location in memory.

To determine the size of an array, use the PROTOTYPE function. For example, if M were defined as

$$M = ARRAY('5,10',0)$$

then   PROTOTYPE(M)

yields   5,10.

C.2
Tables

A table is an array whose elements can be referenced by strings or by integers. For example,

$$ACCOUNT<'M4613'> = 0$$

sets the M4613 element of ACCOUNT to zero.

To define a table use the form:

$$TABLE(n,m)$$

where   n is the initial size of the table.

           m is the number of additional variables provided if more
           are needed.

For example,

$$ACCOUNT = TABLE(30,10)$$

reserves room for 30 elements named ACCOUNT. This is *not* like the definition of a 30 $\times$ 10 array. If the 31st element of ACCOUNT is assigned a value, space for 10 more elements will be allocated, bringing the total up to 40. The next allocation would make the total 50.

The default allocation is n = 10 and m = 10, so the following reserves space initially for only 10 elements.

$$LIST = TABLE()$$

Note that LIST<1> and LIST<'1'> reference *different* elements.

A table may be changed into an $n \times 2$ array, where n is the number of variables in the table. For example,

$$A = CONVERT(LIST,'ARRAY')$$

will make the table named LIST into an array named A. The general term A<I,1> is the Ith referencing argument of the table, and A<I,2> is that element's value.

Conversely, an $n \times 2$ array can be converted to a table using CONVERT in the following way:

$$TAB = CONVERT(A,'TABLE')$$

If A <2,1> = 'MAX' and A <2,2> = 305, TAB<'MAX'> = 305.

C.3
User-defined
Data Structures

In SNOBOL it is possible to define linked lists or other data structures using the DATA function. Its general form is:

DATA(p)

where   p is a string denoting the name of the data type and
             the names of its fields.

For example, to define an atom in a singly linked list, we could write

DATA('ATOM(VALUE,PTR)')

The data type is named ATOM and its fields are VALUE and PTR. Diagrammatically this is:

VALUE	PTR

To create an atom whose value is the string 'XYZ' and whose pointer is null, write

HEAD = ATOM('XYZ',)

To insert an atom at the HEAD of the list, write

HEAD = ATOM('UVW',HEAD)

Then HEAD references an atom with value 'UVW' pointing to the atom whose value is 'XYZ'. Actually, we have created a stack and pushed UVW on top of XYZ. To remove the top of the stack, make

HEAD = PTR(HEAD)

As another example, let us define a data structure to represent a tree in SNOBOL. Assume that each node has three fields: the name (or value) of the node, a pointer to one of that node's successors, and a pointer to another node which has the same immediate predecessor (see Figure C.1). Each node is defined by

DATA('NODE(NAME,SUC,BRO)')

The NAME field gives the node's name, SUC is a pointer to one of its immediate successors, and BRO is a pointer to a node in the filial set of the node's immediate predecessor. This is a good type of organization to represent the user or system files pictured in Figure 6.9. The actual creation of the tree depends upon the application involved, so we will not discuss that here.

(a) Tree

(b) Tree representation
with pointers

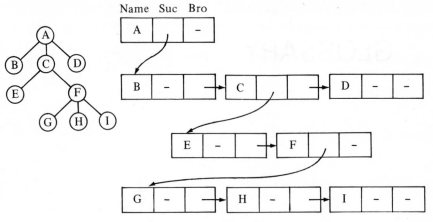

Figure C.1 Tree and a representation with pointers

GLOSSARY

array. An arrangement of elements into one or more dimensions. A one-dimensional array is commonly called a vector; a two-dimensional array is called a table or a matrix.

atom. The elementary building block of data structures. An atom corresponds to a record in a file and may contain one or more fields of data. Also called **node.**

auxiliary memory. Data storage other than main memory; for example, storage on magnetic tape or direct access devices.

average. The statistical mean; the expected value.

average search length. The expected number of comparisons needed to locate an item in a data structure.

backtracking. The operation of scanning a list in reverse.

backward pointer. A pointer which gives the location of an atom's predecessor.

balanced sort. An external tape sort that sorts by merging together tapes, each with an equal number of strings.

binary radix sort. A radix sort in which the sort radix is two.

binary search. In this search method, begin with the middle element and discard half the list. Repeat on sublist until matching key is found or dividing the list produces an empty list.

binary search tree. A binary search accomplished by storing the list in a binary tree. The tree is ordered when constructed or when insertions are made, and this facilitates the search.

binary tree. A tree in which each node has outdegree at most two.

bit. Either zero or one. It is derived from *bi*nary digi*t*.

block search. To accomplish a block search, determine the block the item might be in, then linearly search the block.

bubble sort. Sort by exchanging pairs of keys. Begin with first pair and exchange successive pairs until the list is ordered. Also called **ripple sort.**

buffer. A storage space used to temporarily store I/O data.

buffered I/O. A method of overlapping I/O using two or more buffers.

cascade sort. An external tape sort that sorts by merging strings from all but one tape onto the remaining tape. Subsequent passes merge fewer tapes until one tape contains all items.

character template. A device used to shape an electron beam into an alphanumeric character for CRT display.

circular list. A linked list in which the last element points to the first one. Also called **ring.**

cluster. See **primary cluster, secondary cluster.**

collision. An act that occurs when two or more keys hash to the same address.

column-major order. A method of storing a two-dimensional array in which all elements in one column are placed before all elements in the next column. This method can also be used to store higher-dimensional arrays.

compaction. Packing of data structure to make room in memory.

comparative sort. Sort by comparison of two or more keys.

concatenation. The joining together of two or more strings to form a new one.

connected graph. A graph in which it is possible to get from one node to any other node along a sequence of edges. If the graph is directed, the direction of the edges may be disregarded.

connection matrix. See **incidence matrix.**

contiguous data structure. See **sequential data structure.**

cycle. A path which starts and terminates at the same node.

cylinder. The tracks of a disk storage device that can be accessed without repositioning the access mechanism.

data structure. The relationship between data items.

dense list. A list stored in contiguous locations. Also called **linear list, sequential list.**

density. The ratio of the number of information bits to the total number of bits in a structure.

deque. A double-ended queue. A deque allows insertions and deletions at both ends of a list.

digraph. See **directed graph.**

directed graph. A set of nodes and edges in which an initial and a terminal node determine the direction of the edge. An edge from node A to node B is not an edge from node B to node A.

display register. An internal register in a CRT display terminal.

distributive sort. Sort by partitioning the list and then exchanging items until order exists between partitioned sublists.

dope vector. An atom of a linked list that describes the contents of subsequent atoms in the list.

doubly linked list. A linked list in which each atom contains two pointer fields: one points to the atom's successor, and the other to the atom's predecessor.

dynamic memory management system. A memory system that supplies variable-sized space depending upon the request.

edge. An edge connects two nodes in a graph. An edge may or may not have direction.

empty string. A string containing no characters (has length zero). Also called **null string.**

external fragmentation. Memory loss due to checkerboarding.

external sort. Sort while all or part of a list is stored on an auxiliary storage device.

field. A unit of information.

FIFO. First in, first out queue discipline.

file. A collection of related records treated as a unit.

filial set. A collection of sons descended from a particular node in a tree.

forest. A collection of trees.

forward pointer. A pointer that tells the location of the next item in a data structure. It corresponds to a directed edge in a graph.

fragmentation. Loss of usable memory due to checkerboarding or mismatch in fit. See **internal fragmentation, external fragmentation.**

garbage collection. Release of unused portions of memory from a data structure to make unused areas of memory available for use.

graph. A set containing two types of objects: nodes and edges. This provides a mathematical model for data structures in which the nodes correspond to data items, and the edges to pointer fields.

hashing. A key-to-address transformation in which the keys determine the location of the data.

head. A special data item that points to the beginning of a list. A device that reads or writes data on a storage medium.

heap sort. See **tree sort.**

horizontal distribution. A method of assigning initial strings to tapes when employing the polyphase sort.

Huffman tree. A minimal value tree. See **minimal tree, optimal merge tree.**

incidence matrix. A two-dimensional array which describes the edges in a graph. Also called **connection matrix.**

indegree. The number of directed edges which point to a node.

index. A symbol or numeral which locates the position of an item in an array.

infix notation. A notation where operators are embedded within operands.

internal fragmentation. Memory loss due to mismatch between available space and requested size.

internal sort. Sort made while all items remain in main memory.

IRG. Inter-record gap.

key. One or more fields in a record that are used to locate the record or control its use.

key to address. See **hashing.**

leaf. A terminal node of a tree.

level. A measure of the distance from a node to the root of a tree.

LIFO. Last in, first out stack discipline.

linear list. See **dense list.**

linear search. To accomplish a linear search, begin with the first element and compare until matching key is found or the end of the list is reached.

linked list. A list in which each atom contains a pointer to the location of the next atom.

list. An ordered collection of atoms.

merge sort. Sort which merges ordered sublists to form a larger, ordered list.

minimal tree. A tree with terminal nodes so placed that the value of the tree is optimal. See **optimal merge tree.**

multilinked list. A list in which each atom has two or more pointers.

nil pointer. A pointer used to denote the end of a linked list.

node. See **atom.**

null string. A string containing no characters. Also called **empty string.**

optimal merge tree. A tree representation of the order in which strings are to be merged so that a minimum number of move operations occurs.

oscillating sort. An external tape sort which capitalizes on a tape drive's ability to read forward and backward. The sort oscillates between an internal sort and an external merge.

outdegree. The number of directed edges leaving a node.

overflow. An act that occurs if the allotted memory for a data structure is exceeded.

parsing. The process of separating statements into syntactic units.

path. A path from node n_i to node n_j: a set of nodes n_i, n_{i+1}, . . . , n_{j-1}, n_j and edges such that there is an edge between successive pairs of nodes.

pointer. An address or other indication of location.

polyphase sort. An external tape sort which works best with six or fewer tapes. A Fibonacci sequence of merges is established that maintains a maximum number of active tapes throughout the sort.

pop. The act of removing an element from a stack. Also called **pull.**

postfix notation. A notation in which operators follow the operands that they operate on.

primary cluster. A buildup of table entries around a single table location.

pull. See **pop.**

push. The act of placing an element on a stack. Also called **put.**

put. See **push.**

quadratic quotient search. A hashing algorithm that uses a quadratic offset when probing subsequent table locations.

queue. A list that allows insertion of atoms at one end and deletion of atoms at the opposite end.

quickersort. Sort by partitioning a list into two sublists and a pivotal middle element. All items greater than the pivot go in one sublist and all lesser items go in the other sublist. Sublists are further subdivided until all items are ordered.

radix sort. A distributive sort that uses a number of partitions equal to the sort radix.

random access. A method of retrieving data from a secondary storage device in which the retrieval time is independent of the location of the data. Contrast with sequential access.

record. A collection of related data items. A collection of related records makes up a file.

recursion. A reactivation of an active process; for example, a program segment which calls itself.

replacement-selection. A tournament method of sorting tape files. It produces ordered strings of various lengths which must be merged.

ring. See **circular list.**

ripple sort. See **bubble sort.**

root. The node with indegree zero.

row-major order. A method of storing a two-dimensional array in which all elements in one row are placed before all elements in the next row. See **column-major order.**

scan. An algorithmic procedure for visiting or listing each node of a data structure.

scatter storage. See **hashing.**

secondary cluster. A buildup along a path established by a pattern in a hashing function used for table look-up.

selection sort. Sort by selecting the extreme value (largest or smallest) in the list. Exchange the extreme value with the last value in the list and repeat with a shorter list.

sequential access. An access method for storing or retrieving data items which are located in a continuous manner. The retrieval time of an item depends in part on how many items precede it.

sequential data structure. A data structure in which each atom is immediately adjacent to the next atom. Also called **contiguous data structure.**

sequential list. See **dense list.**

sequential search. See **linear search.**

sort. The process of placing a list in order. See **binary radix sort, bubble sort, comparative sort, distributive sort, external sort, internal sort, merge sort, quickersort, radix sort, selection sort, tree sort.**

sort effort. The number of comparisons or moves needed to order an unordered list.

spanning tree. A subgraph of a graph with two properties: first, it is a tree, and second, it contains all the nodes of the original graph.

sparse array. An array in which most of the entries have a value of zero.

stack. A list that restricts insertions and deletions to one end.

string. A series of characters stored in a contiguous area in memory.

structure. The organization or arrangement of the parts of an entity.

subscript. One of a set of characters used to index the location of item in an array.

synonym. Two or more keys that produce the same table address when hashed.

tail. A special data item that locates the end of a list.

terminal node. A node of a tree which has no successors.

text editor. A program that assists in the preparation of text.

threaded tree. A tree containing additional pointers to assist in the scan of the tree.

token. A code or symbol representing a name or entity in a programming language.

track. The portion of a magnetic storage medium which passes under a positioned read/write head.

traffic intensity. The ratio of insertion rate to the deletion rate of a queue.

transducer. A device that converts information in one form into information in another form.

tree. A connected graph with no cycles. A directed tree is a directed graph that contains no cycles and no alternate paths. A directed tree has a unique node (the root) whose successor set consists of all the other nodes.

tree sort. Sort by exchanging items treated as nodes of a tree. When an item reaches the root node, it is exchanged with the lowest leaf node. Also called **heap sort.**

underflow. An act that occurs when an attempt is made to access an item in a data structure that contains no items. Contrast with **overflow.**

update. A method to modify a master file with current information, according to a specified procedure.

vector. In computer science, a data structure that permits the location of any item by the use of a single index or subscript. Contrast with a table, or matrix, which requires two subscripts to uniquely locate an item.

REFERENCES

BELL, J. R. 1970. "The quadratic quotient method: A hash code eliminating secondary clustering." *Comm ACM* 13, no. 2 (February), pp. 107–109.

BUCHHOLZ, W. 1963. "File organization and addressing." *IBM Syst. J.* 2 (June), pp. 86–111.

BURGE, W. H. 1958. "Sorting, trees, and measures of order." *Inform. and Control* 1, no. 3, pp. 181–197.

CLAMPETT, H. A. 1964. "Randomized binary searching with tree structures." *Comm ACM* 7, no. 3 (March), pp. 163–165.

DAY, A. C. 1970. "Full table quadratic searching for scatter storage." *Comm ACM* 13, no. 8 (August), pp. 481–482.

DAYKIN, D. E. 1960. "Representation of natural numbers as sums of generalized Fibonacci numbers." *Journal London Math. Soc.,* no. 35, pp. 143–160.

FLORES, I. 1960. "Computer time for address calculation sorting." *J. ACM* 7, pp. 389–409.

FLORES, I. 1967. "Direct calculation of k-generalized Fibonacci numbers." *Fibonacci Quarterly* 5, no. 3, pp. 259–266.

GOTLIEB, C. C. 1963. "Sorting on computers." *Comm ACM* 6, no. 5 (May), pp. 194–201.

HARRISON, M. C. 1971. "Implementation of the substring test by hashing." *Comm ACM* 14, no. 12 (December), pp. 777–779.

HIBBARD, T. N. 1962. "Some combinatorial properties of certain trees with applications to searching and sorting." *J. ACM* 9, no. 1 (January), pp. 13–28.

HIRSCHBERG, D. S. 1973. "A class of dynamic memory allocation algorithms." *Comm ACM* 16, no. 10 (October), pp. 615–618.

HOARE, C. A. R. 1961. "Algorithms 63 'Partition' and 64 'Quicksort'." *Comm ACM* 4, no. 7 (July), p. 321.

HOGGATT, V. E. JR. 1968. "A new angle on Pascal's triangle." *Fibonacci Quarterly* 6, no. 4, pp. 221–234.

HOOKER, W. W. 1969. "On the expected lengths of sequences generated in sorting by replacement selecting." *Comm ACM* 12, no. 7 (July), pp. 411–413.

JOHNSON, L. R. 1961. "An indirect chaining method for addressing on secondary keys." *Comm ACM* 5 (May), pp. 218–222.

KNUTH, D. E. 1973. *The Art of Computer Programming*, 2d ed. Vol. 1, pp. 78–96, 435–455. Reading, Mass.: Addison-Wesley Publishing Co.

KNUTH, D. E. 1973. *The Art of Computer Programming*, 2d ed. Vol. 3, Chapters 5 and 6. Reading, Mass.: Addison-Wesley Publishing Co.

LORIN, H. 1971. "A guided bibliography to sorting." *IBM Systems Journal* 10, no. 3, pp. 244–254.

LUM, V. Y.; YUEN, P. S. T.; and DODD, M. 1971. "Key-to-address transform techniques: A fundamental performance study on large existing formatted files." *Comm ACM* 14, no. 4 (April), pp. 228–239.

MARTIN, W. A. 1971. "Sorting." *Computing Surveys* 3, no. 4 (December), pp. 147–174.

MARTIN, W. A., and NESS, D. N. 1972. "Optimizing binary trees grown with a sorting algorithm." *Comm ACM* 15, no. 2 (February), pp. 88–93.

MAURER, W. D. 1968. "An improved hash code for scatter storage." *Comm ACM* 11, no. 1 (January), pp. 35–38.

MILES, E. P. 1967. "Generalized Fibonacci numbers and associated matrices." *Amer. Math Monthly*, no. 67, pp. 745–757.

MINKER, J., *et al.* 1969. "Analysis of data processing systems." Technical Report, pp. 69–99. College Park: University of Maryland.

MORRIS, R. 1968. "Scatter storage techniques." *Comm ACM* 11, no. 1 (January), pp. 38–44.

OMEJC, E. 1972. "A different approach to the sieve of Eratosthenes." *The Arithmetic Teacher* 19, no. 3 (March), pp. 192–196.

PAYNE, W. H. 1969. "Machine, assembly, and systems programming for IBM 360." New York: Harper & Row.

RADKE, C. E. 1970. "The use of quadratic residue research." *Comm ACM* 13, no. 2 (February), pp. 103–105.

RAMAMOORTHY, C. V., and CHIN, Y. H. 1971. "An efficient organization of large frequency-dependent files for binary searching." *IEEE Trans. Comp.* C-20, no. 10 (October), pp. 1178–1187.

SCHAY, G., and SPRUTH, W. G., 1962. "Analysis of a file addressing method." *Comm ACM* 8 (August), pp. 459–462.

SCOWEN, R. S. 1965. "Algorithm 271, Quickersort." *Comm ACM* 8, no. 11 (November), pp. 669–670.

SHELL, D. L. 1959.   "A high-speed sorting procedure." *Comm ACM* 2, no. 7 (July), pp. 30–32.

SHELL, D. L. 1971.   "Optimizing the polyphase sort." *Comm ACM* 14, no. 11 (November), pp. 713–719.

SMITH, B. T. 1970.   "Error bounds for zeros of a polynomial based upon Gersch-gorin's Theorems." *J. ACM* 17, no. 4 (October), pp. 661–674.

SUSSENGUTH, E. H., JR. 1963.   "Use of tree structures for processing files." *Comm ACM* 6, no. 5 (May), pp. 272–279.

VAN EMDEN, M. H. 1970.   "Increasing the efficiency of Quicksort, Algorithm 402." *Comm ACM* 13, no. 11 (November), pp. 693–694.

WINDLEY, P. F. 1960.   "Trees, forests and rearranging." *British Comput. J.* 3, no. 2, pp. 84–88.

ANSWERS TO
SELECTED EXERCISES

Note: In this section exercises are identified by chapter and section.
Thus 2.1.3 is Chapter 2, Section 1, Exercise 3.

CHAPTER 1

1.1.2. Your discussion should include examples of increasing the length of a list by appending to the ends and by insertion in between entries. Alternately, a list can shrink by deleting from the ends or in between. When a list is ordered, it is our responsibility to maintain the order when we insert a new entry.

1.1.4. A graph corresponding to Figure 1.9 is shown below.

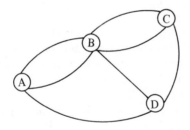

The problem is to cross each bridge only once. To solve the problem, define an IN counter and an OUT counter for each node (A, B, C, and D). In tracing a path of the graph, increment the IN counter each time you enter a node, and increment the OUT counter each time you leave a node. To cross all the bridges only once, you must have OUT − IN = 0 for each node.

CHAPTER 2

2.1.4. This is the way Figure 2.5 would appear with pointers to locate the beginning of each string.

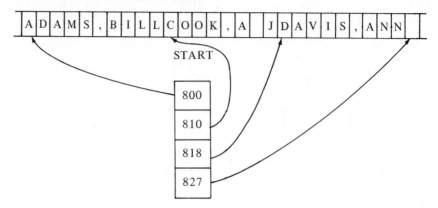

2.2.2. One possibility (there are many others) is to use the storage method described in Figure 2.3 where a dollar sign ($) separates strings, and we include a pointer to the first string. To concatenate the two strings:

1. Locate an area not being used.

2. Locate the first string and copy it into the area, but do not copy the $ character.

3. Locate the second string and copy it into the area following the first string; do copy the $ character.

The original strings would remain intact.

2.2.5. The algorithm must compare each character with an "=" or a "+" sign to determine what is an operator and what is an identifier. Separation is used to split off the = and + characters from the substrings X, A1, and B.

2.3.4. Any algorithm that moves a string in memory risks copying over another string or itself accidentally. Your algorithm must protect the storage areas being manipulated. One protective algorithm works as follows: Create a temporary string long enough to hold the longest string being moved; call this TEMP. Suppose we are to move string SOURCE to string area DESTINATION. Since DESTINATION may actually contain parts of SOURCE, we must copy SOURCE by moving it to TEMP:

$$TEMP \leftarrow SOURCE$$

$$DESTINATION \leftarrow TEMP$$

This destroys anything previously in DESTINATION but guarantees that SOURCE is protected.

CHAPTER 3

3.1.1. 5 bits, since $2^5 = 32$. In general, $\log_2 n$ bits are needed to address n locations. $\log_2 8192 = \log_2 2^{13} = 13$; $\log_2 10,000 = 14$.

3.1.3. $C(i,j)$ is stored in location

$$b + 4(j - 1) + i - 1$$

where b is the location of $C(1,1)$.

3.1.5. The pi-product computes the elements to be skipped to arrive at the proper plane. The summation generalizes plane-skipping to the n-dimensional case. The j_n term indexes into the plane.

3.1.6. Location $= \displaystyle\sum_{r=1}^{n-1} (j_r - l_r) \prod_{s=r}^{n-1} (u_{s+1} - l_{s+1} + 1) + j_n - l_n + 1$

3.1.7. We assumed uniform probabilities, or that $p_k = 1/n$ for every entry. We also assumed that n is a constant, but as you can see, n changes every time an insert or deletion takes place. If n were to fluctuate uniformly randomly from zero to a maximum, say max, the average over all possible lengths would be computed by summing all values of n.

$$m_i = \frac{1}{\max} \sum_{n=0}^{(\max-1)} \frac{n + 1}{2} = \frac{(\max + 1)}{4}$$

$$m_d = \frac{1}{\max + 1} \sum_{n=0}^{\max} \frac{n - 1}{2} = \frac{(\max - 2)}{4}$$

3.1.8. 229.

3.2.2. If there is no HEADER and the list is empty, there is no way to find the list and make an insertion.

3.2.4. Your algorithm may search the entire book one name at a time, in which case you will have to search half the directory (on the average). Your algorithm might take advantage of the alphabetical order by first examining the names at the top and bottom of each page. If the sought-after name does not fall between the top and bottom names, you need not search the page further. A further refinement might be to select any page in the book. If the name you want comes before the names on the randomly selected page, you need not look in the later portion of the book. Repeat the random selection, discarding a part of the book each time. Finally, you will isolate the desired page. This method is quite rapid, surprisingly, and is analogous to browsing. We give the simplest algorithm below.

1. Let P point to the first name.

2. Repeat the following until P is nil:
   (a) If P points to the appropriate name, stop.
   (b) Set P to the pointer of the name referenced by P.

3. Output: "Name not found."

3.2.6. Examine m atoms, where

$$m = \sum_{k=1}^{n} k \cdot p_k$$

and

$$p_k = \frac{1}{n} \text{ for } k = 1, 2, \ldots, n$$

For large values of n, $(n + 1)/2 \approx n/2$.

3.3.3. A ring structure has no nil pointer indicating the end of the list. We must therefore save the address of the first atom so that it may be used as a check in place of the nil pointer of a simple linked list. In deletion, we must be careful not to delete the HEADER.

3.3.4. The total number of bits in each atom of the data structure is $240 + 30 + 16 * 2 = 302$. The number of information bits is $240 + 30 = 270$. For a list of n accounts, the density is (approximately) $270n/302n = 270/302 = 0.9$. The density does not depend on how many entries are included.

3.3.5. A dense list is easily backtracked by decrementing its index variable. A linked list with forward pointers cannot be backtracked without modification. One way to do so is to include a sign bit in the pointer field such that a "+" indicates that the pointer is pointing forward and a "−" indicates that the pointer is pointing backward. While scanning forward, we reverse the FORWARD pointer by pointing it to the atom preceding the atom in which it is kept, and set its sign to "−". In this way we turn the singly linked list inside out while scanning. If we wish to backtrack, we follow the pointers which have a "−" sign since they point to the way back. As we backtrack, we reverse the pointer and set the signs to "+". In a doubly linked list we merely follow the BACKWARD pointers.

CHAPTER 4

4.1.1. Regardless of the size allocated for the queue, there is always a chance that the queue will overflow.

4.1.3. Job PR73 underflows.
Job XA41 is inserted at TAIL = 1.
Job BR11 is inserted at TAIL = 2.
Job XA41 is deleted leaving HEAD = 2, TAIL = 2.
Job BR11 is deleted leaving HEAD = nil and TAIL = nil.

4.1.5. The values of $z = 5$, $\rho = 4/7$ are plugged into the formulas.

$$l = \frac{\lambda}{\mu - \lambda} = \frac{4}{7 - 4} = 1.33$$

$$k = \frac{\log 1/20}{\log 4/7} = 5.35$$

4.1.7. Overflow never occurs in a linked list unless the computer system is unable to provide free space. This is one of the advantages of a linked list. We handle underflow as we did with a dense list. The central problem with a linked list implementation of a queue is that of accessing the HEAD and TAIL. We must either search the full length of the list to find the TAIL (when a single link is used) or employ a doubly linked list structure that contains BACKWARD pointers. If we implement the doubly linked list structure as a ring, the HEADER atom always points to the HEAD of the list (FORWARD) and to the TAIL of the list (BACKWARD).

4.2.1. The modification is made by changing the increment and decrement step sizes. TOP ← TOP + 10 and TOP ← TOP − 10.

PUSH: 1. If TOP is nil, set TOP ← 1.

2. If TOP > N, overflow, else replace STACK[TOP] through STACK[TOP + 9] with the ten elements of the vector.

3. TOP ← TOP + 10.

4.2.3. The operands X, A, B, C, Y, and P are placed on the operand stack in the order in which they are input (left-to-right scan). The − operator is performed first, followed by the ÷ operator and the two × operators. The addition operation is done last.

$$
\begin{aligned}
\text{Start:} \quad & X - A \\
& B \div C \\
& (B \div C)Y \\
& (B \div C)YP \\
\text{Done:} \quad & (X - A) + [(B \div C)YP]
\end{aligned}
$$

4.2.5. In an extreme case the first job stacked will never be output. It will be doomed to the stack base. A queue, on the other hand, guarantees that a job will be processed after an average wait of $1/(\mu - \lambda)$ time units.

4.3.1. 1.   Do only one of the following:

   (a)   If END1 is nil and END2 $= 1$, then overflow, else END1 $\leftarrow$ END2 $- 1$.

   (b)   If END1 $= 1$, then overflow, otherwise END1 $\leftarrow$ END1 $- 1$.

   2.   Insert atom at END1.

   This algorithm will not work for insertion at END2, although that algorithm is similar.

4.3.3. Approximately $(n - k)/2$.

4.3.5. A doubly linked deque is identical to the structure in Figure 3.18, in which the header atom points to one end of the deque and the tail to the other end.

CHAPTER 5

5.1.2. Paths from B to E:

Paths from B to E:	Cycles:
B-E	B-A-C-B
B-D-E	B-C-D-B
B-C-D-E	B-D-E-B
B-A-C-D-E	B-A-C-D-E-B
B-D-B-E	B-A-C-D-B
B-C-B-E	B-C-D-E-B

.
.
.

The graph is connected.

5.1.4. Level 1: Y
   Level 2: X, W, M, N
   Level 3: A, Z
   Level 4: B

5.1.6.

Node	Indegree	Outdegree
M	0	2
N	1	0
O	1	3
P	1	0
Q	1	1
R	1	0
S	1	0

5.1.8. {A, B, C, D, E, F}

5.2.3. The terminal nodes are the only nodes with nil pointers in both left and right pointer fields. The root node is found by looking at the ROOT anchor. Also, we could (tediously) find one or more root nodes by searching for all entries with indegree equal to zero.

5.2.5. The repeated numbers could be inserted in the tree, of course. This would increase the depth of the tree and decrease the update and search speed. Alternately, we could add a repetition field to the fields in each atom. Let REP be a number indicating the number of times each number occurs in the list.

VALUE	LEFT	RIGHT	REP
240		–	3

When deleting a number, we decrement the REP count and actually release the node only if REP = 0. When inserting, we either create a new node with REP = 1 or, if it exists, we increment REP.

5.3.1. NLR-recursive order:A,B,C,G,D,E,F,H
LNR-recursive order: C,G,B,A,E,D,H,F
LRN-recursive order: G,C,B,E,H,F,D,A

5.3.3.

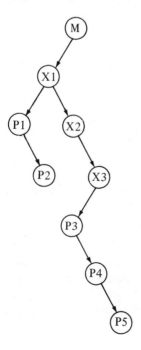

NLR: M, X1, P1, P2, X2, X3, P3, P4, P5

LNR: P1, P2, X1, X2, P3, P4, P5, X3, M

The original tree could be scanned from left to right by a left (L), middle (M), and right (R)-recursive algorithm called the NLMR-recursive order as follows: M,X1,P1,P2,X2,X3,P3,P4,P5. This results in the same order as NLR-recursive. LMNR-recursive order and LNMR-recursive order produce different sequences of nodes, however.

5.3.5. See the solution to Exercise 3.

5.3.7. The tree must be threaded as follows: Left thread points to the root node that is to be output immediately following the terminal node. Right thread links to the next terminal node to be output. The algorithm is in two parts: Part 1: Search the left pointer chain that leads from the root node to the leftmost node. Part 2: Output the current node and the node indicated by the left thread. Follow the right thread until left thread equals nil.

LNR-threaded scan: SCAN(P).

1. Initially P = root node address.

2. Repeat until LEFT pointer is a THREAD:
    (a) Set P ← LEFT of atom at location P.

3. Repeat until LEFT pointer is NIL:
    (a) Output the node at location P.
    (b) Output the node at LEFT thread of atom at location P.
    (c) Set P ← RIGHT thread of atom at P.

4. Output the node at location P.

A sample threaded tree is given below.

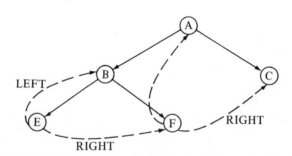

5.3.9. The tree is easily backtracked because threads provide BACKWARD pointers where needed. The threads destroy the definition of a tree, however, because they provide alternate paths to some nodes. Therefore the threads allow cycles in the graph.

The multiattribute file contains multikey records that do not possess unique values.

6.4.2.

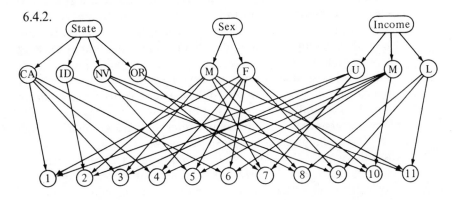

CHAPTER 7

7.1.1. We illustrate a selection sort which sorts the list in ascending order. The first five passes are:

(01)				
19	(11)			
26	26	(19)		
43	43	43	(21)	
92	92	92	92	(26)
87	87	87	87	2
21	21	26	43	87
38	38	38	38	43
55	55	55	55	55
11	19	21	26	38

7.1.2. The conjectured minimal sort effort is $1000 \log(1000) = 3000$.

7.2.3. The algorithm is modified by letting $N = M =$ the length of sublists to be merged. In addition, we must keep track of the subscript on C as it is being filled up by merging A and B. When each pass is completed, we must switch A, B, and C to serve different purposes on subsequent passes.

7.2.4. The discussion on sorting does not consider the size of each record and the corresponding cost to move long records. Names or alphabetic strings tend to be much longer than their sort keys. In considering a sorting method, we should stress the importance of average number of moves and record length. Very long records should be separated from their keys by constructing a directory that contains keys and pointers to the master records. Thus we move only the key and associated pointer, not the entire record.

7.2.6. Tree sort requires as many comparisons as there are edges in the tree structure representing a given pass of the algorithm. Thus in this case there are $n(n - 1)/2 = 15$ comparisons. The number of exchanges are fewer, however, amounting to nine exchanges. The quickersort algorithm, however, bogs down in splitting the list repeatedly because it cannot find elements to exchange. The number of comparisons is roughly $n(n - 1)/2 = 15$ also, but the overhead in splitting requires much more effort.

7.3.2. (a) $t = 4, k = 8$, then
$$a_k^{(i)} = a_{k-1}^{(i)} + a_{k-2}^{(i)} + a_{k-3}^{(i)}$$
$$\text{thus } a_8^{(0)} = a_7^{(0)} + a_6^{(0)} + a_5^{(0)}$$
$$= 105 + 57 + 31$$
$$= 193$$
$$a_8^{(1)} = 24 + 13 + 7$$
$$= 44$$
$$a_8^{(2)} = 37 + 20 + 11$$
$$= 68$$
$$a_8^{(3)} = 44 + 24 + 13$$
$$= 81$$

7.4.2. String 1: 10,20   length = 2
String 2: 15,25,30   length = 3
String 3: 12   length = 1
String 4: 2   length = 1

The minimal binary tree is computed by grouping together the string lengths as follows:

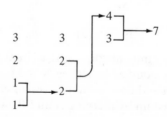

The tree has value of $3(1) + 2(2) + 1(3) = 10$ where level numbers are put in parentheses. The value of 10 represents the number of comparisons performed in merge-sorting the numbers.

CHAPTER 8

8.1.2. A FORTRAN subroutine for computing L, given $c(i)$ and $p(i)$, is as follows:

```
          FUNCTION AVEL (N,C,P)
          DIMENSION C(N), P(N)
          SUM = 0.0
          DO 1 I = 1,N
              SUM = SUM + C(I) * P(I)
     1    CONTINUE
          AVEL = SUM
          RETURN
          END
```

8.2.3. We assumed uniformly random probabilities of access.

8.2.4. This problem is the same as the dense list update problem of Chapter 3.

8.2.5. The access frequency ordering must be extremely skewed to perform like a binary search table. The ordered table is unequaled in its rapid response to searches that reveal *no* key match. The access frequency table will search the entire table when no match is made.

8.2.8.

$$L_{block} = L_b + L_w$$

$$= \log_2(b + 1) - 1 + (s - 1)/2$$

since $b = n/s$

$$L_{block} = \log_2\left(\frac{n + s}{s}\right) + \tfrac{1}{2}(s - 3)$$

8.3.1. See Glossary and Index.

8.3.3. Search and insertion are performed by the linear probe hashing function. The file is divided into buckets with overflow going into the next bucket. Deleted records are marked 'DELETED' so that the hashing chain is not broken for other records. The file is rewritten to remove deleted records only when the ratio of deleted records to total file capacity reaches a threshold of $\sqrt{n}/n$, where n = file size.

8.3.5. The average number of probes is:

$$2 = \cfrac{1}{1 - \cfrac{100,000}{n}}$$

or

$$n = 200,000$$

CHAPTER 9

9.1.2. In either system we may maintain an AVAIL list and an ALLO-CATED list if we reserve a few words in each block of memory for pointers and LENGTH attributes. An AVAIL-HEADER and ALLOCATED-HEADER provide the starting point for two linked lists. A request is filled by scanning the AVAIL list (which links together all free space). A memory release is accomplished by inserting the freed block into the AVAIL list. If a block is not in the AVAIL list, it is in the ALLOCATED list. To provide a variety of block sizes, adjacent blocks are coalesced when possible.

9.2.1. See Exercise 4 of Section 2.3 for a hint.

9.2.2. Scan the linked list for all DELETED atoms. If they are marked DELETED, perform a delete operation on the list and return the free space to the AVAIL list.

9.3.1. Any system that offers its largest block first, followed by exact duplicates of the request sizes, will be better handled by Best Fit method.

		FRAGMENTATION	
AVAIL	*REQUESTS*	*BEST*	*FIRST*
20	15	20 free	15 + 5 free
15	10	15 allocated	10 + 5 free
10	5	10 allocated	5 free
5		5 allocated	5 free

9.3.4. Yes. The Buddy system may not always be able to keep free blocks in buddy positions. For example, in Figure 9.4 the contiguous spaces at locations 8 and 16 are adjacent but not buddies. Thus they cannot be coalesced into a larger block that could satisfy a request for 16 words.

We could measure external fragmentation as the ratio of allocated space to total space. We could measure internal fragmentation as the ratio of requested space to allocated space.

9.3.5. A multilevel system shown below may be more useful than the tree structure in Figure 9.4.

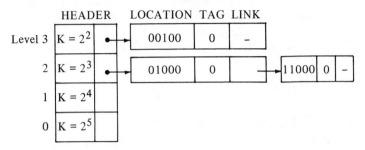

9.4.2. The 2-system is generated from:

$$F_n = F_{n-1} + F_{n-3}$$
$$F_0 = 0$$
$$F_1 = 1$$
$$F_2 = 1$$
$$F_3 = 1$$
$$F_4 = 2$$
$$F_5 = 3$$
$$F_6 = 4$$
$$F_7 = 6$$
$$F_8 = 9$$
$$F_9 = 13$$

9.4.3. Let $F_n = C\alpha^n$ and substitute into the formula:

$$C\alpha^n = C\alpha^{n-1} + C\alpha^{n-k}$$
$$\alpha^{n+k} = \alpha^{n+k-1} + \alpha^n$$
$$\alpha^k = \alpha^{k-1} + 1$$
$$\alpha^k - \alpha^{k-1} - 1 = 0$$

9.5.1. Given n and k, we must start with initial values for $F_0 = 0$, $F_1 = 1$ . . . $F_{k+1} = 1$ and apply the formula repeatedly to get the remaining $(n - k + 1)$ numbers. For $k = 1$ we can do this iteratively or recursively. Iteratively:

```
    F1 = 1;
    F2 = 1;
DO I = 1 TO N;
    F3 = F2 + 1;
    PUT LIST (F3);
    F1 = F2;
    F2 = F3;
END;
```

Recursively:

```
DCL   FN ENTRY (FIXED BINARY) RETURNS (FIXED BINARY);
FN:   PROCEDURE (N) RETURNS (FIXED BINARY) RECURSIVE;
      DCL N FIXED BINARY;
      IF N < 2 THEN
         RETURN (1);
      ELSE
         RETURN (FN(N−1) + FN(N−2));
      END FN;
```

9.5.3. The ALLOCATE and FREE algorithm can be the same as the one proposed in Exercise 5, Section 9.3, except the block sizes are different and the coalesce order is changed. Each block no longer has a buddy; instead each block has a LEFT-BLOCK-COUNT and RIGHT-BLOCK-COUNT that indicate that two blocks can be coalesced. Since $F_{n+1} = 2F_n - F_{n-1}$ we have to search for two F_n blocks for each F_{n-1} block. This requires a more complex FREE algorithm.

9.5.4. The optimal block sizes are determined by solving the state equation for F_{j+1}. Since $cdf(s)$ is:

$$cdf(s) = \int_0^s \frac{e^{-x/m}}{\alpha m} \, dx = (1 - e^{-s/m})/\alpha$$

Therefore:

$$F_{j+1} = F_j + m \left[\exp\left(\frac{F_j + F_{i-1}}{m}\right) - 1\right]$$

This nonlinear equation cannot be easily solved by analytical means. Numerical solutions give F_j when $F_0 = 0$, $F_n = m$.

CHAPTER 10

10.1.1. The algorithm must search the rows to find the jth column and then search the columns to find the ith row. There will be two paths or no path.

10.1.3. A sparse vector may be stored by recording the index of nonzero entries along with the value in a linked list. For example, A(1), A(9), A(17) . . .

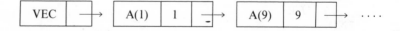

A three-dimensional array requires three links in each atom. A four-dimensional array requires four links in each atom. An m-dimensional array requires m links. Therefore the density of an $n \times n \times n \times \ldots n$ array in m-space is:

$$d = \frac{n^m}{(n + mn/2)^m}$$

Where we have assumed that each pointer field takes up half a word:

$$d = \frac{1}{(1 + n/2)^m}$$

The break-even point is $d \cdot n^m$ nonzero entries or roughly 2^m nonzero elements.

A hashing function could be devised as follows: $H(i,j) = (i - 1)n + j$, where n is the dimension bounds. This hash function results in the same waste as the original data. Suppose we know that the array will never exceed αn^2 nonzero entries. We need a hash table with load factor of α. A possible hash function now is:

$$H(i,j) = \alpha((i - 1)n + j)$$

Collisions are handled by some offset mechanism, and a table of αn^2 locations is allocated instead of n^2 locations.

10.2.2. The INTENSITY field can be expanded to two bits. The code is:

$$00 = \text{off}$$
$$01 = \text{green}$$
$$10 = \text{blue}$$
$$11 = \text{red}$$

10.2.4. A polar coordinate CRT locates a point by a radius r and an angle a. Let a point on the complex plane be re^{ia} where $i = \sqrt{-1}$. The real and imaginary components are located as in Exercise 3.

10.3.1. The expected internal fragmentation is $\overline{w}$.

$$\overline{w} = \int_0^{40} \frac{(40 - x)\, e^{-x/5}}{5}\, dx + \int_{41}^{80} \frac{(80 - x)\, e^{-x/5}}{5}\, dx$$

The expected external fragmentation is calculated from estimating how many strings will exceed 80 characters.

10.3.3. The method is naive in that it does not cope with lines of eighty characters or more. It causes fragmentation as shown in Exercise 1. It is not easy to do inserts and maintain order in the table.

10.4.2. The study should use $-\alpha^{-1} \log_2(1 - \alpha)$ as the benchmark when computing the average comparisons to insert a symbol. The formula $1/(1 - \alpha)$ is appropriate when look-up alone is performed.

10.4.3. The binary search tree uses only the space needed. It keeps the symbols in order. Let us assume this order is 'A', '3', and '5'. The tree is:

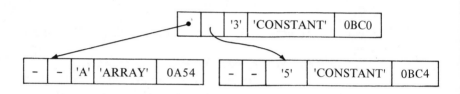

10.4.4. Folding 'B' yields B_{16}. This produces a remainder of 3 and quotient of zero.

10.4.5. To prevent primary clustering when more than one quotient is zero for the same remainder.

10.5.2. The data uses $10 \cdot 20 \cdot 10 = 2000$ words. The dope vector uses $2 + 3 + 3$ words for address, d, M_1 to M_3, I_1 to I_3. If we agree that $M_1 = 1$ always, we need not store it. Therefore seven words are needed in the dope vector. The density is $2000/2007 \approx 0.99$.

10.6.1. See Chapter 2.

10.6.3. The precedence table must be expanded to recognize IF, THEN, and ELSE. Since a true or false condition is tested, we must insert a branch on false in place of the THEN. Unfortunately we do not know the destination of the branch on false until we reach the ELSE clause. A marker must be placed on the stack so we can come back and insert the destination later.

10.7.1. The process time for a buffer load is equal to the size of buffer, e.g., z divided by the processing speed: $(z/40,000)$ seconds. The switch time is given as $(1/40)$ seconds. Therefore the I/O time is:

$$T_{I/O} = \frac{1}{40} + \frac{z}{40,000}$$

The time to fill a buffer is given by the buffer size divided by the I/O rate: $(z/20{,}000)$ seconds. We now solve for z.

$$\frac{z}{20{,}000} = \frac{1}{40} + \frac{z}{40{,}000}$$

$$\frac{z}{40{,}000} = \frac{1}{40}$$

$$z = \frac{40{,}000}{40} = 1000 \text{ bytes}$$

10.7.2. The buffer is overflowed or the next buffer is overwritten. This is called overrun.

10.7.3. Additional buffers can be used to overcome the inevitable overflow. See Chapter 3 for formulas for computing overflow. Instead of switching to a second buffer, we switch to buffer 3, then 4, . . . until we catch up with the data flow.

10.8.1. The routine might be something as follows:

```
DIV: PROC(Q) RECURSIVE;
     DCL X FIXED BINARY;
     IF Q = 0 THEN RETURN;
     X = Q / 10;
     CALL DIV(X);
     PUT(MOD(Q,10) + 48);
END DIV;
```

10.8.2. For n digits, the stack must store $2n$ numbers.

10.9.1. 14.

10.9.3. It might take longer to find the shortest path to node n, but otherwise there is no significant difference. Just pick one of the nodes for the pivotal node.

10.9.5. Each time a node's value changes, record the pivotal node used to calculate the node's value. At the end trace backward from node n to node 1.

CHAPTER 11

11.1.1.
$$A = \{a_1, a_2\}$$
$$P = \{p_1, p_2\}$$
$$I = \{p_1 \sim a_1 \ \& \ a_2, p_2 \sim a_2 \ \& \ a_3\}$$
$$T = \{\text{HEAD, TOP, DATA, LINK}\}$$

$V = \{STACK, 50, VALUE, 60\}$

$\sigma = \{a_1 \sim HEAD, a_2 \sim DATA, p_1 \sim TOP, p_2 \sim LINK\}$

From Figure 11.5(a).

11.1.5. We could use the formalism as a declarative in the language and define the before and after transformations as pseudosubroutines.

11.2.1.

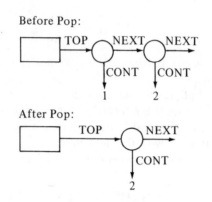

11.2.2.

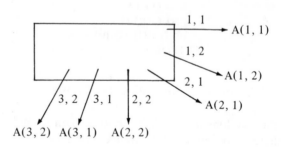

INDEX